Olympic Exclusions

Olympic Games are sold to host city populations on the basis of legacy commitments that incorporate aid for the young and the poor. Yet little is known about the realities of marginalized young people living in host cities. Do they benefit from social housing and employment opportunities? Or do they fall victim to increased policing and evaporating social assistance? This book answers these questions through an original ethnographic study of young people living in the shadow of Vancouver 2010 and London 2012.

Setting qualitative research alongside critical analysis of policy documents, bidding reports and media accounts, this study explores the tension between promises made and lived reality. Its eight chapters offer a rich and complex account of marginalized young people's experiences as they navigate the possibilities and contradictions of living in an Olympic host city. Their stories illustrate the limits to the promises made by Olympic bidding and organizing committees and raise important questions about the ethics of public funding for such mega-events.

This book will be fascinating reading for anyone interested in the Olympics, sport and social exclusion, and sport and politics, as well as for those working in the fields of youth studies, social policy and urban studies.

Jacqueline Kennelly is an Associate Professor in the Department of Sociology and Anthropology at Carleton University in Ottawa, Canada. She is the author of *Citizen Youth: Culture, Activism, and Agency in a Neoliberal Era* (2011) and the co-author (with J. Dillabough) of *Lost Youth in the Global City: Class, Culture, and the Urban Imaginary* (2010). She recently co-edited (with S. Poyntz) *Phenomenology of Youth Cultures and Globalization: Lifeworlds and Surplus Meaning in Changing Times* (2015). Her work has appeared in multiple international academic journals, including *Sociology*, the *British Journal of Criminology*, *Feminist Theory*, *Ethnography*, *Visual Studies*, *Gender and Education*, and the *British Journal of Sociology of Education*.

Routledge Critical Studies in Sport
Series Editors
Jennifer Hargreaves and Ian McDonald
University of Brighton

The Routledge Critical Studies in Sport series aims to lead the way in developing the multi-disciplinary field of Sport Studies by producing books that are inter-rogative, interventionist and innovative. By providing theoretically sophisticated and empirically grounded texts, the series will make sense of the changes and challenges facing sport globally. The series aspires to maintain the commitment and promise of the critical paradigm by contributing to a more inclusive and less exploitative culture of sport.

Also available in this series:

Olympic Exclusions

Youth, poverty and social legacies

Jacqueline Kennelly

LONDON AND NEW YORK

First published 2016
by Routledge
2 Park Square, Milton Park, Abingdon, Oxon OX14 4RN

and by Routledge
711 Third Avenue, New York, NY 10017

Routledge is an imprint of the Taylor & Francis Group, an informa business

British Library Cataloguing-in-Publication Data
A catalogue record for this book is available from the British Library

Library of Congress Cataloging in Publication Data
A catalog record for this book has been requested

ISBN: 978-1-138-96015-2 (hbk)
ISBN: 978-1-315-66041-7 (ebk)

Typeset in Times
by Keystroke, Station Road, Codsall, Wolverhampton

Dedicated to Alex, KaiLin, and Desmond

In *Olympic Exclusions* Jacqueline Kennelly focuses on those in the Olympic city who all too often are ignored. Zeroing in on marginalized populations – youth, the homeless, the poverty-stricken, and working-class people – she shows us how some people are neither invited to the Olympic party nor privy to the Games' social legacies. Drawing from extensive fieldwork on the 2010 Winter Olympics in Vancouver and the 2012 Summer Games in London, Kennelly's nuanced ethnographic inquiry explores the complex, lived experiences of everyday people before, during, and after the Olympic Games. Given that the processes of exclusion typically transpire far from the white-hot glare of the media spotlight, this book is especially important. *Olympic Exclusions* exposes the grim underbelly of the Olympic spectacle. This book is a vital contribution that helps us better understand how ordinary people are affected by the Olympic Games in the twenty-first century.

Professor Jules Boykoff, Department of Politics and
Government, Pacific University Oregon, USA

Olympic Exclusions provides eye-opening accounts of the impact of the Olympic Games on poor urban youth, illustrating poignantly how "legacy" promises for housing and employment are underachieved. Kennelly uses first-hand, ethnographic research to uncover the actual experiences of poor urban youth around the Vancouver Winter Games of 2010 and the London Summer Games of 2012. Kennelly puts these personal stories into a rich framework set by the growing literature on the impact of hosting the Olympics. *Olympic Exclusions* is important reading for anyone seeking to understand how the Olympics can set back, rather than advance, the social goals of a city.

Professor Andrew Zimbalist, Department of
Economics, Smith College, USA

Contents

Acknowledgements

This research began in 2008 as a SSHRC postdoctoral project at the University of Cambridge. It continued on through my early years as a faculty member at Carleton University, with the assistance of a SSHRC Standard Research Grant. It has spanned tenure and promotion, the birth of two children, the dissolution of one marriage, and the beginning of another life partnership. There are thus so many individuals and institutions to thank that I fear I will miss some in the process. I will do my best to capture them all here.

Above all else, my most heartfelt thanks to the youth in Vancouver and London whose experiences are represented in this book. Your honesty, humour, dignity, energy and care for one another are an inspiration and a motivator. Thanks also to the youth workers who helped navigate access to the youth in their care, and to other key informants who helped me make sense of what was going on in each city. This project wouldn't have happened without you.

Dr. Paul Watt, my collaborator on the London portion of the research, deserves a giant round of applause for his collegial support and intellectual presence through the 2010 to 2013 phases of the research. He also has gone above and beyond with feedback on chapters in this book, particularly the London housing chapter. His expertise has made the book better than it could have been otherwise. Paul, it's been a pleasure. Who knew that our chance encounter on the train platform in Harrogate would lead to such things?

Institutionally, thanks are due to Dr. Diane Reay for supervising the initial project when I was a postdoctoral fellow at the University of Cambridge, and to the Faculty of Education at Cambridge for their willingness to host me there. Dr. Jo-Anne Dillabough, my PhD supervisor, provided invaluable assistance in shaping the original project when it was a postdoc application. Carleton University has provided much in the way of institutional support, most importantly through the negotiation of time to write this book during the 2014–15 school year. A special thank you to Neil Gerlach (past Chair of the Department of Sociology and Anthropology) and John Osborne (past Dean of the Faculty of Arts and Social Sciences) for helping that happen.

Funding support for this project has come in large part from the Social Sciences and Humanities Research Council of Canada (SSHRC), initially through a postdoctoral fellowship and then through a Standard Research Grant. I have also benefited from Carleton's professional expense fund and made use of Carleton start-up faculty funding to pay for research assistance, books, and other resources required in the making of a project such as this.

I've had the pleasure of working with a number of talented research assistants throughout this project, without whom this research and the book wouldn't have been possible. In no particular order, big thanks to Trevor White, Christine Meyer, Chris Enman, Amelia Curran, Ryan Boyd, Kevin Partridge, Deborah Conners, Jessica Azevedo, Lynette Schick, and Valerie Stam.

WeiHsi Hu helped me connect with some of the work happening in London around young people and the Olympics, and accompanied me to watch the Opening Ceremonies at a live site in Greenwich. Jules Boykoff provided both intellectual and pragmatic support for this project through cheerful emails and excellent suggestions for publication venues. Kristina Llewellyn deserves credit for the ultimate title of the book, which was a task of great struggle for me. Stuart Poyntz reminded me of the importance of phenomenology at a crucial moment during revisions of the Introduction. Janet Siltanen, Joel Harden, and Deborah Conners provided invaluable feedback on Chapter 1 – it is Janet who gets credit for the phrase 'legitimating discourses.' Marie-Eve Carrier-Moisan and Nick Falvo helped me tighten and refine Chapters 2 and 3. Azim Essaji lent his economic expertise to strengthen Chapter 4. Many thanks to Nora Loreto for thoughtful and careful editing of the entire manuscript. Thanks also to the anonymous reviewers of Chapters 1 and 2 for their ideas and suggestions, and to the editors of the series, Jennifer Hargreaves and Ian Macdonald, for taking on the project. A final round of feedback from Jennifer Hargreaves helped me improve the project as a whole. Thanks to Simon Whitmore, William Bailey, and Cecily Davey for making the publishing process that much smoother and more pleasant, and the entire team at Routledge for seeing the book into print so quickly and professionally.

Special thanks to my writing group, Unit Writers of Ottawa (UWOO): Lara Karaian, Stacy Douglas, Alexis Shotwell, Danielle Dinovelli-Lang, Shoshana Magnet, Jennifer Ridgley, Amrita Hari, Megan Rivers-Moore, Marie-Eve Carrier-Moisan, Rebecca Schein, and others I've probably missed. I wrote (almost) this entire book in 45-minute increments!

Finally, most heartfelt and emotional thanks to my life partner, Alex Campbell, and our children, KaiLin Kennelly Duong and Desmond Kennelly Campbell. You've nurtured me, listened to me rant, come to my presentations, made me laugh, given me the best snuggles, travelled with me to Vancouver and London (Desi in utero!), tolerated my grumpy preoccupations, and just generally made life worth living. Thank you, thank you, thank you.

Introduction

These Games are for who?

Olympic claims to help the young and the poor

> During the implementation phase [of the Vancouver Olympics], steps will be taken to ensure incorporation of the interests of different groups, such as Aboriginal people, women, youth, people with disabilities, people of colour, immigrants and other groups.
>
> (Vancouver 2010 Bid Report)

> Choose London today and you send a clear message to the youth of the world: more than ever, the Olympic Games are for you.
>
> (Sebastian Coe, chair of the London bid committee, in his closing pitch to the IOC)

This is a book about the Olympics, but it is not about sports. Instead, it is about what happens to the people who live in Olympic host cities, and, in particular, about what happens to poor, young people who live in Olympic host cities. It is also about the claims that are made by Olympics promoters to help the young, and the poor, and sometimes the youthful poor. These claims, framed as 'commitments' but without any accountability process to ensure that they are met, have become increasingly central to the bidding process for winning an Olympic Games. This book explores the lived experiences of those who are supposed to be the beneficiaries of these commitments, and poses questions about what it means to win Olympic bids on the basis of such unfulfilled promises.

For example, there is Justine. I met Justine in Vancouver in 2010, the year of the Winter Olympics there. A 22-year-old Aboriginal woman who had grown up in Vancouver, Justine told me she had been excited about the Olympics when she first heard about them, but also nervous that she would be 'run out' of her own city. Although she had managed to stay in Vancouver for the Games, many of her friends had left. She had stayed because her boyfriend had work, and needed to be in the city. She and her boyfriend were housed when I met her, living in the Dunsmuir House. The Dunsmuir was one of the housing options that had been opened in response to federal and provincial pressure to 'clean up the streets' of Vancouver when the Olympics came to town. It has since closed. Before she was housed, Justine was regularly harassed by security guards and the police for sleeping on the streets. She told me during our interview that she had been kicked by security guards on two separate occasions during the previous summer, when she was still homeless. She had noticed the increasing number of security guards and police officers in the period leading up to the Games, and felt cautious about going out on the streets for fear of police harassment. One of her friends had recently been arrested for writing on an Olympic statue, and Justine, who was with her at the time, was also threatened by police with arrest. Though she reported that she generally felt safe in her new neighbourhood, she found the crowds of Olympic visitors overwhelming.

Olu, in London, experienced the Olympics a bit differently. I first met Olu in 2011, during my first round of London fieldwork. Olu is a Black man who had already spent a year in the supportive housing structure where I was conducting my research. He had moved with his family from Nigeria to the UK at age 8; living in a small council housing flat with his father and brother, he decided to move out at age 23 in order to get some distance from a home situation that was becoming increasingly tense. Just turned 24 when we met, Olu had previously completed a training course in Construction, and had a university degree in Architecture. The level of education Olu had attained was unusual for the youth I worked with, most of whom had left school early and had not completed post-secondary schooling. Despite Olu's credentials and eagerness to find work in his field, he had only been able to secure unrelated jobs that paid minimum wage: in retail, as a temporary postal worker, and eventually as an acquisitions officer for a housing development company. When the Olympics infrastructure began to be built in his neighbourhood, he was excited about the potential work he thought he could find, given his skills and training. He had heard about the Olympic commitments made to employ local people, and to provide training programs for youth. Despite his efforts, nothing materialized. At the time of our first interview, he had just been made redundant from one of his jobs, and was working only six hours a week at another. He had recently discovered that his girlfriend was pregnant, and was concerned about being able to financially support her and their child. When we met again in 2012, the year of the London Olympics, his daughter had been born and he had been able to secure a new retail position for 16 hours a week, at slightly higher than minimum wage. He was beginning to resign himself to the fact that he would never find work in his field, and that the Olympic opportunities he had thought he could take advantage of were not to be.

These are but two stories from almost 200 young people (ages 16–25) with whom I spoke before, during, and after the Olympic Games in Vancouver (2010) and London (2012). The experiences of the youth with housing, employment, and policing in their respective Olympic cities are the major themes explored in the book. The backdrop to these stories is the context of twenty-first century Olympic Games, which, I argue, are increasingly positioned by their boosters as a force that will benefit marginalized populations in host cities. The populations in question include young people and homeless or impoverished residents; where these two categories overlap is my focus. Unfortunately, as the Games draw near, such social legacy goals are shed in light of fiscal constraints, the pressure to complete Games-time construction, and unfavourable policy regimes that make the original goals unrealistic in the short term. Host cities often enjoyed widespread public support for their initial bid, due at least in part to promises regarding economic opportunities, regeneration, and the creation of new housing; but after the Games, they are left with an Olympic legacy that exacerbates inequality, amplifies gentrification, and leaves marginalized residents worse off than before. As rising quantities of public funds are allocated to support the hosting of Olympic Games, it is important to take stock of the commitments that are being made, and how the Olympics actually affect those who are supposed to benefit. As succinctly put by London anti-Olympic organizer Martin Slavin, "the Olympics is a brand that doesn't do what it says on the label" (personal communication, July 19, 2011).

While the emerging Olympic focus on marginalized populations is certainly not the only priority – environmental sustainability has been another key emphasis (Holden, MacKenzie, and Vanwynsberghe 2008) – it is one that has gained prominence in twenty-first century versions of the Games. This comes on the heels of significant controversies – and much negative press – regarding the effects of the Olympic Games on impoverished residents of host cities. Bidding committees recognize this focus, and have made strategic use of this knowledge to craft bids that reflect the IOC's recent commitment to social legacy goals. While this book makes the case that the amplified focus on marginalized populations is in some ways a post-millennial phenomenon, it comes with a history that can be traced back to the origins of the modern Olympics. If we understand the new focus on 'helping the poor' as continuous with past modernization aspirations, it becomes clearer that contemporary Games are working for similar goals as did past ones: to promote specific ideals of a modern society, and to legitimate their purpose as a global event of increasing influence and power. The claims made by Olympic proponents for their wider positive effects have always been difficult to prove, and at times have been blatantly false (for example, when Avery Brundage, later to become the IOC president, asserted that the 1936 Olympics hosted by Nazi Germany had promoted international peace). But what contemporary Games share with past Games is a set of claims about how the Olympics can be used to create a 'better world.' That the post-millennial 'better world' is embedded in neoliberal global formations that promote city marketing and gentrification does not change its continuity with the Olympics' past modernizing aspirations. And as the amount of public money going into Olympic Games increase, so too do efforts to legitimate their existence in the name of helping marginalized populations. In other words, contemporary Olympic Games are engaged in both modernization and legitimation efforts that have their roots in the first modern Games held in Athens in 1896.

The Olympics and youth

The origin of Olympic claims to benefit the young in some ways pre-dates even the Olympic focus on creating a 'better world.' As Olympic founder Baron de Coubertin notes in his memoir, the Olympics are "the quadrennial festival of universal youth" (as cited in Guttmann 2002, 1). While Coubertin's vision for the Olympics was always about athleticism, it was primarily as a means to develop the capabilities and capacities of young people. The most notable twenty-first century version of the Olympic emphasis on youth can be seen in the initiation of a Youth Olympics. First proposed in 2007, the first Youth Olympic Games (YOG) was held in Singapore in 2010. With its stated intention being to "inspire young people around the world to participate in sport and adopt and live by the Olympic values" (as quoted in Wong 2011, 1833), it is the most visible manifestation of a long history of Olympic focus on young people. Less visible but still present have been local organizing committees' efforts to engage young people in various ways, from Olympic Youth Camps held in Atlanta in 1996 (Anglin and Mew 2000) and Athens in 2004 (ATHOC and Athens Organizing Committee for the Games 2005) to the Beijing Olympics commitment to create education programs in China that would engage 400 million youth in learning about the Olympic spirit (BOCOG 2008).

Perhaps the most explicit commitment to impoverished youth to date was made by the London bidding committee, which placed East London young people at the very heart of their campaign. In his closing speech to the IOC in Singapore in 2005, London bid chair Lord Sebastian Coe gestured to the 30 East London youth in the audience – invited there by the bid committee to provide an optic that supported their stated commitment to London's youth – and said: "My heroes were Olympians. My children's heroes change by the month. And they are the lucky ones. Millions more face the obstacle of limited resources, and the resulting lack of guiding role models. Today we offer London's vision of inspiration and legacy. Choose London today and you send a clear message to the youth of the world: More than ever, the Olympic Games are for you . . ." (Campbell 2005). This appeal to young people at the bidding stage has been repeated most recently in efforts to win the 2020 Games: both the failed Madrid bid and the successful Tokyo bid for the 2020 Summer Olympics followed London's lead.

> Games full of passion and enthusiasm, both inspiring and providing opportunities for a whole generation of young people and which will be the light of the future.
>
> (Madrid 2020 Bid, cited in Tomlinson 2014, 149)

> And deliver a dynamic celebration that will help reinforce and renew the Olympic Values for a new generation – and so contribute to more young people worldwide sharing the dreams and hope of sport.
>
> (Tokyo 2020 Bid, cited in Tomlinson 2014, 149)

The perennial Olympic focus on young people has more recently come to be intermixed with increasingly complex articulations of the commitments that bid committees make to urban equality and sustainability. Captured well by the stated intentions of the Inner City Inclusive Commitments Statement (or ICICS), which became part of the bid package for the Vancouver 2010 Olympics, Olympic host cities are linking together their legacy commitments to the welfare and well-being of low-income residents with their commitments to youth. As the Vancouver ICICS states:

> The intent is to maximize the opportunities and mitigate potential impacts in Vancouver's inner-city neighbourhoods from hosting the 2010 Winter Games ... steps will be taken to ensure incorporation of the interests of different groups, such as aboriginal people, women, youth, people with disabilities, people of colour, immigrants and other groups.
>
> (VANOC 2009)

Likewise, London based its bid not only on inspiring young people, but also on regenerating London's East End, encompassing some of the poorest boroughs in the UK. The bid for the 2016 Olympics, hosted by Rio de Janeiro, was organized around four main themes: transformation of the city, social inclusion (with a specific focus on homes, training and jobs), youth and education, and sports (Rio 2016 Candidate City, 2009).

The purpose of this book is to unravel both the claims being made and the actual effects of the Olympics on poor youth, focusing on two recent Olympic host cities. Through a detailed comparative, longitudinal, ethnographic study of homeless and marginally housed young people living in the shadow of the Vancouver 2010 and London 2012 Olympic Games, the chapters that follow illuminate the on-the-ground realities of the marginalized young people who symbolically populate the Olympic bidding efforts of the city's elites. Drawing on interviews, focus groups, photo journals and walking tours with almost 200 youth between 2009 and 2013, the major aim of the book is to investigate the legacy claims made by the Vancouver and London bid committees, and trace such claims in relation to the actual lived experiences of the people who were supposed to benefit from hosting the Olympics. The qualitative research is set alongside detailed critical analyses of policy documents, bidding reports, media accounts, and academic studies. With a focus on housing legacies, employment promises, and policing and security, the book provides a comparative analysis of the promises made by bid committees – and subsequently Olympic organizing committees – and how, if at all, such commitments were realized in the lives of the marginally housed and homeless youth with whom I worked.

The youth and the methods

Over the course of five years, two Vancouver-based research assistants, a UK-based colleague, and I spent an accumulated total of approximately 300 hours conducting interviews, focus groups, walking interviews, and generating photo journals with youth living in the host cities of Vancouver and London. In Vancouver, I was fortunate to be able to hire Trevor White and Christine Meyer as research assistants, who were themselves young people familiar with the populations who are at the heart of this project. In London, I collaborated with

Dr. Paul Watt, an urban studies lecturer from Birkbeck, University of London; together, we co-facilitated the focus groups, interviews, photo journals and walking interviews in the London borough of Newham. Because I did some of the research alone, and some of it in collaboration with research assistants or a colleague, I use both 'we' and 'I' throughout the book when describing interactions with the youth.

In each city, fieldwork was conducted the year before, during, and the year following the Olympic Games. In total, we spoke with approximately 200 young people across five years of fieldwork (100 in each city).[1] Due to the transient nature of this youth population, it was generally not possible to do direct follow up interviews with the same young people year after year, though in London we were able to conduct repeat interviews with eight of the youth participants, giving us the opportunity to track their changing experiences as the Olympics passed through their city.

The youth in each city were similar in some ways and different in others. Both groups shared broad demographic characteristics in terms of age (between 16 and 25), education (most had left school early, and very few had any post-secondary training), as well as difficult relations with their families due to poverty, abuse, and/or trauma. In both cities, minority populations were over-represented among the youth I spoke with; in Vancouver, it was Aboriginal youth who were disproportionately present among the homeless youth, and in London, the majority of youth we worked with were in the category referred to in the UK as 'Black and Minority Ethnic' (or BME). The most significant difference between the two groups was in their housing status: whereas the youth in Vancouver were homeless or temporarily housed in emergency shelters, the youth in London lived in a supportive housing complex that provided them with access to youth workers, employment training, and other life skills supports. Although temporary in nature, designed to be no more than two years in length, the youth were often supported into other forms of housing on concluding their time there. This difference reflects the differing trajectories of housing support and social services in their respective countries; whereas Canada cut its federal program for building affordable housing in the 1990s, the UK retains remnants of a highly developed social housing infrastructure. While the latter is under significant threat, it is noteworthy that the youth in these two Olympic cities had significantly different opportunities and life chances, courtesy of these differing housing regimes. This is emblematic of the fact that the potential for realizing legacy is very much shaped by the pre-existing infrastructure and political commitments of the host country in question.

In a typical fieldwork period we would begin with focus groups, as an opportunity to get a broad sense of the youths' experiences as well as allow them the chance to get to know us and learn more about the project. Focus groups were active and interactive, involving various methods designed to get the young people moving and elicit their opinions and perspectives on a range of issues related to the Olympic Games. For instance, at each focus group we conducted an exercise called 'the thermometer,' which involved reading out an opinion statement and asking the youth to align themselves along an imaginary spectrum between 'agree' and 'disagree.' Statements included, 'My neighbourhood has changed since the Olympics were announced,' and 'I believe that the Olympics will benefit my city.' In this way, youth were encouraged to share their perspectives without feeling that there was one right or wrong answer. The kinetic nature of the activities meant that youth were immediately engaged and not 'checking out' as might be the case in more traditional 'talking circle' focus group designs. I also would bring in relevant films and newspaper articles, and ask the youth for their opinions on the issues raised.

After the focus groups, we passed around sign-up sheets for youth to participate in one-on-one interviews. These semi-structured interviews were designed to access more individual demographic and historical information about the youth, as well as to give us a chance to get more details about their experiences with the Olympics in terms of the availability of housing, volunteer and employment opportunities, and encounters with police and security. In one fieldwork period (2010) in Vancouver, the constraints of the youth shelters with which we worked meant that we conducted only interviews with some of the youth and only a focus group with others, without the opportunity to follow up with the youth. But most of the time, youth had the opportunity to participate in both the focus groups and an individual interview; we paid them a modest honorarium of CDN$20 in Vancouver and £10 in London for their participation in each of a focus group and interview. They earned an additional CDN$20/£10 for completing the photo project.

Three youth in Vancouver completed the photo project in 2009, while 13 youth completed the London photo project in 2011. This disparity in numbers has much to do with the institutional supports in place for the respective youth groups. The youth in London, as described above, were housed in a supportive housing structure that had meeting rooms which we could make use of to conduct the project; because the youth were housed there, it was easy to follow up with them and remind them to attend and submit their cameras for photo development. In Vancouver, I made use of the common room of my housing co-op, where I lived in 2009. This required the youth to travel to me, making it less likely that as many of them would be able or willing to participate in the photo project. Youth in both cities were given disposable cameras and asked to take photos of how their city had been impacted by the Olympics. We collected the cameras when they were done and had the photos developed. We then provided them with markers, glue, and paper, and asked them to put their photos together into a photo journal, adding captions as they thought appropriate. One participant in London opted to use his own digital camera and put together his photo journal using the computers available to him through the supportive housing structure in which he lived. Some of the London participants used the cameras to take photos but did not put them into a photo journal; however, they did participate in the follow up focus group in which they discussed the photos and their meaning. In Vancouver, I conducted one-on-one follow up interviews with the three youth to discuss their photo journals; in London, Dr. Watt and I conducted focus groups with the youth who had completed the photo journals in order to learn more about the photos they had taken and what each meant to them.

In London, we also conducted two walking interviews with four of the youth in 2012 (three participated in one walking interview, one participated in another). We opted not to ask them to do another photo project during the Olympics out of fear that they might be targeted by the police for taking photos of Olympic infrastructure during that period, with its heightened level of surveillance of perceived 'terrorist' threats. During the walking interviews, we asked the youth to take us on a tour of their local neighbourhood. They knew that our project was about the Olympics, and were eager to talk about their experiences in the lead up to and during the Games (the walking tours happened five days after the Opening Ceremonies).

Those unfamiliar with the contours of qualitative research may erroneously suggest that the stories of the young people captured in studies such as this one are simply that: stories, which are inescapably subjective and thus untrustworthy as objective accounts of what actually happened. This is a crass mis-reading of what emerges through qualitative research. The epistemology, or theory of knowledge, which lies beneath this study is highly influenced by the work of Pierre Bourdieu and also by phenomenology. Phenomenological approaches to social research recognize that we as researchers can never produce "a transparent picture of the world, including those worlds inhabited by young people today" (Kennelly and Poyntz 2015, 10). Rather, what we aim to do phenomenologically is achieve "a working-through of the meaning-making resources subjects use to orient and constitute their worlds" (Kennelly and Poyntz 2015, 9). Such a project demands a sensitivity to both the words and the embodied knowledges (accessed in part through methods such as walking interviews and photo journals) expressed by the youth. In drawing on phenomenology, I foreground the experiences of the young people whose voices are patently missing from official Olympic documentation and most other research. But, and importantly, their perspectives are not only about *themselves*; they also provide a unique lens into the larger structures of inequality unfolding around them, in which they are caught and towards which they are responding. By hearing from these youth, then, we gain a set of insights on the Olympic phenomenon that would otherwise be unknowable to those of us who are not young and poor in an Olympic host city.

In keeping with my effort to represent the experiences of young people, I have opted to retain in the excerpts from transcripts some (though not all) of the colloquialisms and language patterns used by the youth. Those familiar with the cadence of the accents in each region will perhaps be able to 'hear' the rhythm of the youths' words, which I find to be poetic in their own right. But those who are not familiar, or perhaps not imaginative enough, might read their words as somehow reflecting an inherent incapacity or lack of insight. This is why I have chosen to 'clean up' their language to a limited extent, in order to enhance the readability of the verbatim quotes, and also in recognition that a transcript can never be a faithful rendering of spoken language. But I have not done so to the extent that the uniqueness of their language gets disappeared, opting to leave in some of the 'innits' and 'you know what I means' from East London, and the 'likes' and 'you knows' from Vancouver. I have also included in each chapter at least one vignette that provides more detail about the lives of individual youth. I do this with some trepidation, concerned that these young people who are already so marginalized will be further dismissed should I not manage to convey the complexity of their stories – and their stories are always complex, and I am never able to do justice to them. But it is important, also, to see into the group called 'youth' here and understand that within this group are individual stories and trajectories. This does not change the sociological weight of their collective experiences, which were broadly similar along a number of themes. But it perhaps will serve to further humanize them and their struggles, against the backdrop of both the Olympic behemoth and the wider context of state disinvestment and apparent disinterest in their well-being.

In addition to the extensive fieldwork with young people before, during, and after the Olympics in each city, I also conducted 'key informant' interviews with people connected either to the Olympics or who worked with young people in each city. These included interviews with civil society actors who were trying to leverage the Games for local benefits; government officials working to implement the Olympic commitments in each city; and support workers who engaged directly with the youth participating in our project. Both key informants and youth were assigned a pseudonym (youth were given the option to choose their own), though in the case of some key informants I sought their permission to use their real names if the statements they were making were already part of the public record (for example, Am Johal of the Impacts of the Olympics on Communities Coalition (IOCC) in Vancouver, Martin Slavin of Games Monitor, and Neil Jameson of London Citizens).

Olympic resistance from the young and the poor

Although the focus of the book is not on anti-Olympic activism (see Boykoff 2014 for an excellent discussion of resistance to the Olympics in Vancouver and London), it is worth noting here some instances of resistance against the Games by impoverished people and youth in both cities. Critical and anti-Olympic organizing has contributed in its own way to the emerging emphasis on Olympic legacies aimed towards assisting marginalized populations and youth, though the specific manner in which these commitments manifest tend to bear little resemblance to the initial justice claims made by community organizations and activists. Examples of this dynamic at work are documented in subsequent chapters of the book; here, I will touch briefly on some of the relevant resistance movements that came from the young and the poor in Vancouver and London.

There were many creative and engaging activist responses to the Olympics in both cities. In Vancouver, the Carnegie Community Action Project, in collaboration with the Vancouver Area Network of Drug Users (VANDU), Raise the Rates, Streams of Justice, and the BC Persons with AIDS Society, put on the Poverty Olympics in 2008, 2009, and 2010 – the last one happening just a few days before the 2010 Winter Games began (Iromoto 2008; Hui 2010). In 2009, the Poverty Olympics introduced their three mascots: Itchy the Bedbug, Creepy the Cockroach and Chewy the Rat (press release for Poverty Olympics 2009). With such poign-antly humorous events as the Welfare Hurdles, the Poverty-Line High Jump, and Long Jumps over Bedbug-Infested Mattresses, the Poverty Olympics highlighted the crisis levels of poverty in the city and the province, as well as the absurdity of hosting a major sporting event in the midst of such inequality. A similar event was hosted by Youth Fight For Jobs in London in 2012. The Austerity Games, as they were called, included a 100 Meter Race to the Bottom, Hardship Hurdles, the Deficit Discus, and the Toss a Tory Shot Put (Boykoff 2014). Both cities also had protest events and rallies in the period leading up to the Games and during the Games themselves (though this was policed with particular ferocity in London, preventing, for example, a Critical Mass bike ride from passing close to the Olympic stadium during the Opening Ceremonies. I stumbled across this as it unfolded, and had the infuriating experience of helplessly witnessing the cyclists being corralled into a double decker bus by police, where they were subsequently held for many hours (for more, see "Arrests in Critical Mass Bike Ride near Olympic Park" 2012; Richards 2013)).

Despite the presence of these events in their community, and the relevance of the issues raised, the majority of youth I worked with did not engage in these anti-Olympic actions; this is due in part to the fact that they were focused primarily on survival without the requisite time and energy for activism. It is also due to the culturally and politically marginalized position occupied by activism and social movements in liberal democracies, where activists are portrayed by mainstream media outlets as rowdy and out-of-control or dismissed as ridiculous, and also where activists increasingly face draconian police responses (Kennelly 2009; 2011). This means that, if youth have not been exposed to the counter-messages available through activist subcultures, that they will likewise see the protests as ineffective or unnecessary, despite the fact that such events were attempting to raise awareness about issues they also had identified as important. This contradic-tion was reflected in responses from youth in Vancouver; most had not attended the protests, and those who did wondered about their effectiveness. They were also concerned about the likelihood of being arrested.

Leila: I don't believe in protesting like that. I don't think that it does very much. Yes, it gets people's voices heard. And their opinions stated but I don't know that it does anything and I don't like the violent aspect to it. And I wouldn't want to get involved in something where I'm going to get in trouble for it.

Charlie: I've gone to a couple of protests. I haven't done anything illegal yet. But I've gone to a couple of protests. I left when the riot squad showed up. [Laughs.] I got the hell out of there.

In London, the youth in 2012 were still feeling the effects of the anti-police riots that had broken out in Tottenham the previous summer, and the police crackdown on anything resembling protests that had then occurred. Although the Austerity Games organized by Youth Fight For Jobs had been held in neighbouring Hackney,

**NO OLYMPICS
ON
STOLEN
NATIVE
LAND
2010
BULLSHEET**

2009 March 27th

Figure i.1 The cover page for Trot's photo journal, created one year before the
Vancouver Olympics.

the youth we spoke with in Newham did not mention participating in these or any
other anti-Olympic events.

Another important locus of resistance to the Vancouver Olympics came from
First Nations communities. One prominent slogan of the anti-Olympics move-
ment in the city was 'No Olympics on Stolen Native Land' (Boykoff 2014); this
same sentiment was captured in Trot's photo journal cover created in 2009 for
this research (see Figure i.1). There was also support for the Games from
Aboriginal communities in BC, reflected in part by the agreement between the
Vancouver Organizing Committee (VANOC) and the Four Host First Nations
Society (FHFN), representing the Lil'wat, Musqueam, Squamish and Tsleil-
Waututh First Nations. While the Vancouver Olympics may have "generated
economic, infrastructural, and cultural opportunities for sanctioned Aboriginal
participants," the VANOC/FHFN relationship also "obscured tensions, uneven
power dynamics and/or structural inequality over time" (Silver, Meletis and Vadi
2012, 303). This confluence of opposition and support resulted in a 'complex
context' in relation to Aboriginal peoples and the Vancouver Winter Olympics
(Silver, Meletis, and Vadi 2012). This complexity was reflected in the experiences
of the youth with whom I spoke, a disproportionate number of whom were

Aboriginal. TomTom told me that her family had participated in the Opening Ceremonies, which featured traditional Aboriginal dancing, and that she and her mother had been able to watch her cousins dancing on television. This was a high-light of the Games for her. However, the remainder of the Aboriginal youth with whom I spoke did not feel that the Olympic Games benefitted themselves or their communities.

Overview of chapters

The first chapter sets the conceptual context for the rest of the book, by tracing the evolution of modernizing and legitimating discourses that have accompanied the modern Olympic Games since 1896. Building on Maurice Roche's (2000) work in *Mega-Events and Modernity*, the chapter outlines how modernization efforts have coincided with Olympic aspirations, and how these modernization efforts have gradually shifted to become a focus on assisting marginalized populations. Such shifts reflect the ramping up of neoliberal pressures on cities to engage in city marketing strategies, techniques which include being perceived as liberal and humanitarian, in order to attract international investment and development. As more public money is spent on the Olympic Games, in pursuit of the neoliberal goal of competing on the global stage, so too do the legitimating discourses increase to justify the Olympic expense and imposition on host city populations.

The chapters that follow draw on the fieldwork with youth living in Vancouver and London before, during, and after the Olympic Games in their respective cities. Chapters 2 and 3 focus on the housing promises made, and then broken, in Vancouver (Chapter 2) and London (Chapter 3), and how these impacted the homeless and marginally housed youth living there. Vancouver's Olympic housing story turned out to be one of temporary emergency shelters, rather than the prom-ised "affordable housing legacy" specified in the Inner City Inclusive Commitments Statement. This reality was reflected by the youth with whom I worked, who found themselves pressured into short term HEAT (Homeless Emergency Action Team) shelters that did nothing to relieve their longer term needs for sustainable housing – though they did serve to 'hide' the rampant homelessness in Vancouver from curious tourists' eyes during the Olympics. London's Olympic housing story was one of gentrification and the displacement of working class populations from East London. Hinging on an important policy shift away from 'social rents' (set at 50% of market rates) and towards 'affordable rents' (set at 80% of market rates), the effect was to make the local housing stock in Newham inaccessible to the youth I worked with. In addition, the youth had been hard hit by substantial cuts to housing and employment benefits introduced by the Conservative-Liberal Democratic coalition as part of austerity measures. The net effect for youth in both cities appears to have been a worsening, rather than an alleviation, of their housing situations.

Another significant claim made by the Vancouver and London Olympic committees was related to the number of jobs that were to be generated by the Olympics. Both cities made explicit commitments to youth employment and jobs for the long-term unemployed and/or inner-city residents. Chapter 4 traces the respective commitments and outcomes in each city, and the experiences of the youth I spoke with there. The year before the Olympics in Vancouver and London, the youth were excited about their job prospects, having heard about the promises that were made regarding jobs and training opportunities. Once the Olympics began, however, they found themselves largely left out of such employment opportunities. Findings from my study suggest that, while *some* young people were able to secure Olympic-related employment during the period immediately before and during the Games, such employment was typically short-term, insecure labour that paid minimum wage. Job opportunities were also significantly gendered; some young men benefitted from opportunities in construction or security, for example, but young women as a group received very few employment opportunities related to the Games. Such a finding is consistent with broader research on employment opportunities for low-income youth, which has found that young women tend to be more precariously employed than young men, and receive less income for their paid work (O'Grady and Gaetz 2004; Klodawsky, Aubry, and Farrell 2006). Such a finding is perhaps not surprising in the context of the neoliberalization of cities, where those at the bottom of the social ladder are hard-pressed to find meaningful work or ways out of poverty; however, it flies in the face of the feel-good rhetoric produced by both bid committees and the International Olympic Committee in terms of legacies of the Games. For example, the IOC published a Vancouver Facts and Figures 'Factsheet' in 2011 which claimed, among other economic benefits, that "Employment in BC was given a bump up in February 2010 according to Statistics Canada. This amounted to 8,300 positions with average weekly earnings, including overtime, of CAD 843.91" (International Olympic Committee 2011). Such broad figures disguise the details of who obtained such employment, what kind of employment was generated, and whether these opportunities were permanent or temporary.

Chapters 5 and 6 turn to the experiences of the youth with policing and security, particularly before and during the Olympics. As noted by Bennett and Haggerty (2011, 5) in a recent volume on the topic, "Security has become an integral part of the Olympic ritual." An increasing body of literature has emerged documenting the intensification of policing and security at the Olympics (Boyle 2011; Yu, Klauser, and Chan 2009) but such accounts remain largely theoretical in nature and do not provide insight into the actual lived experiences of host city populations. Chapter 5 documents the experiences of the youth in Vancouver, who reported a ramping up of interactions with police and private security during the year prior to the Games, but a precipitous drop when the Olympics began. The policing prior to the Games was substantially focused on moving youth out of visible tourist sections of the downtown area and into the Downtown Eastside, the low-income and drug-ravaged neighbourhood that many of them were seeking to escape. The drop in police–youth interactions during the Games was particularly noteworthy given that *15 times* the normal number of policing personnel were on Vancouver's streets, courtesy of the Vancouver Integrated Security Unit (VISU), which brought together military, private security, and federal and municipal police units from across the country. One explanation for this is consistent with the city marketing thesis, whereby the city was attempting to look tolerant and liberal when the global media focus was at its most intense during the Games. In London, the youth were subject to 'dispersal orders' which meant that they were not permitted to be in public spaces in groups of two or more. Such infringements on their civil liberties were met with helpless outrage but also resignation to the fact that policing seemed to be directed towards protecting tourists rather than themselves. A high profile murder of one of their peers at the nearby Westfield mall just prior to the Olympics confirmed for many of them that the police and security which had become a very visible presence prior to the Games were not there for them. Ongoing tensions between police and members of ethnic minority communities, particularly young Black men, were marked among the youth we spoke with; this is consistent with research documenting the disproportionate degree to which young Black men are stopped by the police in London more generally.

The book concludes by revisiting the opening conceptual frame concerning the role of the young and the poor in the Olympics' current versions of modernizing and legitimating discourses. Taking into account the empirical evidence that has been provided throughout the intervening chapters, the concluding chapter considers the implications of unfulfilled legacy commitments and the effects of security and policing for host city populations, especially for young people living at the urban margins. The book concludes with suggestions for future potential host cities to ask of their local governments and bidding committees, to assist in mitigating the problematic effects of future Olympic Games on their host cities. It also concludes with suggestions for future research and directions that academics might take, to build on the existing evidence regarding the actual effects of Olympic Games on host city populations.

Note

1 I use 'approximately' as a caveat here because some of the focus groups involved young people coming and going from the group, making it difficult to provide an exact count. Also, the interviews conducted by my Vancouver research assistants were on audiotape, and where one interview ended and the next one began was not always clear in the transcripts.

Bibliography

All website URLs were accessed between September 2014 and December 2015.
Anglin, Jacqueline, and Tommy Mew. 2000. "Global Village: Art of the Olympic Youth." *School Arts*, 42–43.
ATHOC, and Athens Organizing Committee for the Games. 2005. "Official Report of the XXVIII Olympiad." The Games. Greece. http://library.la84.org/6oic/OfficialReports/2004/or2004b.pdf.
BBC News. 2012, July 28. "Arrests in Critical Mass Bike Ride near Olympic Park." www.bbc.com/news/uk-england-london-19023104.
Bennett, Colin J., and Kevin Haggerty, eds. 2011. *Security Games: Surveillance and Control at Mega-Events*. New York: Routledge.

BOCOG. 2008. "Bid Documents and Analysis: Passion Behind the Bid." Beijing Olympic Games Official Report Volume One. China. http://library.la84.org/6oic/OfficialReports/2008/2008v1.pdf.

Boykoff, Jules. 2014. *Activism And The Olympics: Dissent At The Games In Vancouver And London*. New Brunswick, New Jersey: Rutgers University Press.

Boyle, Philip, and Kevin Haggerty. 2011. "Civil Cities and Urban Governance: Regulating Disorder for the Vancouver Winter Olympics." *Urban Studies* 48 (15): 3185–201.

Campbell, Dennis. 2005. "The Day Coe Won Gold." *The Guardian*, July 10, sec. Sport. www.theguardian.com/uk/2005/jul/10/olympics2012.olympicgames6.

Guttmann, Allen. 2002. *The Olympics: A History of the Modern Games*. 2nd edition. Illinois History of Sports. Urbana and Chicago: University of Illinois Press.

Holden, M., J. MacKenzie, and R. Vanwynsberghe. 2008. "Vancouver's Promise of the World's First Sustainable Olympic Games." *Environment and Planning C: Government and Policy* 26 (5): 882–905.

Hui, Stephen. 2010. "Poverty Olympics to Be Held in Vancouver Days before 2010 Winter Games." *Georgia Straight Vancouver's News & Entertainment Weekly*. January 15. www.straight.com/article-281132/vancouver/poverty-olympics-be-held-vancouver-days-2010-winter-games.

International Olympic Committee. 2011. "Factsheet. Vancouver Facts & Figures." www.olympic.org/documents/games_vancouver_2010/factsheet_vancouver_legacy_february_2011_eng.pdf.

Iromoto, Goh. 2008. "Downtown Eastside's Poverty Olympics." *The Dominion: News from the Grassroots*, March 13. www.dominionpaper.ca/articles/1766.

Kennelly, Jacqueline. 2009. "Good Citizen/Bad Activist: The Cultural Role of the State in Youth Activism." *The Review of Education, Pedagogy and Cultural Studies* 31 (2–3): 127–49.

Kennelly, Jacqueline. 2011. *Citizen Youth: Culture, Activism and Agency in a Neoliberal Era*. New York: Palgrave-MacMillan.

Kennelly, Jacqueline, and Stuart R. Poyntz. 2015. "Introduction: Phenomenology of Youth Cultures and Globalization: Lifeworlds and Surplus Meaning in Changing Times." In *Phenomenology of Youth Cultures and Globalization: Lifeworlds and Surplus Meaning in Changing Times*, edited by Stuart R. Poyntz and Jacqueline Kennelly. New York; London: Routledge.

Klodawsky, Fran, Tim Aubry, and Susan Farrell. 2006. "Care and the Lives of Homeless Youth in Neoliberal Times in Canada." *Gender, Place, and Culture* 13 (4): 419–36.

O'Grady, Bill, and Stephen Gaetz. 2004. "Homelessness, Gender and Subsistence: The Case of Toronto Street Youth." *Journal of Youth Studies* 7 (4): 397–416. doi:http://dx.doi.org.proxy.library.carleton.ca/10.1080/1367626042000315194.

"Press Release for Poverty Olympics 2009." 2009, February 7. Carnegie Community Action Project. https://ccapvancouver.wordpress.com/2009/02/07/be-sure-to-check-out-the-poverty-olympics-on-feb-8th/.

Richards, Tom. 2013, March 18. "How the Met Police Criminalised the Critical Mass Bike Ride." *The Guardian*. www.theguardian.com/environment/bike-blog/2013/mar/18/police-activism.

Rio 2016 Candidate City. 2009. "Candidature File for Rio de Janeiro to Host the 2016 Olympic and Paralympic Games." www.rio2016.com/en/organising-committee/transparency/documents.

Roche, Maurice. 2000. *Mega-Events and Modernity: Olympics and Expos in the Growth of Global Culture*. London: Routledge.

Silver, Jennifer J., Zoë A. Meletis, and Priya Vadi. 2012. "Complex Context: Aboriginal Participation in Hosting the Vancouver 2010 Winter Olympic and Paralympic Games." *Leisure Studies* 31 (3): 291–308. doi:10.1080/02614367.2011.645248.

Tomlinson, Alan. 2014. "Olympic Legacies: Recurrent Rhetoric and Harsh Realities." *Contemporary Social Science* 9 (2): 137–58. doi:10.1080/21582041.2014.912792.

VANOC. 2009. "Vancouver 2010 Bid Report." Vancouver: Vancouver Organizing Committee of the Olympic and Paralympic Games.

Wong, Donna. 2011. "The Youth Olympic Games: Past, Present and Future." *The International Journal of the History of Sport* 28 (13): 1831–51. doi:10.1080/09523367.2011.594687.

Yu, Ying, Francisco Klauser, and Gerald Chan. 2009. "Governing Security at the 2008 Beijing Olympics" 26 (3): 390–405.

1 Modernizing aspirations and legitimation rationales *or* why the Olympics claims to help the young and the poor

The modern Olympic Games have always been about more than amateur sports. Initially existing mainly as a side show to the more popular World Fairs, the Olympics have played a significant role in broader efforts to promote distinctive ideas about society, whether those be aspirations for technological advancement or visions for peace and prosperity in a world teetering on the brink of war (Horne and Whannel 2012; Roche 2000). In *Mega-Events and Modernity,* Maurice Roche (2000) looks back at the twentieth century in order to develop his analysis of modernization in relation to mega-events such as the Olympic Games and World Fairs. Near the end of his book, he poses the question: "As we enter the early part of the twenty-first century, what are some of the main elements of the sociological role played by mega-events in the development of world society in our period?" (Roche 2000, 217). This is the key question to which I offer a partial response in this book. I argue that twenty-first century Olympics are promoting specific ideas of what a 'better world' looks like, continuous with modernization claims from previous Games. What is distinct in the contemporary period is that claims to improve the lives of the young and the poor (among other social legacy goals) are used to win bids; bid commitments are then used to leverage public funds. Public funds are spent to support the Games, while accountability processes to ensure that the legacy promises are fulfilled are notably lacking. In other words, when post-millennial Olympic Games promoters claim that the Olympics will boost employment, provide housing, and help young people at both a local and global scale, they are participating in a modernization discourse that has roots in the past, but also carries distinct qualities, unique to the post-millennial period. One unique quality is the context of neoliberalism; another important piece is the level of public funding now dedicated to the Games.

Neoliberalism, in short, is a political, economic, and cultural rationality that emphasizes self-reliance over dependence on the state, and is attended by a whole suite of policy initiatives designed to prevent or reduce individuals' reliance on state systems such as education, welfare, and health care. It privileges the free market, and glorifies competition as the means to create the best outcome. There is an enormous body of academic literature across a range of disciplines describing and analysing neoliberalism in all of its forms (see, for example, Brown 2005; J. Dean 2009; M. Dean 2012; Harvey 2007; Rose 1999). Within critical Olympic and urban sociological literature, a consensus has emerged regarding the intense pressure that cities are under, generated by neoliberal political and ideological commitments, to compete with one another on the global stage for tourism and investment income (Brenner and Theodore 2011; Peck and Tickell 2002; Vanwynsberghe, Surborg, and Wyly 2013; Short 2008; Horne and Whannel 2012). The Olympics have become the primary hallmark event by which cities attempt to better position themselves within this global competition. Ironically, the post-millennial version of Olympic-driven neoliberalization of cities requires vast expenditures of public money on what is essentially a private venture, taking place in a period of ever-expanding austerity. This is why Jules Boykoff (2014b) has identified the Olympics as the prima facie example of what he calls 'celebration capitalism,' which centrally relies on public investment in private ventures in order to shore up capitalist interests. The Olympics have become "a celebratory spectacle that is more about economic benefit for the few than economic prosperity for the many" (Boykoff 2014b, 2).

The recent Olympic emphasis on social responsibility dovetails with the neoliberal imperative to engage in city marketing, in that cities attempting to attract foreign investment have a stake in appearing liberal and tolerant (McCann 2009). However, the public expenditures on recent Olympic Games have been leaving cities and nations *more* vulnerable financially, as well as resulting in subsequent cuts to social services and other forms of public disinvestment. While the numbers are notoriously difficult to pin down,[1] the Vancouver Olympics were estimated to have cost CDN\$7.7 billion (US\$6.76 billion), of which approximately 60% was covered by various levels of government (Vanwynsberghe and Kwan 2013).[2] This means that approximately CDN\$4.6 billion (US\$4.04 billion) of public funds were dedicated to the Vancouver Games. As a point of comparison, the British Columbia provincial government, the province in which Vancouver is located, budgeted about CDN\$4.6 billion in 2010 for public education (BC Ministry of Education 2010). The London Games are estimated to have cost about £11 billion (US\$17.2 billion), £9.3 billion of which was public money (US\$14.6 billion), or about 85% (Rogers 2012).[3] The public money dedicated to the London Games falls somewhere between the amount spent on the UK Ministry of Justice in 2011–12 (£8.55 billion) and the national cost of policing and security through the Home Office in 2011–12 (£10.1 billion) (Rogers 2012). In contrast, London's 1948 Olympics cost £732,268, or about £20 million (US\$31 million) in today's money (The Economist 2013) – in other words, the 2012 London Games cost about 550 times more than the previous London Olympics. Such staggering sums of public money have significantly shifted the landscape in which contemporary Olympic Games are held, and also the discursive terms that are used to legitimate their existence.

Examining some of the early Olympic modernization claims (pre-1984) will help to historicize contemporary social legacy promises made by Olympics promoters, demonstrating that what we are seeing today has not emerged from nowhere. While early Olympics espoused abstract commitments to peace and global progress, the tone and tenor of Olympic modernization claims shifted substantially with the Los Angeles Games of 1984. Widely identified as a turning point in the history of the modern Games, the 1984 Games were the first Olympics to *not* rely on public funds, and were also the first to bear a significant profit, in large part due to a shift in their broadcasting and corporate sponsorship formulas (Kitchin 2012). The LA Games in 1984 were thus a watershed moment for the Olympic movement, and the effect they had on subsequent Olympics was to re-energize the Games as a profitable venture for certain private interests. Also important in this segment of the Olympic story is the emerging public relations disaster associated with the forced displacement of marginalized residents from host cities (most notably Seoul '88 and Atlanta '96), and the publication of international reports condemning the Olympics' impact on marginalized populations. By the year 2000, we begin to see concrete efforts by the IOC to incorporate social legacy goals into the Olympic movement, setting the stage for the social commitments that went into the bids for the Vancouver and London Games.

The evolution of Olympic modernization efforts

One of the early motivations for the modern Olympics was grounded in Coubertin's desire to ensure that the youth of France would be strong enough to successfully engage in battle with neighbouring Germany. Humiliated by the defeat of the French by the Prussians in 1870, Coubertin became obsessed with ensuring that French youth would receive more vigorous physical education as part of their schooling (Guttmann 2002). This early emphasis on athletics as a means to develop stronger soldiers later gave way to the more widely known early Olympic focus on peaceful internationalism. Coubertin crafted the opening and closing ceremonies of the first Olympic Games, held in Athens, Greece in 1896, to reflect this focus. As Allen Guttmann (2002, 18) notes in his detailed history of the Olympic Games, "The modern games were inaugurated in style, with the ritual and fanfare that Coubertin felt was essential to their social purpose." The specifics of this 'social purpose' were indelibly shaped by the history, geography, and politics of Coubertin's time, reflecting elitist aspirations towards peaceful co-existence that were grounded in a distinctly Western, liberal, individualistic framework with substantial overtones of imperialism. This manifested as a focus on the "[d]evelopment of the sovereign individual, both mentally and physically," which was presumed to result in "the cumulative advancement of humanity" (Real 2010, 222). Coubertin's vision has been widely identified as blind to the contours of social class, race, sexuality, and gender – if not outright exclusionary along these axes – and he presumed as obvious that the colonial powers of Europe would be the leaders in Olympic organizing (Horne and Whannel 2012; Guttmann 2002). He thus selected the first representatives to the inaugural International Olympic Committee (IOC) from among his monied and aristocratic peers.

While Coubertin's belief in the value of athleticism originated in its benefits for young people, another important quality was its connection to nineteenth century chivalry, "as a counter-value to the materialist values of commercialism and the grey egalitarianism of socialism" (Allison 2012, 26). The sporting ethic that motivated Coubertin and the founding of the modern Olympics can perhaps best be summarized by his own poem, entered into a poetry competition at the 1912 Stockholm Games under a pseudonym. The poem begins with the exclamatory "O Sport, delight of the Gods, distillation of life!" and goes on to equate sport with "Beauty . . . Justice . . . Daring . . . Honour . . . Joy . . . Fecundity. . . Progress. . . and Peace" (Allison 2012, 30). This mélange of ecstatic qualities closely matches the ethic of nineteenth century European elites, and the modernization discourses that were prominent at that time. Particularly noteworthy are the twin concepts of 'progress' and 'peace' – these two ideals have recurred throughout Olympic history and continue to echo in contemporary Olympic rhetoric. For instance, the current Olympic charter declares itself as being at the service of "the harmonious development of humankind, with a view to promoting a peaceful society concerned with the preservation of human dignity" (Olympic Charter 2014, 12).

Through both economic necessity and the convergence of shared ideas and goals, the early Olympic Games were closely linked to World Fairs, particularly in 1900, 1904 and 1908 (the second, third, and fourth Modern Olympic Games). It was not until after the Second World War that the Olympics were to become a fully fledged mega-event in their own right (Horne and Whannel 2012). The World Fairs, even more explicitly than the Olympic Games, were designed to promote a modernist vision of society that saw technological advancement as inevitable, and inevitably beneficial, and promoted a social Darwinist narrative of progress that understood white European and North American society as being at the pinnacle of social evolution. Non-white cultures were positioned as the 'savage other' against which the thousands of World Fair attendees might measure their own superiority. This was most evident through the inauguration of 'Anthropology Days' as a central part of the Olympic Games that were associated with the early World Fairs. The St. Louis World Fair in 1904 and its Olympic Games staged 'Anthropology Days' that organized 'races' between members of the ethnic groups who were part of the 'living displays' at the World Fair, and European and American athletes. The ostensible goal of such a repulsive exhibition was to measure "the performances of 'savages' against 'civilised' men" (Horne and Whannel 2012, 89). To be fair, Maurice Roche (2000) argues that these 'human displays' were neither approved nor appreciated by Coubertin and others involved in the Olympic movement. Roche suggests that the 'Anthropology Days' may have been part of the reason that the Olympics were separated from World Fairs in subsequent iterations. However, the next Olympic Games were associated with the Franco–British Exhibition in 1908, held in London; Coubertin was the central advocate and organizer for these Games. Though they did not include the controversial 'Anthropology Days,' the Exhibition was still "structured around an imperial ideology of civilisation, brought to savage peoples, for their betterment" (Horne and Whannel 2012, 94).

Other modernizing aspects of the early Olympic Games are associated with their form. The rationalization and bureaucratization of the Games under

Coubertin's leadership reflected emerging ideas about modernity at the turn of the twentieth century, with a focus on systematization, institutionalization and quantification. The very establishment of an international sporting body was the beginning of globalizing processes that continue to echo today – some of the first international bodies were sports-related ones, including the IOC (Horne and Whannel 2012). After the First World War, the IOC sought to associate itself with the League of Nations, seeing in it a comparable international association that was attempting to create order out of the chaos that had preceded and then been exacerbated by the First World War (Roche 2000). This form of association continues today, as the IOC was granted special observer status at the United Nations' General Assembly in 2009 in recognition of their efforts to "achieve common human rights goals" (Dahill 2010, 1134).

As sports underwent an internationalization and modernization process at the beginning of the twentieth century, largely at the behest of the IOC, it was matched by the rapid development of transport and communication systems, particularly radio in the 1920s (Roche 2000). This convergence of events provided the fodder from which grew an ever-expanding national and international interest in large sporting events. It also laid the groundwork for the evolution of the Olympic Games into a powerful venue for promoting nationalist propaganda. The potential for this first became apparent in the so-called 'Nazi Games' of 1936, which were used unabashedly to demonstrate the strength and organizational capacity of the German Nazis under Hitler. The fact that the Nazis suspended certain aspects of their institutionalized racism in order to permit Black and Jewish athletes (from other countries) to compete prompted Avery Brundage, who would be elected IOC president in 1952, to state that "once again this great quadrennial celebration has demonstrated that it is the most effective influence toward international peace and harmony yet devised," and that it had succeeded in "fulfilling the vision of its founder, Baron Pierre de Coubertin" (as quoted in Guttmann 2002, 70).

Alongside modernizing aspirations connected to promoting Western ideals of internationalism, peace and progress has come a somewhat puzzling insistence by Olympic proponents that the Games are in no way political. A quote from Avery Brundage in 1937 is characteristic of this position: "[I]t is difficult to keep the public clear on the point that politics have no part in the Olympic movement" (as quoted in Guttmann 2002, 73). He makes this statement in the context of the awarding of the 1940 Games to Japan, in the face of Japan's ruthless imperialist expansion into China. (Japan would ultimately withdraw from hosting the Olympics, in order to focus on its military expansion; the 1940 Games, which had been hastily reorganized to take place in Finland, would be cancelled in 1939 after the Germans invaded Poland and the Soviet Union invaded Finland.) The IOC's consistent denial of political involvement flies in the face of the overtly political motivations that inspired the Games from the beginning, and can only be seen as genuine if 'political' is understood in its narrowest and most particular sense. Olympic historian Allen Guttmann (2002, 4) puts the point succinctly: "[T]he Olympics have, indeed, been what their founders wanted them to be: political. To lament the 'intrusion of politics into the world of sports' is naïve."

The current IOC President, Thomas Bach, seems to have taken this critique to heart. Since taking office in 2013, he has spoken out about the importance of recognizing the relationship between politics and sport. However, he continues to insist that the goal of the Olympic Movement is to remain 'neutral' – an assertion that realigns him with Avery Brundage's earlier position that 'politics have no place in sports' (Dorsey 2014).

The political aspirations of not only the IOC but also of athletes and participating countries have had significant consequences over the years. Three events in the period between the Second World War and the LA Games of 1984 highlight how the Olympics has been explicitly implicated in political processes, from the level of the IOC, to actions by competing nations, to the athletes themselves. The first example is the IOC's opposition to South African apartheid throughout the 1960s, 70s and 80s; the second is the Black Power salute made by American athletes Juan Carlos and Tommie Smith from the podium of the Mexico City Games of 1968; and the third is the boycotting of the Moscow and Los Angeles Olympics by their respective Cold War enemies.

In 1964, during its 62nd session, the IOC voted to suspend the South African Olympic Committee (SANOC) on the basis that the South African government's policy of racial discrimination contravened the core Olympic principles of inclusion and respect for human dignity. This decision coincided with a gradual and intentional expansion of the 'Olympic movement' into newly independent African countries, an effort that was actively supported by IOC president Avery Brundage (Guttmann 2002). These initiatives have arguably resulted in a mixed legacy – on the one hand, efforts by the IOC to this day have sought to make Olympic sports more accessible to impoverished African countries; on the other hand, the definition of sports remains insistently Western, with little to no recognition of regionally specific athletic practices (Real 2010). That aside, the boycotting of South Africa by the IOC was a significant act in the cultural isolation of South Africa during the apartheid era, and represented "an important denial of international recognition to a racist state" (Roche 2000, 203). The boycott was vehemently resisted by Avery Brundage, who ultimately conceded to it in the face of international and activist pressure (Boykoff 2014a).

In 1968, the Mexico City Summer Olympics were preceded by a police massacre of unarmed student protesters in the Plaza de las Très Culturas in the Tlatelolco section of Mexico City. The students had made the link between the escalating poverty in Mexico and the expense of the Olympic Games, and raised chants like 'Justice, yes! Olympics, no!' (Lenskyj 2000; Shaw 2008). When African-American athletes Tommie Smith and John Carlos won the gold and bronze medals, respectively, for the 200-meter race, they used their visibility on the podium to signal their opposition to racism in the United States and their solidarity with the slain Mexican students (Shaw 2008). As Jules Boykoff (2014a, 45–6) notes:

Their choreographed symbology pointed to the macrosocial issues they wished to address. Their shoeless feet and black socks represented poverty.

The black scarf and gloves signified black pride. Carlos's open jacket symbolized the working class that included his parents. Around their necks they wore beads that represented their African heritage as well as thick strings signifying the ropes of lynching in the US South. They sported human rights pins on their coats and were joined by silver-medal-winning Australian Peter Norman who wore a political button in solidarity.

Smith and Carlos raised black-gloved fists during the playing of the American national anthem, generating an image that has become iconic in the intervening decades. The event outraged Avery Brundage and members of the IOC, who summarily evicted Smith and Carlos from the Athlete's Village and from the Games themselves (Shaw 2008).

In 1974, when Moscow was awarded the 1980 Olympics by the IOC, forty US congressional representatives protested (Guttmann 2002). When the Soviet Union threatened to intervene in Afghanistan in 1979, US President Jimmy Carter's response was to present the following ultimatum: "Soviet withdrawal from Afghanistan or an American boycott of the 1980 Summer Games" (Guttmann 2002, 150). President Carter persuaded other countries to follow suit, including Canada, West Germany, Israel, Japan, and the People's Republic of China. In the end, 62 nations boycotted the Moscow Games while 81 participated, resulting in far fewer athletes attending the Games than at each of the previous three Olympics (Guttmann 2002). In a direct tit-for-tat response to the Moscow boycott, the Soviet Union and sixteen of its allies stayed away from the 1984 Olympics hosted by Los Angeles, while 140 teams attended (Guttmann 2002).

As these examples demonstrate, political goals are inextricable from Olympic organizing at all levels, though the notion of the Olympics as a political vehicle has been vehemently denied by its proponents. Since the inception of the modern Olympics in 1896, aspirations to create a better world have been a central aspect of Olympic goals. Early versions of this focused on peaceful co-existence, following a specifically Western, liberal, and individualized notion of how this ought to be understood. This peaceful co-existence was not extended to colonized and racialized 'others' such as those subject to scrutiny in the 'Anthropology Days.' Imperial logics and the dynamics of colonialism were deeply embedded in the early Olympic project. Peace and progress were envisioned as an outcome of orderly institutions and internationalization, reflected in the IOC's own organizational form. Internationalization combined with technological advances to set the stage for the large-scale promotion of nationalist ideals, such as occurred under Hitler's leadership at the 1936 Berlin Games. The IOC imposed a boycott of South Africa because their apartheid policies were a blatant breach of Olympic rules (Guttmann 2002). At each moment of political intervention, the IOC drew on its position as a global body to shape the world in a manner that matched its aspirations – specifically, its particular ideas of what 'peace' and 'progress' might look like. Nations and athletes have likewise made use of the Olympics as a political platform to generate social change, or to shape the world as they think it ought to be. Sometimes these efforts are aligned with broader social movements and *have* created a better world – that is, a world that is more just and equitable (for instance, the anti-apartheid boycott of South Africa). But at other times Olympic interventions have served to exacerbate inequalities. This is particularly true in the period after the LA Games of 1984.

From corporatization to homeless expulsions: Los Angeles 1984 to Atlanta 1996

Los Angeles was the only city to bid for the 1984 Olympic Games. Compare this to the most recent bidding competition: six cities submitted a bid for the 2020 Games, which were ultimately awarded to Tokyo. The London and Vancouver Games, which are the focus of this book, had nine cities and eight cities respectively submitting a bid. But at the time of the selection process for the 1984 Olympics, cities willing to take on the costs and controversies of the Games were scarce. What has changed between then and now?

It is widely agreed that cities were reluctant to host the 1984 Olympics as a direct result of what Tomlinson (2014) calls the 'M crises': – Mexico 1968, where government forces had massacred student protesters ten days before the Olympics; Munich 1972, during which Palestinian terrorists murdered eleven Israeli athletes in the Olympic Village; Montreal 1976, which resulted in a debt so large that it took the City of Montreal 30 years to pay it off; and Moscow 1980, with its US-led anti-communist boycott. After a decade of controversial, expensive, and deadly Olympic Games, it is no surprise that cities kept their bidding committees at home by the time the 1984 Games were to be awarded.

Because LA was the only city to bid, they were able to make demands of the IOC that would otherwise have been ignored. One such was a unique agreement stating that the city would not be responsible for any fiscal deficit accrued with the Games. LA also amended their city charter so that no public money could be spent on the Olympics. This set the stage for what came to be known as the 'entrepreneurial Games,' and significantly shifted the conditions for Olympic host cities for decades to come (Boykoff 2014b; Burbank, Andranovich, and Heying 2001).[4] The LA Games represented an about-face in terms of profitability, generating a US$225 million surplus (Burbank, Andranovich, and Heying 2001). They also provided a validation to neoliberal policies that Ronald Reagan made substantial use of during his 1984 presidential campaign (Gruneau and Neubauer 2012). Most of this profitability has been attributed to their privatized model that drew substantially on corporate sponsorship, but it is important to highlight that the LA Games, despite the rhetoric, *did* ultimately draw on public funds, specifically for transport infrastructure, policing, and security (Horne and Whannel 2012).

Nonetheless, the spectre of inevitable Olympic debt for host cities was dissipated with the hosting of the LA Games; this opened the door to ever more competitive bidding processes for subsequent Olympics, a trend that continues to this day. It also set the conditions for a new kind of modernization discourse to come to the fore in Olympic rhetoric: the efficacy of a free market, capitalist approach to managing mega-events.

The trumpeting of capitalism was a somewhat unexpected turn for the Olympic movement to make, though in hindsight it may seem inevitable. Prior to the LA Games, the IOC had expressed a distinct distaste for the trappings of capitalism, particularly in the form of corporatization. Both Baron de Coubertin and later Avery Brundage were clear in their disdain for the role of money in sporting, seeing it as polluting the purity of amateur athleticism which laid at the heart of their vision for the Games (Mcfee 2012).[5] When the LA Olympic organizing committee developed a scheme requiring all bidders for television rights to submit a refundable US$500,000 deposit, IOC President Lord Killanin reprimanded them for acting in a manner that contravened the Olympic spirit (Boykoff 2014b). But by this time the tide had turned, and capitalist ideals of free market entrepreneurialism had a firm hold on the Olympic movement.

Alongside this capitalist turn emerged another key concept that is now so tightly entwined with Olympic rhetoric that it is hard to imagine the Olympics without it: legacy. Alan Tomlinson (2014) traces the emergence of this concept, noting that its first use in the context with which we now associate it took place in LA in 1984, at the IOC meeting held there on the eve of the Summer Olympics. It was Frank King, chairman of the 1988 Winter Olympics in Calgary, who made a solemn pledge to ensure a positive legacy of the Games, specifically with reference to "Olympic facilities fully paid for" (as cited in Tomlinson 2014, 138). This emerging focus on legacy, while still at this point referring to Olympic infrastructure and financing, also marks the beginning of the shift towards concepts of social sustainability that have become so integral to post-millennial Olympics and their bidding competitions. John Horne (2012, 38) denotes the importance of the rhetorical device of 'legacy' to considering social consequences of the Games: "Legacy is a warm word, sounding positive, whereas if we consider the word 'outcomes' it is a more neutral word, permitting the discovery of both negative and positive outcomes."

The success of the Los Angeles Games happened too late to effectively shape the bidding process for the 1988 Summer Olympics, which went to Seoul, Korea. Only one other city bid for those Games in the 1981 bidding competition. But by the time decisions were being made for the 1992 Olympics, the success of LA was beginning to manifest. Six cities submitted bids for those Summer Olympics, which were ultimately awarded to Barcelona. Since that time, the bidding process has become ever more competitive, with a high of eleven cities bidding for the 2004 Games, awarded to Athens.[6]

The Summer Olympics in Seoul, Korea, inadvertently played an important role in the evolution of Olympic modernizing discourses towards a focus on marginalized peoples and social responsibility. It did so through its *disregard* for such concerns. As documented in a report published by the Centre on Housing Rights and Evictions (COHRE 2007), Seoul forcibly evicted 720,000 people to make way for Olympic venues.[7] Seoul's city beautification campaign, which was undertaken specifically to prepare the city for the arrival of the Olympic Games and its associated Western tourists and media, was condemned by the UN Habitat conference in 1987 as "one of the world's most physically violent and brutal housing relocation policies" (COHRE 2007, 79). Conducted in order to 'Westernize' the city so as to attract international financial investment and enhance tourism and service industries (COHRE 2007), Seoul used the presence of the Olympics as an added leverage to undertake a larger project of urban transformation (Davis 2011). In other words, the displacement of Seoul residents might have occurred without the Olympics being present, but the hosting of the Games spurred the Korean government on to more ambitious relocation projects, amplifying the human rights disaster that ensued.

The 1992 Olympics, in Barcelona, Spain, were marginally better – at least in the sense that they did not perpetuate quite the whole-scale human rights abuses that had taken place in Seoul. But they still resulted in widespread displacement of marginalized populations, particularly Roma communities, in and around the Olympic venues and related infrastructure. They also created gentrification so rapid and intense that low-income earners were forced to leave the city, leaving an elite, high-income core of neighbourhoods around the former Olympic venues (COHRE 2007).

The Barcelona Olympics were held under the auspices of IOC President Antonio Samaranch, himself a member of the Spanish elite, and a keen supporter of bringing a more financialist perspective to the Olympics (Boykoff 2014b). Indeed, some felt that it was no coincidence that Barcelona won the Olympics under Samaranch's leadership, quietly whispering of undue favouritism (Guttmann 2002). Although the Barcelona Games are often touted as a model for urban redevelopment (see for example Gold and Gold 2010), such approbation disregards the fact that 624 families were dislocated, directly or indirectly, by Olympic development; the majority of these were of Roma ethnicity, and were thus already substantially marginalized within the city (COHRE 2007). The coming of the Olympics to Barcelona worsened their circumstances, often displacing them to neighbourhoods with less services and amenities, as well as leaving them vulnerable to increased hostility from communities that were not interested in welcoming Roma into their midst. While the displaced families were offered alternative housing or compensation, there was no mechanism for citizen participation in the decision-making process; citizens were regarded as "passive subjects, who were expected to accept the urbanisation process established by technicians and politicians" (COHRE 2007, 112). Combined with the gentrification effects of the Olympic redevelopment, the Barcelona Olympics succeeded in making Barcelona friendlier for tourists, but less accommodating for marginalized peoples living within its boundaries.

When the Olympics returned to the United States in 1996, it resulted in a notable convergence between corporate capitalism and the displacement of marginalized populations. Impressed by the success of the LA Games, the city of Atlanta sought the 1996 Olympics in an effort to boost its national and global reputation (Burbank, Andranovich, and Heying 2001). It had stiff competition from other cities, including Greece which was the sentimental favourite for this centennial of the first modern Olympic Games. But Atlanta won out on the strength of its being one of the birthplaces of the American Civil Rights movement, and also on the technological advantage offered by, for instance, CNN being headquartered in the city (Burbank, Andranovich, and Heying 2001). It also didn't hurt that Coca Cola, an Olympic sponsor since 1928, had its head offices in the city. Indeed, the IOC was criticized for choosing television rights and corporate sponsorship over tradition and heraldry when it selected Atlanta over Greece for the 1996 Summer Games (Guttmann 2002).

The Atlanta Olympics, when they ultimately happened in 1996, were critiqued for what was perceived as their crass commercialism as well as for their negative effects on marginalized populations within the city (Gold and Gold 2010). Criticism was such that then-President of the IOC Antonio Samaranch withheld his traditional congratulatory statement at the end of the Games, where he typically declared them 'the best games ever.' One of the most substantial public critiques of the Games related to the treatment of poor and homeless populations in the city of Atlanta. The headline of a widely cited newspaper article published by the New York Times on July 1, 1996 declared that the 'homeless are not feeling at home in Atlanta' (Smothers 1996). Atlanta officials quoted in the article stated that there had been no city policy to eject homeless people from the city, conveniently forgetting, perhaps, the ordinances passed in 1991, one year after Atlanta won the Olympic bid. These ordinances made it illegal for 'suspicious-looking' people to be in a parking lot without having a car there, to beg 'aggressively,' or to enter vacant buildings (Quesenberry 1996). These anti-homeless municipal policies resulted in 9,000 arrest citations issued to homeless people in Atlanta in 1995 and 1996 (COHRE 2007). The Centennial Olympic Park, built from US$50 million in private corporate funding, replaced three homeless shelters (which had held 10% of the city's shelter beds) and one large single occupancy hotel, previously used as housing for low-income people (Quesenberry 1996). The renovation of Woodruff Park, a favoured gathering place for homeless people in Atlanta, further redeveloped the city in favour of tourists over local homeless populations. Populated with benches designed to prevent people from lying down, intermittent sprinklers, and a lack of public washrooms, the park was clearly designed to prevent homeless people from making further use of it (Burbank, Andranovich, and Heying 2001). But perhaps the most infamous decision made by the city of Atlanta came in the form of a program non-ironically called 'Homeward Bound,' which offered one-way tickets out of town to homeless people who signed a statement declaring that they would never return (Quesenberry 1996; AP: Duluth News-Tribune 1996). The spectre of 'homeless busses' resonates to this day; even the hint of a similar policy surrounding Olympic Games is eagerly sought out by media outlets seeking a spectacular story.[8]

One of the other major negative effects of the Atlanta Olympics on the city's poor came in the form of the destruction of 2,000 public housing units, resulting in the displacement of nearly 6,000 residents (COHRE 2007). The Techwood/ Clark Howell public housing project was the oldest in the United States before being bulldozed to make room for the Olympic Village dormitories designed to house the athletes. The dormitories later became a mixed-income gated community; the destruction of this public housing thus resulted not only in the displacement of its largely Black and poor residents, but also fundamentally changed the character of the neighbourhood (Burbank, Andranovich, and Heying 2001; Vale and Gray 2014). This was the explicit end goal of the redevelopment, justified by the hosting of the Olympic Games. As then CEO of the Atlanta Housing Authority stated in later reminiscence:

> These things are fortuitous, or sometimes you can say they are God-ordained, or however you want to put it, but with the Olympic dormitories being right across the street [from Techwood], it "wasn't no prettyin' it up"; you couldn't have painted it enough or locked it down enough. It was just right there. All of the world's TV cameras were going to be there. You couldn't help but ask, "Well I know we're here at the Olympics but what the heck is all that over there?" So something had to be done.
>
> (As quoted in Vale and Gray 2013, 10)

The destruction of Techwood/Clark Howell was only the beginning; the U.S. Department of Housing and Urban Development (HUD) ultimately helped to "finance a dramatic change in the landscape of public housing in Atlanta" (Burbank, Andranovich, and Heying 2001, 118). Burbank, Andranovich, and Heying (2001) note that one of the major 'Olympic legacies' in terms of housing in Atlanta has been substantial physical improvements in the housing landscape, but at the cost of the displacement of an estimated 16,000 of the city's lowest-income residents. The Centre for Housing Rights and Evictions, which conducted its own independent study of the effects of the Olympics on housing in Atlanta, puts the number even higher. They conclude that "approximately 30,000 poor families and other individuals, [were] forced from their homes by Olympic gentrification, the demolition of public housing, rental speculation, and continuing urban renewal" (COHRE 2007, 113).

The social history of the Olympic Games since LA 1984 has been matched by an evolving set of discourses produced in official Olympic documents. A close examination of the post-Olympic official reports of each host city from 1984 onwards reveals a significant rhetorical shift towards social responsibility and the protection of marginalized populations.[9] This shifting emphasis involves a move away from abstract promises of peace and development through sport and towards specific commitments to protect marginalized populations from displacement and ensure social legacies for host communities. Also apparent is an ongoing rhetorical commitment to children and youth. Tomlinson's (2014) point about the emergence of 'legacy' as an Olympic keyword since the 1988 Games in Calgary is a piece of this story. 'Legacy' appears ten times in the text of Volume 1 of the Official Report of the Calgary Games, known as the XXV Olympiad (Calgary Olympic Organizing Committee 1989). Its use in the Calgary official report is generally reserved for references to athletic and sporting legacies, as well as the obligatory abstract legacy of "the seeds we sow in the hearts of our children" (1989, 5). The report also notes that "the Games are a modern mega-project in both economic and social terms" (1989, 5). This signals the emergence of a focus on social impacts that is tightly connected to the notion of 'legacy.' The Summer Games, held in Seoul in the same year, generated an official report that noted 'legacies' six times, but with a much stronger emphasis on the traditional modernization discourses of peace and progress (Seoul Olympic Organizing Committee 1989). One irony of the Seoul official report is the claim to have brought "diverse peoples [together] in an atmosphere of harmony" (1989, 46) without any mention of the 720,000 residents who were displaced by the Games.

'Legacy' recedes somewhat in the official reports of Barcelona and Albertville, hosts to the 1992 Summer and Winter Olympics, respectively (COOB 1992; Organizing Committee of the XVI Olympic Winter Games of Albertville and Savoie 1992). Lillehammer, host to the Winter Olympics in 1994 (the first Winter Games to be held separately from the Summer Games, as the IOC switched from a four-year cycle to a two-year cycle), makes no mention of legacy, and has very little to say about the social impacts of the Games (Lillehammer Olympic Organizing Committee 1994). But the official report for Atlanta 1996 marks a significant shift. With a whopping 61 references to 'legacy' in Volume 1, the report prefigures future emphases on social responsibility and commitments to marginalized populations (ACOG 1996). As with Seoul, the irony here is that Atlanta has become known as the Games that had one of the worst impacts on marginalized communities. Given that the official reports were written after the Games happened – and after the worst of the media attention had already occurred – it is possible that the writers of the official report were attempting to recoup Atlanta's battered reputation after the fact. Equally likely, on the other hand, is that the 'official version' of events has an official blindspot to the negative impacts of the Games, as Olympic boosters are unable or unwilling to concede that the Olympics have been bad for marginalized residents in their city. For instance, when making reference to the Techwood/Clark Howell public housing project, the report manages to erase the fact of the destruction of this community:

> When the US Housing and Urban Development Department announced it would provide a redevelopment grant to the Atlanta Housing Authority for Techwood and Clark-Howell Homes, one of the nation's oldest public housing projects . . . ACOG saw the opportunity to link the site of the Olympic Village with the GWCC and Omni Coliseum through the creation of a park. The area would include a large gathering place for the Games. A smaller park would remain as a legacy of the 1996 Games.
>
> (ACOG 1996, 81)

The phrasing here implies that Techwood/Clark Howell was 'redeveloped' (rather than destroyed), and that the residents subsequently had access to a lovely park as a 'legacy.' Likewise, in discussing the issue of displacement, the report fails to mention the closing of three homeless shelters and instead states that "a major success story was the relocation of the Sheltering Arms Day Care Center from within the park area to a site less than two blocks away" (ACOG 1996, 82).

And of course nowhere in the report does it mention the 9,000 arrest citations issued to homeless residents of Atlanta in 1995 and 1996 (COHRE 2007).

The Nagano Winter Games of 1998 make few references to legacy, and fewer still to the notion of supporting marginalized populations – though, like every official report, they make an abstract promise to "inspire grand dreams in children – who are our future – and foster in them an understanding of the importance of peace" (Nagano Olympic Organizing Committee 1998). It is with the Sydney Games of 2000 that the commitments to marginalized populations returns, in force. The section below explores what I am calling the 'post-millennial Games' and the emergence in the twenty-first century of Olympic claims to help the young and the poor.

Post-millennial Games: Olympic interventions for the young and the poor

As the twentieth century gave way to the twenty-first, the discourse of positive social legacy became increasingly enshrined in Olympic documentation. In 1999, the IOC adopted the Olympic Movement *Agenda 21: Sport for Sustainable Development*, which incorporated commitments to combat social exclusion, including fighting poverty and integrating disadvantaged groups (Rolnik 2009). In 2002, the Olympic Charter was amended by the IOC to formally incorporate the concept of 'legacy,' emphasizing the importance of leaving a positive legacy for the host city and country (Tomlinson 2014). In 2006, the Torino Winter Games developed a 'Charter of Intent' as one of its 'Olympic legacies'; the Charter established the "ethical, social, and environmental principles to be followed in implementation of the Olympic Programme" (Torino Organizing Committee of the Olympic Games 2006, 49). The Torino Organizing Committee intended for this Charter to be used by future Olympic Games organizers. It is clear that the notion of social rights and protections have increasingly come to the forefront of Olympic rhetoric; but why?

The high profile displacements of marginalized communities during and prior to the Olympics in Seoul 1988 and Atlanta 1996 created a public image problem for the Olympic Games. It also generated critical interest in the negative social impacts of the Olympics, resulting in the Centre on Housing Rights and Evictions (COHRE) report of 2007. COHRE was a non-profit organization located in Geneva, Switzerland, not far from Lausanne, where the International Olympic Committee is housed. It closed in 2012. Before its closing, it played a significant role in promoting the human right to housing internationally and raising awareness about forced displacements throughout the world. COHRE staged a workshop on the issue of mega-events and displacement in June 2007, which was attended by the UN Special Rapporteur on housing (Rolnik 2009). From this flowed the publication of the 2009 annual report of the UN Special Rapporteur on housing, who at that time was Raquel Rolnik. The report focuses on mega-events and their impacts on housing in host cities; it suggests that the IOC has taken some important steps to protect host cities from the negative social impacts of hosting the

Olympics, but that they have not yet gone far enough. Specifically, the report notes that "the bidding and selection process offers many opportunities for addressing the right to adequate housing at an early stage," but the commitment to housing does not appear in the letters of guarantee, host city contracts, or the Rules of Conduct applied to cities wishing to organize the Olympic Games (Rolnik 2009, 15). In other words, cities are strongly encouraged to incorporate commitments to marginalized communities when they are attempting to win the Olympics, but no mechanisms are in place to ensure that such commitments are enacted.

One initiative undertaken by the IOC that may have been intended to remedy this deficit is the recent introduction of the Olympic Games Impact (OGI) reports, required of host cities since the 2008 Beijing Olympics (Dubi and Felli 2006). Rob Vanwynsberghe, the academic lead on the Vancouver OGI, suggests that the role of the OGI is to contribute "towards a framework for measuring whether or not bids translate into hosting efforts that represent positive social change towards sustainability" (2015, 3), where 'sustainability' here refers to social, environmental, and economic issues. Through his experience conducting the Vancouver OGI, he concluded that a key element missing from the assessment process is a "standard of acceptability" that would indicate if and when the Games were fulfilling a positive social role in terms of legacy; he also points out that the current OGI Technical Manual "does not outline how host context can be incorporated into data analysis and interpretation" (2015, 7). In other words, the social impact of a Games, which is tightly linked to pre-existing conditions in the host city and country, cannot be adequately measured if the pre-existing context of the host is not taken into account. He also notes that other researchers have suggested that the OGI measures, being quantitative in nature, do not capture the qualitative experiences of local residents impacted by the Games. The OGI, whether effective as a measurement tool or not, is part of the over-arching shift towards social legacy goals within the Olympic movement. While it is designed to measure such impacts, it is not, in itself, a mechanism to ensure that such commitments are met.

While the rhetoric of social legacy has been enshrined in Olympic documentation since the turn of the millennium, its incorporation into post-millennial Olympic Games has been uneven to date. The Sydney Summer Games actually pre-figured the Olympic emphasis on social responsibility, incorporating into their 1992 candidature files explicit commitments to integrating indigenous peoples, engaging different cultural communities, and employment and training programs for the long-term unemployed (Minnaert 2012). This is likely due to the negative public relations generated by the poor treatment of homeless and marginalized populations in Atlanta and Seoul. By the time of Sydney's 1992 bid, the impacts of Seoul's displacement policies were widely known. When the 2000 Games occurred, the failures of Atlanta were fresh in the minds of Olympic organizers; this may have been the motivation for the establishment of a *Homelessness Protocol*, introduced during the Sydney Olympics and designed to "ensure that homeless people on 'Olympics Live Sites' in the Sydney central business district and surrounding precincts were treated sensitively and appropriately" (New South

Wales Department of Community Services 2003). The *Homelessness Protocol* was revised and expanded in 2003 and continues to be in use, prompting Olympics scholar Lynn Minnaert to identify it as "a lasting legacy of the Sydney 2000 Olympics for socially excluded persons in the host community and wider region" (Minnaert 2012, 369).

Not all agree, however. As Helen Lenskyj (2002) points out, additional laws were passed in Sydney in 1999 to facilitate the removal of homeless peoples and others deemed to be 'disorderly' from public spaces. *The Homebush Bay Operations Regulation 1999* dramatically extended police powers and also gave powers to those authorized by the Olympic authority at the Homebush Bay Olympic site. Those so authorized were permitted to remove anyone who contravened the regulation, trespassed or caused an "annoyance or inconvenience" within the site (Lenskyj 2002, 55). The COHRE (2007) report identifies the Sydney Olympics as part of the New South Wales government's efforts to cast Sydney as a 'world class' or 'global' city, and points out that the Olympics were used to fast-track urban development that resulted in rapid gentrification and the escalation of housing costs in Sydney, effectively reducing the access of low-income people to affordable housing within the city.

The Salt Lake City Winter Olympics of 2002 had neither an explicit focus on social legacy commitments, nor a measurable positive social legacy; there were, however, some minor initiatives directed towards youth and the homeless (Minnaert 2012). The Athens Summer Olympics of 2004 incorporated social and environmental legacy commitments into their bid (ATHOC, and Athens Organizing Committee for the Games 2005), though much of their bid was focused on the 'legacy' of returning the Olympics to its birthplace and the subsequent effects on Greek pride (Karamichas 2012). The main emphasis of the Greek bid was on infrastructural legacy, which was then presumed to benefit local Greeks' quality of life (Minnaert 2012). One of their infrastructure commitments was to social housing, which would be accommodated by the Athlete's Village; the legacy of that commitment has been mixed, as residents have raised frustrations about the lack of essential facilities within the new community, such as schools and recreational sites (Karamichas 2012). The Torino Winter Games of 2006 focused more on environmental sustainability than social legacies, though they also linked the two concepts throughout their bidding documents (Minnaert 2012; Torino Organizing Committee of the Olympic Games 2006). The Beijing Summer Olympics of 2008 emphasized the integration of Beijing and China into the global community (BOCOG 2008); they did not emphasize social legacy goals, though the IOC justified their choice of Beijing in part by suggesting that hosting the Olympics would result in the improvement of human rights in that country (Kidd 2010). This was very much *not* the case, as government crackdowns on dissidents, journalists, and the poor were documented by Amnesty International and Human Rights Watch (Canaves 2008; Kidd 2010).

The focus on social legacy re-emerged powerfully with the Vancouver 2010 Winter Games and the London 2012 Summer Games. The Vancouver bid incorporated its Inner City Inclusive Commitments Statement as part of its candidature file, signed by the bid committee and all three levels of government (VANOC 2009). The commitments included preventing Games-induced homelessness, protecting social housing stock, and building employment opportunities for low-income residents in Vancouver's Downtown Eastside. The London bid placed low-income East London youth at the centre of its bid, and built in regeneration of the economically deprived Olympic host boroughs as part of its Olympic legacy, including commitments to social housing and employment for previously workless East London residents. The emphasis on both social legacies and on youth has continued into bids for future Games, including the successful bid for Rio 2016:

> Brazil enjoys one of the youngest demographic profiles of any nation in the world. Recent initiatives by the Brazilian Olympic Committee, the government and non-governmental organisations to develop youth-oriented programmes based on Olympic values have had a dramatic impact, demonstrating the tangible power of sport as a transformation tool for social inclusion and education.
>
> (Rio Candidature Acceptance Application, 11,
> as cited in Minnaert 2012, 369)

As Lynn Minnaert (2012, 369) notes, "A trend towards a greater emphasis on social sustainability is noticeable" among bids to host the Olympic Games since the turn of the twenty-first century. This commitment to social legacies might be seen as a progressive move on the part of the International Olympic Committee and the host city Organizing Committees, except for one important factor: the commitments are not being met. In fact, the Olympics continue to have a negative impact on marginalized populations. The Athens Games of 2004 negatively affected 2,700 Roma, through forced evictions and the abandonment of previous commitments to relocate communities to settlements with basic services and facilities (COHRE 2007). The Beijing Games of 2008 resulted in the displacement of at least 1.25 million people (COHRE 2007). The London Olympics was the catalyst for the demolition of over 400 homes in the Clays Lane housing estate (Watt 2013), and the Vancouver Olympics created developmental pressure that directly and indirectly resulted in the closure of at least 1,400 low-income rental units in the Downtown Eastside in the lead-up to the Games (Eby and Misura 2006). Clearly, social legacy commitments are not sufficient to ensure that marginalized populations are not harmed by Olympic Games.

Conclusions

The publication of two reports about the negative effects of mega-events on the right to housing, by COHRE and the UN Special Rapporteur on Housing, signalled the increased international profile of social impacts created by the Olympics. The IOC is aware of these reports – indeed, they were substantially consulted for the production of the UN report. It is thus reasonable to assume that the higher profile of social legacies within the Olympic Movement can be traced at least in part to the increasing international attention being given to the negative effects. The shift in discourse towards an expanded focus on social responsibility is thus not an accident; rather, it is a strategic and intentional move to respond to (or perhaps to curb) criticism of Olympic practices. The ongoing lack of enforceable accountability measures combined with the ever-mounting social scientific evidence of harms to marginalized populations in host cities raises an important question: what role are these claims to social legacies playing within the Olympic movement?

It is useful here to return to the concept of modernization discourses and the manner in which they can be used as legitimation rationales. If we understand the Olympics as more than a sporting event, and instead see it as part of modernizing efforts employed by host cities and the IOC to promote specific ideas of the 'good society,' then the incorporation of notions of social responsibility into Olympic rhetoric can be seen in a different light. While earlier Olympic visions for a 'better world' focused on international peace and liberal notions of individualized freedom, the Olympics since the LA Games of 1984 have adopted not only the dominant Western discourse of the efficacy of capitalism and the free market, but also a new focus on supporting marginalized populations. Legitimation rationales can help us make sense of this: while the Olympic movement has always based its claims to being something bigger than just sports on notions of creating a better world, the specificity of those claims have increased in the same historical timeframe as the reliance on public funds has risen. As Alan Tomlinson (2014, 139) notes, from the new millennium on, "the escalating and consistently uncontrollable costs of [Olympic] staging would be increasingly rationalised by the appeal to legacy, in realms from the economic to the environmental, participation to regeneration, diplomacy to public health, national pride to global harmony."

So why do Olympic bid committees incorporate social legacy goals? Because they need to do so in order to win the IOC's favour, but also because they need the support of the public, both fiscally and symbolically, to successfully run the Olympic Games. This is intricately related to neoliberalism, and the pressure on cities to compete at a global scale. When cities are using the Olympic Games to position themselves as 'world class' or 'global cities,' as Olympics scholars agree is the norm, they are employed in an effort to make their cities *appear* a certain way. One of the qualities of a world-class, cosmopolitan city is that it be seen as a place that is humane, liberal, and progressive – whether or not the truth of the situation matches the image. This is why so many of the Olympics' negative effects have to do with displacement of homeless and marginalized populations; when Olympic tourists arrive, the organizers do not want them to get the impression of a city that neglects its residents, an impression they would surely receive were they to be accosted by panhandlers or faced with Roma tents. That displacement pressures are facilitated by efforts to engage in 'city cleansing' or 'city beautification' makes the message clear: cities are not seen as clean or beautiful when they have visibly poor people in the vicinity of Olympic venues. Ironically, Olympic commitments to help the urban poor may be having the opposite effect:

by permitting bidding committees to win the prize of the Olympic Games, they end up exacerbating the inequality faced by the very people to whom they made social legacy commitments in the first place.

Notes

1 Horne and Whannel (2012) discuss why this is, pointing to the variability in the elements that are included in various Olympic estimates. For instance, some estimates will include expenses that are incurred due to the pending Olympic Games, such as new transportation infrastructure, whereas others would leave this out.

2 These numbers are drawn from the Olympic Games Impact Study for the 2010 Olympic and Paralympic Games, a recently mandated reporting mechanism now required by the IOC of all Olympic organizing committees. Beginning with the Beijing Olympics in 2008, Vancouver was the second organizing committee required to submit a series of four reports following IOC-specified methodology. The reports are intended to measure the impact of an Olympic Games on its host city (Dubi and Felli 2006).

3 Interestingly, the final Olympic Games Impact Study for the London 2012 Games did not include any estimates regarding public money spent on the Games, and so I was not able to use this as a comparable source to the Vancouver Games.

4 It is important to note that the exemption given to LA regarding fiscal responsibility for the Olympics was not extended to future bid cities.

5 McFee (2012) does mark an important distinction between Brundage's and Coubertin's interpretation of amateurism in relation to the sponsorship of athletes. He argues that Brundage equated the two in a relatively simplistic relationship that suggests that anyone profiting materially from their sporting participation could not be considered an amateur. Coubertin, on the other hand, saw the benefit of sport as being about its *educational* value, and particularly its capacity to impart *moral education*. So the question in that case became less about whether a person might gain financially from sport, and instead whether their participation in sport was 'for its own sake' rather than 'just' for money.

6 It is interesting to note that the numbers of bids for Olympic Games is slowly dropping again, though they are still substantial (e.g. six bids for the 2020 Games). But will this downward trend continue, and is it at all related to the plethora of critical scholarship analyzing the Olympics and its negative effects on cities?

7 This report by COHRE has arguably played its own key role in the evolution of the Olympics towards claims to promote social responsibility, as shall be discussed further in the next section.

8 I encountered this phenomenon in 2010 when I was speaking to the media about my research on the effects of the Olympics on homeless youth in Vancouver. I was repeatedly asked if Vancouver homeless people had been bussed out of the city, a claim that I was unable to substantiate (although some of my participants had reported hearing about such a policy). For an interesting discussion on the ways in which the media's questions shape reporting on social issues related to the Olympics, see Lenskyj (2008).

9 I would like to make a special acknowledgement here of the outstanding work done by one of my research assistants, Deborah Conners, in coding and summarizing the official reports of the Olympic Games from 1988 to 2012, and the bidding document for 2016.

Bibliography

All website URLs were accessed between September 2014 and December 2015.
ACOG. 1996. "The Official Report of the Centennial Olympic Games, Volume 1: Planning and Organizing." The Atlanta Committee for the Olympic Games.

Allison, Lincoln. 2012. "The Ideals of the Founding Father: Mythologised, Evolved or Betrayed?" In *Watching the Olympics: Politics, Power and Representation*, edited by John Sugden and Alan Tomlinson, 18–35. London and New York: Routledge.

AP: Duluth News-Tribune. 1996. "Olympics – Atlanta 'Cleanup' Includes One-Way Tickets For Homeless." *The Seattle Times*, March 22. http://community.seattletimes. nwsource.com/archive/?date=19960322&slug=2320280.

ATHOC, and Athens Organizing Committee for the Games. 2005. "Official Report of the XXVIII Olympiad." The Games. Greece. http://library.la84.org/6oic/OfficialReports/ 2004/or2004b.pdf.

BC Ministry of Education. 2010. "Operating Grants Manual." BC. www.bced.gov.bc.ca/ k12funding/funding/10-11/estimates/operating-grants-manual.pdf.

BOCOG. 2008. "Bid Documents and Analysis: Passion Behind the Bid." Beijing Olympic Games Official Report Volume One. China. http://library.la84.org/6oic/OfficialReports/ 2008/2008v1.pdf.

Boykoff, Jules. 2014a. *Activism And The Olympics: Dissent At The Games In Vancouver And London*. New Brunswick, New Jersey: Rutgers University Press.

Boykoff, Jules. 2014b. *Celebration Capitalism and the Olympic Games*. London and New York: Routledge.

Brenner, Neil, and Nik Theodore, eds. 2011. *Spaces of Neoliberalism: Urban Restructuring in North America and Western Europe*. 1st edition. Maiden, MA: Wiley-Blackwell.

Brown, Wendy. 2005. *Edgework: Critical Essays on Knowledge and Politics*. Princeton, New Jersey: Princeton University Press. http://public.eblib.com/EBLPublic/PublicView. do?ptiID=445457.

Burbank, Matthew J., Gregory D. Andranovich, and Charles H. Heying. 2001. *Olympic Dreams: The Impact of Mega-Events on Local Politics*. Explorations in Public Policy. Boulder and London: Lynne Rienner Publishers.

Calgary Olympic Organizing Committee. 1989. "Official Report of the Games of the XXIV Olympiad."

Canaves, Sky. 2008. "Beijing's Olympic Cleanup Sends Migrants and Homeless Packing." *The Wall Street Journal*, August 5. www.wsj.com/news/articles/SB121788405 566611245.

COHRE. 2007. "Fair Play for Housing Rights: Mega-Events, Olympic Games and Housing Rights." Centre On Housing Rights and Evictions (COHRE). www.ruig-gian.org/ ressources/Report%20Fair%20Play%20FINAL%20FINAL%20070531.pdf.

COOB. 1992. "Official Report of the Games of the XXV Olympiad Barcelona 1992."

Dahill, Elizabeth Hart. 2010. "Hosting the Games for All and by All: The Right to Adequate Housing in Olympic Host Cities." *Brooklyn Journal of International Law* 36: 1111.

Davis, Lisa Kim. 2011. "International Events and Mass Evictions: A Longer View." *International Journal of Urban and Regional Research* 35 (3): 582–99. doi:10.1111/ j.1468-2427.2010.00970.x.

Dean, Jodi. 2009. *Democracy and Other Neoliberal Fantasies: Communicative Capitalism and Left Politics*. Durham: Duke University Press.

Dean, Mitchell. 2012. "Rethinking Neoliberalism." *Journal of Sociology*, April, 1440783312442256. doi:10.1177/1440783312442256.

Dorsey, James. 2014. "IOC President's Call for Transparency Challenges Middle Eastern/Asian Political Dominance of Soccer." *Huffington Post*. September 21. www. huffingtonpost.com/james-dorsey/ioc-presidents-call-for-t_b_5857000.html.

Dubi, Christophe, and Gilbert Felli. 2006. "What Is the Olympic Games Global Impact Study?" *Olympic Review: Official Publication of the Olympic Movement*. International

Olympic Committee (IOC). www.olympic.org/Documents/Reports/EN/en_report_1077. pdf.

Eby, David, and Christopher Misura. 2006. "Cracks in the Foundation: Solving the Housing Crisis in Canada's Poorest Neighbourhood." Vancouver: Pivot Legal Society.

Gold, John R., and Margaret M. Gold. 2010. "Olympic Cities: Regeneration, City Rebranding and Changing Urban Agendas." In *The Olympics: A Critical Reader*, edited by Vassil Girginov, 271–86. London and New York: Routledge.

Gruneau, Rick, and Robert Neubauer. 2012. "A Gold Medal for the Market: The 1984 Los Angeles Olympics, the Reagan Era, and the Politics of Neoliberalism." In *The Palgrave Handbook of Olympic Studies*, edited by Stephen Wagg and Helen Lenskyj, 134–62. New York: Palgrave Macmillan.

Guttmann, Allen. 2002. *The Olympics: A History of the Modern Games*. 2nd edition. (Illinois History of Sports.) Urbana and Chicago: University of Illinois Press.

Harvey, David. 2007. *A Brief History of Neoliberalism*. Oxford: Oxford University Press.

Horne, John. 2012. "The Four 'Cs' of Sports Mega-Events: Capitalism, Connections, Citizenship and Contradictions." In *Olympic Games, Mega-Events and Civil Societies: Globalization, Environment, Resistance*, edited by Graeme Hayes and John Karamichas, 31–45. (Global Culture and Sport.) New York: Palgrave Macmillan.

Horne, John, and Garry Whannel. 2012. *Understanding the Olympics*. London and New York: Routledge.

International Olympic Committee. 2014. "Olympic Charter." Lausanne, Switzerland. www.olympic.org/Documents/olympic_charter_en.pdf.

Karamichas, John. 2012. "A Source of Crisis? Assessing Athens 2004." In *The Palgrave Handbook of Olympic Studies*, edited by Stephen Wagg and Helen Lenskyj, 163–77. New York: Palgrave Macmillan.

Kidd, Bruce. 2010. "Human Rights and the Olympic Movement after Beijing" 13 (5): 901–10.

Kitchin, Paul. 2012. "Chapter 6 – Financing the Games." *Routledge Online Studies on the Olympic and Paralympic Games* 1 (36): 131–47. doi:10.4324/9780203840740_chapter_6.

Lenskyj, Helen Jefferson. 2000. *Inside the Olympic Industry: Power, Politics, and Activism*. Albany: State University of New York Press.

Lenskyj, Helen Jefferson. 2002. *The Best Olympics Ever?: Social Impacts of Sydney 2000*. Book, Whole. Albany: State University of New York Press.

Lenskyj, Helen Jefferson. 2008. *Olympic Industry Resistance: Challenging Olympic Power and Propaganda*. Albany: State University of New York Press.

Lillehammer Olympic Organizing Committee. 1994. "Official Report of the Lillehammer Winter Olympic Games, Volume 1."

McCann, E. J. 2009. "City Marketing." In *International Encyclopedia of Human Geography*, edited by Rob Kitchin and Nigel Thrift, 119–24. Oxford: Elsevier. www.sciencedirect.com/science/article/pii/B9780080449104010440.

Mcfee, Graham. 2012. "The Promise of Olympism." In *Watching the Olympics: Politics, Power and Representation*, edited by John Sugden and Alan Tomlinson, 36–54. London and New York: Routledge.

Minnaert, Lynn. 2012. "An Olympic Legacy for All? The Non-Infrastructural Outcomes of the Olympic Games for Socially Excluded Groups (Atlanta 1996–Beijing 2008)." *Tourism Management* 33 (2): 361–70. doi:10.1016/j.tourman.2011.04.005.

Nagano Olympic Organizing Committee. 1998. "Official Report of the XXVIII Olympiad, Volume 1."

New South Wales Department of Community Services. 2003. "Protocol for Homeless People in Public Places: Guidelines for Implementation."

Organizing Committee of the XVI Olympic Winter Games of Albertville and Savoie. 1992. "Official Report of the XVI Olympic Winter Games of Albertville and Savoie."

Peck, Jamie, and Adam Tickell. 2002. "Neoliberalizing Space." *Antipode* 34 (3): 380–404. doi:10.1111/1467-8330.00247.

Quesenberry, Preston. 1996. "The Disposable Olympics Meets the City of Hype." *Southern Changes. The Journal of the Southern Regional Council, 1978–2003* 18 (2): 3–14.

Real, Michael R. 2010. "Who Owns the Olympics? Political Economy and Critical Moments in the Modern Games." In *The Olympics: A Critical Reader*, edited by Vassil Girginov, 221–38. London and New York: Routledge.

Roche, Maurice. 2000. *Mega-Events and Modernity: Olympics and Expos in the Growth of Global Culture*. London: Routledge.

Rogers, Simon. 2012. "London Olympics 2012: Where Does the Money Come from – and Where's It Being Spent?" *The Guardian*, July 26 (Sport section). www.theguardian.com/sport/datablog/2012/jul/26/london-2012-olympics-money.

Rolnik, Raquel. 2009. "Special Rapporteur on Adequate Housing as a Component of the Right to an Adequate Standard of Living, and on the Right to Non-Discrimination in This Context." United Nations General Assembly. www.ohchr.org/en/issues/housing/pages/housingindex.aspx.

Rose, Nikolas S. 1999. *Powers of Freedom: Reframing Political Thought*. Cambridge, United Kingdom; New York: Cambridge University Press.

Seoul Olympic Organizing Committee. 1989. "Official Report: Organization and Planning, Volume 1."

Shaw, Christopher A. 2008. *Five Ring Circus: Myths and Realities of the Olympic Games*. Gabriola Island, BC: New Society Publishers.

Short, John R. 2008. "Globalization, Cities and the Summer Olympics." *City* 12 (3): 321–40. doi:10.1080/13604810802478888.

Smothers, Ronald. 1996. "As Olympics Approach, Homeless Are Not Feeling at Home in Atlanta." *New York Times*, July 1. www.nytimes.com/1996/07/01/us/as-olympics-approach-homeless-are-not-feeling-at-home-in-atlanta.html.

The Economist. 2013. "Why Would Anyone Want to Host the Olympics?," September 8. www.economist.com/blogs/economist-explains/2013/09/economist-explains-0.

Tomlinson, Alan. 2014. "Olympic Legacies: Recurrent Rhetoric and Harsh Realities." *Contemporary Social Science* 9 (2): 137–58. doi:10.1080/21582041.2014.912792.

Torino Organizing Committee of the Olympic Games. n.d. "Olympic Winter Games Official Report Torino 2006." www.olympic.org/Documents/Reports/Official%20Past%20Games%20Reports/Winter/EN/2006_Torino_Vol_3.pdf.

Vale, Lawrence, and Annemarie Gray. 2014. "The Displacement Decathlon: Atlanta 1996 to Rio 2016." http://placesjournal.org/article/the-displacement-decathlon/.

VANOC. 2009. "Vancouver 2010 Bid Report." Vancouver: Vancouver Organizing Committee of the Olympic and Paralympic Games.

Vanwynsberghe, Robert. 2015. "The Olympic Games Impact (OGI) Study for the 2010 Winter Olympic Games: Strategies for Evaluating Sport Mega-Events' Contribution to Sustainability." *International Journal of Sport Policy and Politics* 7 (1): 1–18.

Vanwynsberghe, Robert, and Brenda Kwan. 2013. "Olympic Games Impact (OGI) Study for the 2010 Olympic and Paralympic Winter Games: Post-Games Report," October. http://circle.ubc.ca/handle/2429/45295.

Vanwynsberghe, Robert, Björn Surborg, and Elvin Wyly. 2013. "When the Games Come to Town: Neoliberalism, Mega-Events and Social Inclusion in the Vancouver 2010 Winter Olympic Games." *International Journal of Urban and Regional Research* 37 (6): 2074–93. doi:10.1111/j.1468-2427.2012.01105.x.

Watt, Paul. 2013. "'It's Not for Us': Regeneration, the 2012 Olympics and the Gentrification of East London." *City* 17 (1): 99–118. doi:10.1080/13604813.2012.754190.

2 Olympic housing legacies in Vancouver

Clearing the streets with short-term shelters

Cuts in funding for programs – for overage housing workers, for underage housing workers, for outreach supports for people who are living on the streets. [All] have been cut. A whole bunch of programs aimed at helping the people of the Downtown Eastside have been cut. But they're like, "We'll open some shelters for you. We'll throw [CDN]$50,000 for, you know, to open a church that we had open on the weekends and during the day anyway."

(Marianne, Vancouver youth participant, 2009)

I met Marianne the day after her 24th birthday. She would stop the interview periodically to settle her 3-year-old daughter, who was busy getting into desk drawers and drawing on herself while her mom spoke with me. Marianne had been given up into foster care at age 2, and had started running away from her foster parents' home at age 14. She briefly mentioned that she had been abused at home, but didn't go into details. She would be picked up on the streets of the Downtown Eastside (DTES) and returned home until the age of 16, when she was kicked out permanently for her addiction to crack cocaine. Of Aboriginal ancestry, Marianne was connected to some of her extended family of nineteen half-siblings and various cousins, though she had no contact with her birth parents. When we met, she was living with one of her cousins in social housing in a quiet residential neighbourhood away from the DTES. She spoke fondly of the residents of the DTES who had helped her survive on the streets there for five years, and who had ultimately given her the money she needed to get out of that scene and break free of her addiction. An astute observer of the changes that had happened at street-level as Vancouver prepared for the Olympics, her intent was to leave the city during the Games the following year.

Marianne's description of the state of supports for homeless people in Vancouver succinctly summarizes the nature of the housing policies implemented in the period before, and during, the Olympics. Rather than funding outreach programs designed to help people move off the street in a sustainable and long-term fashion, the bulk of housing related expenditures in Vancouver before and during the Olympics was for short-term shelters designed to hide the rampant homelessness from tourists. This was despite the fact that the Vancouver organizing committee

(VANOC) had made explicit commitments to ensuring a housing legacy as a result of the Olympic Games. Consistent with the post-millennial Olympic emphasis on social benefits for marginalized populations, they wrote into their bids specific goals in relation to housing; these commitments contributed to their success at winning the Olympics.

In this chapter, I trace the impacts of the Vancouver Olympics on housing, and what these impacts meant for the homeless and marginally housed young people who were supposed to be at the receiving end of a housing legacy produced by the Games. I begin with an overview of the Vancouver 2010 housing commitments and the evolution of these commitments away from an affordable housing legacy and towards short-term shelters. I place this shift in the wider context of many decades of federal and provincial disinvestment in social housing. The outcome of the focus on short-term and emergency shelters leading up to the Vancouver Olympics was effectively a 'cleaning the streets' approach to housing, rather than the promised 'affordable housing legacy.' I also look at commitments made to protect existing rental stock and prevent gentrification from displacing residents or exacerbating homelessness, two other housing promises that were directly relevant to the youth with whom I worked. Finally, I consider the legacy of the Vancouver Athlete's Village and its relation to Olympic housing commitments.

Vancouver housing commitments: 'Provide an affordable housing legacy and start planning now'

When the Vancouver bid committee was drawing up its bid in 1999, the failures of a previous Vancouver mega-event were still relatively fresh in the minds of residents and organizers: Expo '86. Boosters for the 1986 World Fair (formally titled the 'World Exposition on Transportation and Communication'), which had been timed to coincide with the city's centennial, saw it as an opportunity to redevelop parts of the formerly industrial False Creek area while simultaneously putting Vancouver 'on the map' in terms of global reputation and status – goals that were later echoed in the 2010 Olympic bid. Located adjacent to the DTES, the development of the Expo '86 buildings on the North side of False Creek had a direct impact on this historically impoverished yet culturally rich neighbourhood. Real estate speculation was one of the culprits in this, as was the desire of single residence occupancy (SRO) hotel owners to take advantage of tourists' needs for short-term stays. These two forces combined to drive the eviction of between 500 and 950 residents, and the conversion of between 1,000 and 1,500 lodging house rooms into tourist rental units (Olds 1998). The evictions generated significant negative publicity, and were immortalized in the words of the song 'Profiteers,' by Vancouver band Spirit of the West:

> here's a cold wind blowin' through the old east side
> it cuts with the devil's curse
> they're turning our people into the streets, while

the landlords line their purse
with the greenback dollar of the tourist trade
there's a fortune to be had
make way for the out-of-towners, for
the tenants it's just too bad[1]

The Expo '86 evictions generated not only public distaste for mega-event-induced displacement; they also provided the impetus for broad-based organizing between community groups and the City of Vancouver, spearheaded by the Downtown Eastside Residents' Association (DERA) under the leadership of Jim Green (Olds 1998). There was thus a great deal of both public and institutional memory in Vancouver about the negative effects of mega-events by the time the bid for the 2010 Winter Olympics was beginning to gain momentum.

By the time of the Olympic bid in 2002, the homelessness crisis in Vancouver was a highly visible aspect of the urban landscape. In that same year, a group of homeless people and activists set up a squat in and around the former Woodward's department store building, located in the heart of the Downtown Eastside. The building had sat empty for nine years, and became the focus of demands for affordable housing and to stop the gentrification of the DTES that had accelerated

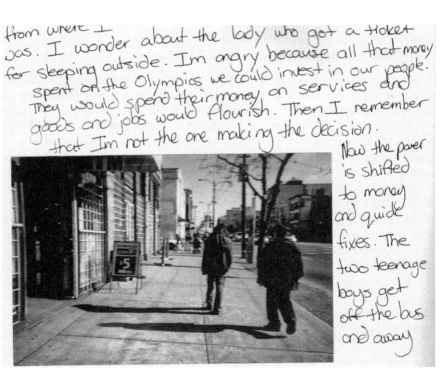

Figure 2.1 An excerpt from Allison's photo journal, with an image from Vancouver's Downtown Eastside.

since Expo '86 (Barnholden and Newman 2007). It received widespread popular support and lasted for nearly three months ("Woodward's Squat" 2011). That year, the number of homeless people documented through the Greater Vancouver Homeless Count was between 1,181 and 1,206; this estimate was gathered through a one-day count of people in 40 emergency shelters, transition and safe houses as well as street homeless individuals at 45 locations across the region where homeless people congregate during the day (Greater Vancouver Regional District 2002). This was the first count of its kind of street homeless people in Vancouver (Greater Vancouver Regional District 2002); it is widely acknowledged to be an under-representation of the actual numbers (Paulsen 2007). The report also documented what they characterized as an "alarming increase" in the number of households and persons at-risk of homelessness, which they attributed to population growth, increasing rents, and a decline in incomes (Greater Vancouver Regional District 2002).

It was in this context that a group of activists, unions, academics, and community organizations came together to form the Impacts of the Olympics on Communities Coalition (IOCC). The IOCC focused on "maximizing the positive impacts of the 2010 . . . Games for the host city and surrounding regions, while minimizing negative impacts" (as quoted in Edelson 2011, 810). In the beginning, their aim was to remain politically neutral, avoiding advocating for or against the Olympics and instead focusing on leveraging the Games to win important benefits for Vancouver's most marginalized residents. As Am Johal, one of the founding members of the Coalition, recalled:

> [We were] aware of Expo '86 and the evictions that had happened at that time. So in that summer [2001] we began the process of organizing and discussing what we needed. We knew that the bid was going forward. We knew that it was wildly popular and there wasn't a lot of opposition to it at the time. Not public opposition. So we were trying to get some NGOs together to at least begin the process of raising the issue of having community economic development, employment in the inner city, principles like that built in. Sustainability. Housing. Stopping evictions.
>
> (Personal communication, 2009)

Johal listed the groups involved in this coalition as including: "Tenants Rights Action Coalition, Better Environmentally Sound Transportation, other people like Jim Green, who used to be the executive director at DERA [Downtown Eastside Residents Association]. The Vancouver and District Labour Council I think at some point. The Building Trades. CUPE [Canadian Union of Public Employees] was around. And we had a few academics as well: people like Jim Frankish, Rob Vanwynsberghe and others." As he notes, "[I]t was a fairly mainstream, NGO kind of intervention, acting as a watchdog trying to reform the bid and trying to get some promises extracted from them."

The efforts of the coalition were prefigured in part by another important city-level initiative to address the long-term housing, mental health, and addictions issues that plagued the DTES. Termed the 'Vancouver Agreement', it brought together all three levels of government (municipal, provincial, and federal) to fund and implement a variety of projects designed to address the four priority areas of "Economic Revitalization, Safety & Security, Housing, and Health & Quality of Life" (Western Economic Diversification Canada 2010, i). The relationships formed through the Vancouver Agreement were later instrumental in the multi-level governmental cooperation required for both winning the bid and for hosting the Olympic Games (Edelson 2011). The Vancouver Agreement also formed the backdrop to early conversations about how the Olympics might best be leveraged for positive social legacies (Am Johal, personal communication, 2009).

Within the context of the ever-increasing pressure for Olympic bid committees to incorporate commitments to social legacies, it was in the Vancouver bid committee's interest to engage with this fledgling organization in order to claim that they had worked with the community, and to secure concrete commitments to socially responsible legacy goals. And in the beginning, they did so engage (Edelson 2011; Vanwynsberghe, Surborg, and Wyly 2013). Collaborating with the IOCC, as well as representatives from the three levels of government, the Vancouver bid committee developed the Inner City Inclusive Commitments Statement (ICICS), "an unprecedented bid-level effort to include community concerns in Games planning" (Vanwynsberghe, Surborg, and Wyly 2013, 2076). Incorporating 14 themes of social responsibility, including accessibility for people with disabilities and commitments to protect civil liberties, the document also incorporated five housing-related commitments:

- Protect rental housing stock
- Provide as many (sic) alternative forms of temporary accommodation for Winter Games visitors and workers
- Ensure people are not made homeless as a result of the Winter Games
- Ensure residents are not involuntarily displaced, evicted, or face unreasonable increases in rent due to the Winter Games
- Provide an affordable housing legacy and start planning now

("2010 Winter Games Inner-City Inclusive
Commitment Statement" 2013)

These commitments, though offering some specificity, were not nearly as specific as the IOCC wanted. As Am Johal notes,

> At the time the housing program in the province was 1,200 units a year. BC and Quebec were the only two provinces to build social housing after the federal government cutbacks. And so what we said is not only should we maintain the existing social housing program but we should have a legacy of 2010 new units. That was the position that we were taking but they did not include that into the document. So a lot of people keep referring to the Inner City Inclusive Commitments Statement and its kind of

vague promises but in terms of what we were pushing for, they were not vague. They were very specific things. And having a no-eviction policy in the lead up to 2010.

(Personal communication, 2009)

Although the Inner City Inclusive Commitments Statement did not incorporate the level of specificity that the IOCC requested, the relationship between this broad-based coalition and the Vancouver bid committee remained amicable – until Vancouver won the bid. The International Olympic Committee selected Vancouver to host the Games in 2003, at which time the bid committee was transformed into the Vancouver Organizing Committee for the 2010 Olympic and Paralympic Games (VANOC). One of the conversations that had been happening prior to the success of the bid was that a formal 'watchdog' would be funded by VANOC, to ensure that their commitments were followed through. Members of the IOCC reasonably expected that this role would fall to them. But after they had won the bid, VANOC refused to fund such a body; nor did they invite any members of the IOCC to be part of their board. As Nathan Edelson (2011, 814) notes,

This lack of transparency became a major point of contention for members of the IOCC, who had played a moderating role in the public debate leading up to the bid. They felt their credibility had been undermined as they were not given appropriate information in a timely manner, and they had to continue to volunteer many hours to help protect the interests of the low-income community and others whose interests had been reflected in the inclusive commitments.

The IOCC had already come under attack by activist organizations who felt that they had been co-opted by the Olympic movement, and lent it legitimacy that it otherwise would not have had. This belief led Chris Shaw, a leader in the Vancouver 'No Games' movement, to derisively label the IOCC a 'watch poodle' (Shaw 2008). But, as Am Johal points out, despite the IOCC's efforts to remain politically neutral and to ensure the social legacies of the Games were realized, they were still shut out of the process:

What's interesting is that we as an organization have been attacked by people like VANOC and government and portrayed as being on the fringe and periphery of society. And also by media organizations. On the other hand, the activist organizations who are in opposition to the Games view us as in bed with VANOC and government partners. Selling out the communities. So in that sense it's like we've gotten it on both sides, yet we've had no funding. We've tried to play this role and maintain public credibility and try to get things done and push for reform. We're cognizant of the way that we're situated. But at the same time it's interesting that we've gotten criticism from across the map. And we're still not at the table. So you know, I think that the level of polarization in this city about the Olympics has a lot to do with the fact that even the moderate organizations didn't get to the table and exact concessions that would have been fairly small and achievable.

(Personal communication, 2009)

With no funding to support them, the IOCC continued to play a 'watchdog' role, issuing report cards that were designed to bring attention to the degree to which VANOC and its government partners were or were not keeping their social commitments. In their 2007 report card, issued 1,000 days before the start of the 2010 Games, the IOCC assigned VANOC and the three levels of government involved in organizing the Games a grade of D- for their efforts to date in meeting their Inner City Inclusive Commitments Statement. In terms of housing, they note:

Vancouver is following historical patterns of Games related evictions. With just two and a half years until the Games begin, little or no government construction of promised legacy social housing has commenced for low income singles, suggesting that very little, if any, new legacy-related housing will be available prior to 2010 for this group, which is most at risk of displacement and homelessness.

(Impacts of the Olympics on Communities Coalition 2007, 6)

They urged VANOC and the municipal, provincial, and federal governments to engage in dialogue with themselves and other members of the community in order to more effectively move forward to reach their Inner City Inclusive Commitments Statement goals.

Despite the efforts of the IOCC and other concerned community organizations, VANOC followed an unfortunate but perhaps predictable trajectory towards shedding their much-touted social inclusion commitments as the Games drew nearer. As Vanwynsberghe, Surborg and Wyly (2013, 2082) note, "By 2006 . . . VANOC began to downplay its role in many of the ICICS objectives and to drop some of them entirely." In their own Sustainability Report of 2007, VANOC notes that "only half" of the ICICS commitments fall "within our decision-making scope. The rest, such as homelessness, involve public policy issues that exceed our authority or capacity to act" (as quoted in Vanwynsberghe, Surborg, and Wyly 2013, 2082). While this may be true to a certain extent, it begs the question as to why they included such commitments in their original bidding documents. It also does not respond to the question of why commitments that *were* within their remit, such as funding a watchdog organization, were not met.

Short-term shelters to 'get people off the streets'

In the face of VANOC's gradual withdrawal from their housing commitments, efforts continued in order to ensure that the goals of the ICICS were implemented – but these efforts were largely exerted by government. As a City of Vancouver staff person told me in 2009, "With VANOC we have a pretty good working relationship, but in a lot of ways they're like, this isn't [our mandate] – our mandate is to organize the Games. It's the government's responsibility to do all this other stuff, so, you know, it's your fault [laughs]. So sometimes trying to bring them along is a bit challenging." VANOC's Olympic housing plan overlapped almost exactly with the housing commitments already underway through the City's pre-existing 'Homeless Action Plan'; but with the Olympics coming to town, at the level of policy "everything is because of the Olympics but nothing is because of the Olympics" (senior City of Vancouver staff, 2009 interview). Although the City staffer reported a strong working relationship with the province in terms of housing, particularly through BC Housing, she noted that "the federal government, when it comes to the housing related work, they just have other priorities."

The federal government of Canada at the time did, indeed, have other priorities. Starting in 1993, in the last budget of the Conservative government led by Brian Mulroney, the federal government withdrew funding for the development of new social housing units, funding that has never been replaced (Klein and Copas 2010). The recently defeated Conservative government, led by Stephen Harper and in power for ten years, focused its housing spending on mortgage stimulus packages in the context of the 2008 economic downturn, rather than on funding to address unmet housing needs in the country (Pomeroy and Falvo 2013). In terms of housing policy for non middle-class individuals, federal funding since 1999 has focused on emergency shelters and transitional housing, under successive Liberal and then Conservative governments (Pomeroy and Falvo 2013). This focus has been mirrored at the provincial level; in BC, the province where Vancouver is located, there has been a shift towards what Klein and Copas (2010, 3) call a 'Housing Plus' approach, "meaning, all funding for new units has gone toward housing with supports – either supportive housing for homeless people with addictions and/or mental health challenges, or assisted living for seniors." While such housing is needed and welcomed, "it has come at the expense of basic (and less costly) social housing for those who simply struggle with low incomes" (ibid.).

It was in this context of federal disinterest in long-term housing solutions that the City of Vancouver worked, largely without the support of VANOC, to implement the commitments to housing that had helped Vancouver win the bid in the first place. City staff were cognizant of this dynamic, and conscious of using the Olympics to 'leverage' funding for portfolios that they had already prioritized (on the strategy of Olympic-related 'social leveraging' by government, see Vanwynsberghe, Derom, and Maurer 2012). However, such a strategy was substantially constrained by both the lack of federal support for social housing and the realities of the 2008 global economic crash. While advocates and government staff, particularly at the municipal level, tried to make the most of the opportunities ostensibly connected to the Olympic commitments to social legacies, the results of their efforts were significantly *not* "an affordable housing legacy." Instead, the majority of housing spending in the years leading up to the Olympic Games were focused on three areas: rental assistance supplements, new emergency shelter beds, and the purchase of existing Single Residence Occupancy (SRO) hotels (Klein and Copas 2010).

The BC government invested significant housing dollars between 2006 and 2010 into short-term emergency shelters. In 2008/09, one year prior to the opening ceremonies of the 2010 Olympics, the number of emergency shelter beds in the province almost doubled, from 1,320 spaces to 2,170 spaces (Klein and Copas 2010). While one City staff member told me that she did not think these shelter spaces had anything to do with the pending Olympics, when viewed in the wider political context of the desire of urban elites to ensure that their city 'looked its best' when the 'world was watching', it is hard not to believe that such initiatives were undertaken at that time with the Olympics firmly in mind.

This conjecture is supported by the findings of an unrelated report, published in 2013 in the journal *Social Science and Medicine* (Macnaughton, Nelson, and Goering 2013). The focus of this study was on the implementation of policy at the federal level, with a focus on the At Home/Chez Soi project, "the largest mental health services trial ever mounted in Canada." As a Canadian expert in the field of homelessness, I had been asked to comment on a video produced for this project by the National Film Board of Canada.[2] The project followed a 'housing first' model that I had noticed was coming to the forefront of policy discussions and advocacy in my research with homeless youth in Ottawa. I was thus interested in the project and its genesis. I was surprised to find, upon reading the report published in *Social Science and Medicine*, that one of the driving factors behind the implementation of this project was the Vancouver Olympics. Drawing on key informant interviews with those who had implemented the project, the report documents the links between the federal government's embarrassment about Vancouver's crisis level of homelessness, the pending Olympic Games, and the federal policy decision made to fund an unspecified "project for homeless people with mental illness in Canada" (Macnaughton, Nelson, and Goering 2013, 103). As noted by a "federal policy key informant," "[The situation was discussed politically] . . . in the context of the Vancouver 2010 Winter Olympics, which was a very important factor to acquiring the funding" (Macnaughton, Nelson, and Goering 2013, 103). Due to the political sensitivity of being seen as funding a project because of the Olympics, the public relations optic required that the project be started across multiple cities: "If you're going to do a demonstration project, you've got to do it across the country or you get killed politically . . . Politically, if a pilot project is run in only one area, and if the area you picked is Vancouver, then it looks like the government is pandering only to the Olympics" (Macnaughton, Nelson, and Goering 2013, 104). The former Senator who helped design the project was given 'carte blanche' to initiate a project, as long as it addressed homelessness in Vancouver and framed it in terms of mental illness.[3] The result was an innovative demonstration project across five cities in every region of the country, using a 'housing first' framework to address mental health and homelessness.

While the results of this fortuitous combination of funding and choice of leaders has resulted in a hopeful turn in Canadian conversations about housing, what is interesting for our purposes is that there were clearly decisions being made by the federal government to address homelessness in order to prevent public embarrassment before the Vancouver 2010 Games. In other words, public funding for addressing homelessness was focused on a 'cleaning the streets' mentality in light of the anticipated media focus on Vancouver as an Olympic city, rather than on actual documented social need for housing. It certainly was not about meeting the ICICS commitment to 'provide an affordable housing legacy.'

At the provincial and municipal level, the housing focus on short-term emergency shelters resulted in the opening of five HEAT (Homeless Emergency Action Team) shelters prior to the Winter Olympics.[4] The City of Vancouver, under Mayor Gregor Robertson, situated these as part of a longer-term strategy to end street homelessness by 2015. As a senior city staffer told me in 2010: "We're trying to get creative and think of ways we can get people off the street. [So we asked] what kind of interim housing solutions can we provide until more permanent housing is built?" Thus the focus on temporary housing was seen by the City as part of a longer-term plan to provide more permanent housing – except that the City relies on provincial and federal cooperation in order to successfully implement such a plan. Funding provided by the federal government for housing has been focused on short-term bandaids and, in the context of the Olympics, funding projects that would help reduce the 'embarrassment' of street homelessness. BC focused its housing dollars largely on rent supplements and 'supportive housing,' as well as substantial funds for emergency shelters (Klein and Copas 2010).

The youth I spoke to in 2009, 2010 and 2011 made the connection between the new shelters being put up and the desire to hide Vancouver's homeless population:

2009 Focus Group discussion:

Woman 1: If you look at the map and you literally put down where all the new shelters are, it's off the path from where Olympic vehicles and traffic is going to be.

Woman 2: Yeah, totally. They don't give a shit about making the problem better. They just want to put it away. Because the shelters don't make any sense. For the cost of what people need when they go to the hospital [due to health problems from being on the street], they can do low income housing. It's not going to be that expensive. It doesn't make any sense what they're doing right now with the shelters.

2010 interview:

Shelby: And they have all these shelters, like all these homeless shelters, that are all funded for the Olympics. And as soon as the Olympics are gone are they going to have any shelters? Not a chance. They're going to be all closed down and it's all going to be back the way it was. You know? They just hide people out.

The homeless won't be enjoying the Olympics.

Figure 2.2 Stephanie's image captures a flyer advertising a festival for homeless people in Vancouver's DTES, and also reflects her thoughts about how homeless people will feel during the Olympics.

2011 interview:

Colvin: I just think it's sad how leading up to the Games they had this like cold weather homeless shelter thing. Yeah. That was bullshit. That was like, let's hide the homeless people from all the people who are coming to Vancouver.

The HEAT shelters have become an ongoing emergency response to Vancouver's homelessness crisis, with the temporary shelters re-opening each winter. While four new shelters were added in 2012 (City of Vancouver 2012), at least four others were closed in 2014 (RainCity Housing 2015).

Although VANOC had largely divested itself of its commitments to providing housing, even they channelled funds towards temporary shelter beds for homeless youth. On January 13, 2010, one month before the opening ceremonies, the province of BC issued a media release announcing the joint funding between the federal government, the provincial government and VANOC of "32 new transitional housing beds with support services for homeless and at-risk youth." The funding went to the downtown location of Covenant House, a popular resource centre and shelter for homeless youth in the city. Interestingly, VANOC positioned their support as providing a "permanent housing legacy" (Ministry of Housing and Social Development 2010), perhaps overlooking the fact that the shelter beds are designed to be temporary in nature. Or, more likely, they are using the notion of 'housing legacy' to mean something very different than providing permanent long-term housing solutions for homeless people in the city.

The HEAT shelters and other short-term housing did provide more spaces for the youth during the Games and in the year immediately following. This was reflected in the interviews, where youth in general reported that it was difficult to find shelter spaces in 2009, moderately difficult to easy in 2010, and fairly easy or pretty much the same in 2011. These impressions are matched by the statistics gathered through homeless counts. The 2008 Greater Vancouver Homeless Count, the third of its kind, noted that street homelessness had increased by 137% since the first count in 2002 (Greater Vancouver Regional Steering Committee on Homelessness 2008). The 2015 Vancouver Homeless Count notes that 2011, on the other hand, marked the low point for unsheltered homeless people in the city (Thomson 2015), likely due to the higher number of emergency shelter beds put in place for the Olympic Games. This was part of the reason that the youth were having trouble finding shelter space in 2009, but found shelter fairly easily in 2010 and 2011. In a 2009 conversation with a young woman accessing one of the emergency shelters, she noted both the lack of shelter space and the probable cause:

Erin:	Shelters are full. You can't really find space anywhere.
Interviewer:	Have they always been full?
Erin:	No. When I first came here [two years ago] it was like, which one do you want to go to? And now you can't find a bed anywhere. Like it's really good luck if you get a bed.
Interviewer:	What do you think that's about?
Erin:	There hasn't been any more shelters put up, which seems ridiculous in two years. I haven't heard of any [new shelters], the ones that I used to call are still there and there's no new ones.
Interviewer:	So why do you think they're filling up now?
Erin:	I think it's that there are more homeless people and there's less shelter space.

The tenor of these conversations had changed, however, in our 2010 interviews. As Leila commented in 2010, "I think there's more shelters open right now." While the youth reported more shelters being available during the Games, the state of these shelters left much to be desired, according to our participants. Often consisting of mats on the floor or church benches, and subject to consistent over-crowding, many of the youth remarked that they would rather sleep outside. The shelters that were specifically for young people, such as Covenant House or

Directions, were identified as positive places to be. But these were age-limited, meaning the youth could only access them until they reached a certain age, typically 24.

One advantage of the HEAT shelters was that they were 'low-barrier' housing; that is, there were less prohibitions in place to ensure that as many people as possible could access the shelters. For example, HEAT shelters permitted street youth to bring in their pets (often dogs), whereas many of the other shelters would not. This change was commented on by a director of one of the youth centres in 2011:

> I think there was a definite ease for people who have dogs to access places. For people who had [shopping] carts to access places. So, typically, some of the previous ways that things were running is there might have been beds, but they weren't eligible, cause the barriers were there. The intake barriers existed. We talked to youth, "do you want to go there?" "Well I can't go there because I have a dog." "I can't go there because I have a cart." And those eligibility criteria were widened or softened, and then the actual number of opportunities seems to have gone up. Suddenly there was almost, you couldn't swing a dead cat without hitting a worker saying "yeah, we got space."

The problem, however, remained: the housing that was being provided was largely (though not entirely) temporary in nature. A few new housing initiatives were opened; one that was mentioned by several of the youth in 2010 was the Dunsmuir House, a former hotel that had been converted into interim housing and was being run by RainCity Housing (the same not-for-profit organization that ran some of the HEAT shelters). The Dunsmuir, leased from private development company The Holborn Group, was put in place to replace the controversial Howe street HEAT shelter, which had been plagued by issues and complaints from nearby condo owners. It, too, while more permanent in nature than the HEAT shelters, was designed as an 'interim solution' until more permanent housing was available (Bula 2009). It has since closed.

In a group interview with youth workers in 2010, they reflected on the dilemmas presented by the state of housing in the city, with which they were intimately familiar given their efforts to find housing for the youth with whom they worked:

Youth worker 2:   There were probably some programs that came about that were good. They were because of the Olympics, not some altruistic motive. But in that sense they were okay. And the HEAT shelters … they're okay. They're not housing though. They're not reasonable, or good housing.

Youth worker 1:   Yeah, but neither are the SROs.

Youth worker 2:   Well none of them are.

Youth worker 1:   Yeah, none of the affordable housing is.

Figure 2.3 Cover image for Allison's photo project, illustrating her sense of the impact of the Olympics on Vancouver housing – i.e., 'home' will be a cardboard box

Rent increases and the loss of SROs

Single-Room Occupancy (SRO) hotels are an important part of the housing story in Vancouver, particularly in the DTES. Historically, SROs in the nineteenth and early twentieth century largely served single, working class men who travelled to the city seasonally in search of fishing and logging work. They were also utilized by Chinese labourers who were largely excluded from other parts of the city, thanks to racist policies and practices (Antolin 1989). The City of Vancouver describes contemporary SROs as follows:

> Single-room occupancy (SRO) buildings are rooming houses and residential hotels containing small single rooms, usually about ten by ten feet in size. Residents share common bathrooms and sometimes cooking facilities. These SRO units represent the most basic and the lowest cost housing provided by the private market – very little other market housing is available in the same price range.
>
> (Housing Policy Community Services Group 2010, 3)

In recognition of the fact that SROs would be under pressure for conversion prior to the Olympics, as had happened during Expo '86, the City of Vancouver introduced an updated law to protect the existing stock from conversion. The Single Room Accommodation By-Law (or SRA) was introduced in 2003, and was designed to regulate the demolition and conversion of SROs and thus prevent homelessness in the period prior to the Olympics (Chan 2014). However, significant loopholes existed in the policy that permitted owners of these buildings to work around the regulations' intended effects (Pivot Legal Society 2008).

SROs are widely regarded as poor quality, last resort housing. The fact that they are considered within wider conversations about affordable housing at all highlights the paucity of options in the region. As documented above, the policy focus on housing at the federal level for decades has been decidedly *not* on providing long-term affordable housing. Instead, it has been a crisis response approach to the chronic levels of homelessness that have arguably been a direct result of the original cuts to the federal provision of social housing in 1993. One consequence has been the gradual regression of official notions about what counts as 'suitable' housing. The SROs in Vancouver are a case in point. As a public nurse working at one of the youth shelters told me in 2010:

> In the 90s SROs weren't considered acceptable housing. So if you got an intent to rent from welfare, SRO didn't count. That was unacceptable housing, it didn't count. Then what happened, they [government] lowered their [welfare] rates, and then they gave up. Then they said: "well now we have to . . ." So it wasn't like anyone decided all of a sudden that SROs are reasonable housing, it's just that we don't give you enough to get anything but that.

The province of BC purchased 26 SRO hotels in the years leading up to the Games (24 of which were in Vancouver) (Klein and Copas 2010). The purchase of SROs were signalled to me by various City staff as a significant 'win' for the City in terms of affordable housing. One senior staffer noted that this helped to "protect the existing stock," which had been one of the commitments of the ICICS. A former city planner suggested that, "the province wouldn't have bought those SROs if it weren't for the Olympics." Original plans to refurbish and upgrade them were abandoned, however, in the context of the 2008 economic crash. As explained to me in 2012 by a long-time advocate for the homeless in Vancouver:

> The bad part was this was, what, 2006–2007, in there [that the SROs were purchased]. They made the purchase, they put not-for-profits in charge of the buildings, they pulled back and worked to do renovations that were going to reduce the number of rooms slightly, but would mean that each tenant had their own bathroom, right? Really important for quality of life stuff. So it would have been a good thing. And then we had this massive crash, the economic crash, and all of a sudden there was no money. And so they did a spit and polish renovation. A little bit of paint, a little bit of this, a little bit of that. But no major renovations.

The descriptions of the youth we spoke to, many of whom had stayed in the SROs at various points, paint a vivid picture of the state of this housing:

Erin: Yeah, I've stayed in a lot of them. I've never actually had one of them on my own. Friends are like, most of my friends are in those crappy places. And it's disgusting. It's really, really disgusting. It's like, so gross. Bedbugs. Just dirty. Just disgusting. Like, eww. Just gross. And like so small and cramped. It's just a bad scene.

Interviewer: How much do people pay for those?

Erin: Three seventy-five. That's what welfare covers, right?

Richard, who had lived in SROs, told me that the spaces shouldn't have even been rented out. With bedbugs, termites, rats and cockroaches as the norm, he said that the spaces were unliveable. Yet, he notes, "They're still renting out of it and that was, like, a year ago that they were supposed to not be."

Klein and Copas point out that the purchase of SROs does not, in fact, provide additional affordable housing. Instead, it 'rescues' such housing from the possible fate seen during Expo '86, of being converted into higher-end units for tourists or more affluent residents. In a survey conducted from April to June of 2010, Wendy Pederson and Jean Swanson of the Carnegie Community Action Project (CCAP) found that a net loss of SRO rooms had occurred between 2009 and 2010 – even with the opening of the new SRO spaces that had been bought by the province:

CCAP found that 67 affordable rooms closed and the number of rooms in hotels that rent all their rooms for [CDN]$375 or less fell by 415. Only 12% of the privately owned rooms surveyed by CCAP are now affordable to DTES residents on income assistance, disability and basic pension.

Even though 2010 was a really good year for newly built units and provincially owned hotel rooms opening up, the number of newly affordable units was 112 less than the number of closed hotels plus hotel rooms lost to rent increases above $375.

(Pederson and Swanson 2010, 2)

Loss of low-income housing due to rent increases occurred not only in SROs but also throughout the city. In a report that documents housing and rental prices across Metro Vancouver between 2004 and 2013, the Metro Vancouver Housing Data Book notes that rents increased at a rate of 30% over this 10 year period, or 3% per year (Metro Vancouver 2014). Over the same period, Vancouver's price index increased by 1.7% per year, and average wages increased by only 2.5% per year, meaning that rents have increased at a rate higher than both inflation and incomes (ibid.). The increase in rental prices in the period leading up to the Olympics was one of the reasons given by some of the youth we spoke to about their own homeless status. In 2010, Matthew noted the following:

Interviewer: What did you think when you heard the Olympics were coming to Vancouver?

Matthew: I didn't like it. I was homeless at the time so it's really hard to find a place. . . . Anything that was low income got raised way, way higher. Like what we have to pay for a two-bedroom is ridiculous. Right now we pay [CDN]$1,400 for a two bedroom.

And in 2011, during a focus group, the following conversation took place:

Jeffrey: There was one thing. I had a place before the Olympics, I had my own place, I was paying my own rent. And, the simple fact was as soon as the Olympics started coming to town, when it got closer to that time of year, my landlords, and I know quite a few of my friends that had landlords that raised the rent, significantly, because of the Olympics. And we're talking, like, I was paying [CDN]$650 for my place, and then it went up to, like, $1,200. And we're like "what the fuck?" And yeah, it was ridiculous. And I go back and look at it, because it was for rent again, and it was still, like, $900 because the Olympics were gone. But still, I can't afford that.

Property owners also attempted to profit from the Olympics by renting out their units for short-term stays during the Games; this also had an impact on some of the youth in my research. In 2011, a group of housing support workers described the challenges they faced trying to help youth find housing during the Olympics:

Youth worker 1:   I remember looking, we'd often use Craigslist, so we would sit down and all the ads would be like, oh this is [CDN]$400, that sounds affordable. And then it was like, oh, but it's for a night. So it's like, sorting through this list and trying to see what is housing and what is somebody renting out.

Interviewer: Is this during the Olympics?

Youth worker 1:   Yeah.

Youth worker 2:   A lot of people thought that they could cash in on the Olympics by doing short-term rentals.

While rent increases are theoretically limited by the Residential Tenancy Act, in practice the Act contains policy loopholes that landlords were able to exploit prior to the Olympics (Chan 2014), allowing them to increase rents above affordable levels for the youth in my study. It is quite likely that rent increases and the loss of low-income stock in the form of SRO rooms were part of the reason for the substantial increases in homelessness leading up to the 2010 Games.

Olympic housing legacy: The Vancouver Athlete's Village

One of the spaces that had been promised as part of the affordable housing legacy claimed by the bid committee was the Athlete's Village. I touch on this here simply to round out the picture of Vancouver housing commitments and their failed implementation. The youth I spoke with saw the Athlete's Village as outside of their circle of concern, as a place they heard about in the media but not as a place where they could imagine themselves finding housing, even if the original commitments to social housing were met. Given that the wait list for BC Housing as of May 2008 had over 13,400 applicants (Klein and Copas 2010), this sense was a realistic one. But it is worth touching on the fate of the Athlete's Village in Vancouver, not least because it will offer a point of comparison to the London Athlete's Village.

The Vancouver Athlete's Village was built on the Southeast shore of False Creek, across the water from the Expo '86 developments of two decades earlier. The City of Vancouver entered into a unique lease agreement with Millennium Developments company, the company that was ultimately selected to complete the Athlete's Village. Under this agreement, the City kept the land title before and during the 'Olympic exclusive-use period' in order to maintain control over the development of the project and ensure that it would meet its commitment to VANOC that the project be completed by November 1, 2009 (Scherer 2011). In exchange, Millennium contracted to "design, finance, and construct over 800 units of market housing (and other commercial space), as well as additional city-owned buildings (252 units of social housing, a community centre, and a childcare facility)" (Scherer 2011, 785). However, when Millennium was refused further funding and their loan agreement was broken by the New York-based hedge fund Fortress Investment Group after the 2008 economic crash, the City of Vancouver was left to cover the company's cost overruns. City Council made their decision during an in-camera meeting on October 14, 2008, where they agreed to advance CDN$100 million of public money to the private developer (Scherer 2011). This decision was made public three weeks later by an article in the national newspaper, *The Globe and Mail*. The public outcry that ensued played a definitive role in the defeat of the right-leaning NPA during the next municipal election, and the win of Vision Vancouver mayor Gregor Robertson (Scherer 2011).

In 2010, the left-leaning Vancouver city council, under the leadership of Gregor Robertson, voted to reduce the number of social housing units that had been part of the original plan from 252 units to half of that. The other 126 units would be sold at market rates (CBC 2010). This left 126 social housing units mixed in with 1100 market-rate condominiums to be sold privately. As of 2011, the project looked poised to lose over CDN$230 million (Scherer 2011). It was thus with obvious relief that Mayor Gregor Robertson recently announced that the remaining condominium units had been sold to Aquilini Group for CDN$91 million, permitting the City to retire the outstanding portion of the original CDN$630 million that they had borrowed commercially to complete the project (Lee 2014). In the meantime, reports have been surfacing of the discomfort felt by residents living in the few social housing units that were preserved in the Olympic Village, now called the Village on False Creek. As one media report notes, low-income tenants were being 'forced out' due to the high cost of utilities; they were also discouraged from forming a tenants' association to advocate for themselves with the City, who are still the owners of the buildings in which the social housing units are located (Vulliamy 2013).

Conclusions

The original commitments to housing that were part of the Vancouver bid for the 2010 Games focused on preserving existing housing stock, ensuring residents were not made homeless, and leaving an affordable housing legacy. While some efforts were made to preserve SROS – themselves substandard housing that ought not to even be considered 'housing stock' – these efforts were largely unsuccessful. More low-income SRO units were ultimately lost then preserved, despite the 26 buildings that were purchased by the province. Homelessness in Vancouver more than doubled between 2002 and 2010; while it is difficult to assess how much of this was due directly to the Olympic Games and how much to other factors such as the economic crash of 2008, it is clear that speculation and gentrification pressures on the housing market in Vancouver were connected to the Olympic Games, and likely played a role in increasing homelessness. Finally, the efforts to provide housing – which was done by government, since VANOC stepped away from these commitments by 2007 – focused almost exclusively on short-term and emergency shelters, a strategy that arguably has more to do with 'cleaning the streets' to make the city 'look good' than providing an affordable housing legacy. In other words, the Vancouver Olympics are a prima facie case of post-millennial Olympic social promises being made, and then broken, with impunity.

Five years after the Games, it is apparent that Vancouver mayor Gregor Robertson's commitment to end homelessness by 2015 has not been achieved. In fact, the number of unsheltered homeless people in Vancouver has risen steadily since 2011, with a slight dip between 2014 and 2015. This speaks to the rising overall level of homelessness in the city, where the emergency shelters that were the real housing legacy of the Games cannot keep up with the ever-increasing need. The rate of overall homelessness has increased by 2% since 2010, but the rate of increase of homelessness is now rising: homelessness went up by 4.5% per year between 2013 and 2015. The number of homeless children and youth has also risen since the Olympic Games, representing 21% of the homeless population in 2014, and 17% of the homeless population in 2015. This is in contrast to 2010, where the number of children and youth counted represented 13% of the total homeless population (all statistics in this paragraph are from Thomson 2015). The 2002 promise of 'an affordable housing legacy' as a result of the Olympic Games is almost laughable in the face of such statistics. While the Olympics have come and gone, homeless people in Vancouver, and homeless youth in particular, are now worse off than they were before the bid.

Notes

1 "Profiteers" by J. F. Mann/G. Kelly – Spirit of the West – Lyrics used by permission. All rights reserved. Administered by SOCAN.

2 See http://athome.nfb.ca/athome/blog/?p=11182#more-11182 for my blog post on the project and the Vancouver-based video.

3 As the report notes, this coincided with the Conservative government's ideological commitments to linking homelessness to mental illness rather than, say, lack of affordable housing.

4 One of these HEAT shelters, the Howe street shelter, ultimately closed due to public pressure, particularly from nearby condominium owners who did not like the behaviour of the shelter's inhabitants. Another HEAT shelter, the Granville street shelter, was closed in 2009 and then re-opened shortly before the Olympic Games (Bula 2009; CBC News 2010).

Bibliography

All website URLs were accessed between June 2013 and December 2015.

"2010 Winter Games Inner-City Inclusive Commitment Statement." 2013. http://themainlander.com/PDFs/ICI.pdf.

Antolin, Mercedes Mompel. 1989. "Single Room Occupancy Housing: Two Cases, Vancouver and Toronto." http://circle.ubc.ca/handle/2429/29919.

Barnholden, Michael, and Nancy Newman. 2007. *Street Stories: 100 Years of Homelessness in Vancouver*. Vancouver: Anvil Press.

Bula, Frances. 2009. "Controversial Vancouver Homeless Shelter to Close." *The Globe and Mail*, July 30. hwww.theglobeandmail.com/news/national/controversial-vancouver-homeless-shelter-to-close/article4213510/.

CBC. 2010. "Vancouver Cuts Olympic Village Social Housing." April 23. www.cbc.ca/1.882070.

CBC News. 2010. "Controversial Homeless Shelter Reopens." January 5. www.cbc.ca/1.892539.

Chan, Sophy. 2014. "Unveiling the 'Olympic Kidnapping Act': Examining Public Policy and Homelessness in the 2010 Vancouver Olympic Games." *University of Western Ontario – Electronic Thesis and Dissertation Repository*, July. http://ir.lib.uwo.ca/etd/2195.

City of Vancouver. 2012. "Four New Temporary Cold-Weather Shelters in Vancouver." Text/xml. October 24. http://vancouver.ca/news-calendar/four-new-temporary-cold-weather-shelters-in-vancouver.aspx.

Edelson, Nathan. 2011. "Inclusivity as an Olympic Event at the 2010 Vancouver Winter Games." *Urban Geography* 32 (6): 804–22. doi:10.2747/0272-3638.32.6.804.

Greater Vancouver Regional District. 2002. "Research Project on Homelessness in Greater Vancouver." www.metrovancouver.org/planning/homelessness/ResourcesPage/Volume1_Executive_SummaryL.pdf.

Greater Vancouver Regional Steering Committee on Homelessness. 2008. "Still on Our streets . . . Results of the 2008 Metro Vancouver Homeless Count." Vancouver. www.metrovancouver.org/planning/homelessness/ResourcesPage/HomelessCountReport 2008Feb12.pdf.

Housing Policy Community Services Group. 2010. "2009 Survey of Low-Income Housing in the Downtown Core." Vancouver: City of Vancouver.

Impact of the Olympics on Community Coalition. 2007. "Olympic Oversight Interim Report Card: 2010 Olympic Games."

Klein, Seth, and Lorraine Copas. 2010. "Unpacking the Housing Numbers: How Much New Social Housing Is BC Building?" Canadian Centre for Policy Alternatives

BC Office. www.policyalternatives.ca/sites/default/files/uploads/publications/2010/09/CCPA-BC-SPARC-Unpacking-Housing-Numbers.pdf.

Lee, Jeff. 2014. "Aquilini Group Buys Remaining Olympic Village Condos for $91 Million, Retiring Vancouver's Debt." *Vancouver Sun*, April 28. www.vancouversun. com/business/Aquilini+Group+buys+remaining+Olympic+Village+condos+million+retiring+Vancouver+debt/9784174/story.html.

Macnaughton, Eric, Geoffrey Nelson, and Paula Goering. 2013. "Bringing Politics and Evidence Together: Policy Entrepreneurship and the Conception of the At Home/ Chez Soi Housing First Initiative for Addressing Homelessness and Mental Illness in Canada." *Social Science & Medicine (1982)* 82 (April): 100–107. doi:10.1016/j. socscimed.2013.01.033.

Metro Vancouver. 2014. "Metro Vancouver Housing Data Book." Vancouver. www. metrovancouver.org/planning/development/housingdiversity/HousingDataBook Documents/MV_Housing_Data_Book.pdf.

Ministry of Housing and Social Development. 2010. "News Release: 32 New Shelter Beds Open for Homeless Youth." www2.news.gov.bc.ca/news_releases_2009-2013/2010 HSD0003-000019.htm.

Olds, Kris. 1998. "Urban Mega-Events, Evictions and Housing Rights: The Canadian Case." *Current Issues in Tourism* 1 (1): 2–46. doi:10.1080/13683509808667831.

Paulsen, Monte. 2007. "More Homeless than Athletes in 2010." *The Tyee*. May 28. http://thetyee.ca/News/2007/05/28/Homeless1/.

Pederson, Wendy, and Jean Swanson. 2010. "Pushed Out: Escalating Rents in the Downtown Eastside." Vancouver: Carnegie Community Action Project (CCAP).

Pivot Legal Society. 2008. "Submissions of Pivot Legal Society to the UN Office of the High Commissioner for Human Rights For the Universal Periodic Review of Canada." http://lib.ohchr.org/HRBodies/UPR/Documents/Session4/CA/PLS_CAN_UPR_S4_2009_PivotLegalSociety.pdf.

Pomeroy, Steve, and Nick Falvo. 2013. "Pragmatism and Political Expediency: Housing Policy under the Harper Regime." In *How Ottawa Spends, 2013–2013: The Harper Government: Mid-Term Blues and Long-Term Plans*, edited by C. Stoney and B. Doern, 184–95. Montreal: McGill-Queen's University Press.

Raincity Housing. 2015. "Emergency Housing." Accessed July 17. www.raincityhousing. org/what-we-do/emergency-housing/.

Scherer, Jay. 2011. "Olympic Villages and Large-Scale Urban Development: Crises of Capitalism, Deficits of Democracy?" *Sociology* 45 (5): 782–97. doi:10.1177/003803851 1413433.

Shaw, Christopher A. 2008. *Five Ring Circus: Myths and Realities of the Olympic Games*. Gabriola Island, BC: New Society Publishers.

Thomson, Matt. 2015. "Vancouver Homeless Count 2015." M. Thomson Consulting. http://vancouver.ca/files/cov/vancouver-homeless-count-2015.pdf.

Vanwynsberghe, Robert, Inge Derom, and Elizabeth Maurer. 2012. "Social Leveraging of the 2010 Olympic Games: 'sustainability' in a City of Vancouver Initiative." *Journal of Policy Research in Tourism, Leisure and Events* 4 (2): 185–205.

Vanwynsberghe, Robert, Björn Surborg, and Elvin Wyly. 2013. "When the Games Come to Town: Neoliberalism, Mega-Events and Social Inclusion in the Vancouver 2010 Winter Olympic Games." *International Journal of Urban and Regional Research* 37 (6): 2074–93. doi:10.1111/j.1468-2427.2012.01105.x.

Vulliamy, Claire. 2013. "Last Low-Income Tenants at Olympic Village Are Being 'Forced Out.'" *The Mainlander*. March 21. http://themainlander.com/2013/03/21/last-low-income-tenants-at-olympic-village-are-being-forced-out/.

Western Economic Diversification Canada. 2010. "Evaluation of the Vancouver Agreement." www.wd.gc.ca/images/cont/12531_eng.pdf.

"Woodward's Squat." 2011. *Vancouver Media Co-Op*. http://vancouver.mediacoop.ca/olympics/woodwards-squat/6356.

3 Olympic housing legacies in London

Gentrification and displacement of working class communities

> Because of the Olympics and the interest in the Stratford area, Stratford and Newham as a whole have become more expensive to live, even food and stuff is just really, really expensive . . . so myself and my sister were looking to basically move out of the area . . . because the [housing] council are telling us now that if we do want help that they can place us anywhere in the UK and we just have to up and leave regardless whether we want to or not.
>
> (Angelica, London youth participant, 2013)

We first met Angelica in 2012, one month after the birth of her son. She had left home when she became pregnant at age 21, following her sisters into the supportive housing structure where we were doing our research. Angelica and her sisters had relocated to Britain from St. Lucia as children, a few years after their mother had moved there in order to earn money to send back to her young family. Her mother had worked as a cleaner since arriving in the UK. Though Angelica's mum had insisted she could no longer live with her once Angelica was pregnant, they remained on good terms; her mum was excited about the birth of her first grandson. Angelica was ambivalent about staying in Stratford. She was concerned for her mixed-race son and whether he'd be able to build a good life for himself in an area of the city that she described as dangerous. She didn't want him to feel that he'd have to 'prove' himself to his Black peers, a phenomenon she'd witnessed among mixed-race men of her own age. But her mum lived in the area, and Angelica knew it would be hard on her mum if she and her sisters moved away with their children. Angelica had looked at various housing options in the area, including private rentals. With a housing allowance from social assistance of £635 per month, even the most run-down one bedroom flats she could find in Stratford were not accessible to her, with rents set at £700 to £800 per month. The new rules in place for the social housing waiting lists meant she had to accept flats outside of London; she had thus resigned herself to leaving Stratford, and was even looking forward to moving to a part of the UK that she thought might be a better area to raise a child – despite the fact that this meant leaving behind her mother and the supports with which she was familiar.

Angelica's situation was typical of many of the young people we spoke to in London. Stratford, now the site of the 2012 Olympic stadium and the associated

Westfield Mall, had become an increasingly desirable, and expensive, place to live. For young people who lived there, many of whom had grown up in the area, this meant facing the likelihood of leaving the neighbourhood – either because they were being priced out or due to pressure from the social housing system to accept housing elsewhere in the country. These were different pressures than those faced by the youth in Vancouver, who were already homeless. Whereas the Vancouver youth were pushed into short-term shelters in order to 'clean the streets' for the sake of the Games, the youth in London, who would have been homeless but for the temporary housing in which they lived, faced pressure from multiple sites to move out of the neighbourhood they knew best. The differences between their respective housing stories has to do with the wider social context in which each bid and Olympic Games took place. Whereas Vancouver's housing interventions focused on short-term and emergency shelters – consistent with federal and provincial policy directions from the preceding two decades – London continued an already established policy trajectory of 'regeneration' that ultimately translated into gentrification for the working class communities who traditionally resided in East London. It is these differences – between short-term shelter stays, and gentrification pressures – that were revealed most directly through interviews with the youth who lived in each city.

There were also some striking similarities between the 2012 London Olympics housing story and what occurred in Vancouver. Both bidding committees were influenced by civil society organizations, each of which provided the social responsibility blueprint that became key to their respective wins. Both cities made clear commitments in their bid to provide a housing legacy, and both cities ultimately built less housing than earlier estimates had led the public to believe. Both cities converted their Athlete's Village into housing, and both cities provided significant government bailouts for private developers when the 2008 economic crash happened. In what follows, I discuss the genesis of the commitments made to social housing by the London bid committee, aligned with the twenty-first century emphasis on social legacies for Olympic Games. I then discuss the erosion of these commitments, thanks in part to a shifting policy terrain that replaced 'social' rents (at 50% of market rent) with 'affordable' rents (at 80% of market rent). This shift would be key to the gentrification of the neighbourhood and the pushing out of the young people with whom I worked. Finally, I consider the creation of contrasting areas of Stratford, divided economically and aesthetically into 'old Stratford' and 'new Stratford,' and how this division was experienced by the youth.

London housing commitments: 'The regeneration of an entire community for the direct benefit of everyone who lives there'

The original London bid was supported by then Mayor Ken Livingstone only on the basis that it be used to enhance the existing urban regeneration agenda in the East end of London (Poynter 2009). East London had been the centre of urban regeneration policy and projects for at least the preceding 30 years, the most significant of these being the London Docklands and the Thames Gateway project. Neither of these regeneration projects had a good track record for benefitting the area's local working class communities: the London Docklands development, not far from the London 2012 stadium, resulted in increased social polarization between the populations who had previously lived there and those who moved into the newly built housing; Thames Gateway prioritized owner-occupied units for young, childless couples, rather than much needed family housing (Bernstock 2009). The Olympic regeneration project was effectively built over top of pre-existing plans for the area, originally outlined in the Mayor's 2004 London Plan; transport schemes and the development of the Westfield's mall at Stratford station were already underway when the Olympic bid was won (Davis and Thornley 2010). Thus, regeneration of the area was already in the cards; adding it to the Olympics bid had the dual result of ensuring the bid's success with the IOC, and linking regeneration to the tempo and priorities of the Games (Davis and Thornley 2010).

There were six official Olympic Host boroughs in East London: Newham, Hackney, Tower Hamlets, Waltham Forest, Greenwich, and Barking and Dagenham. Four of these boroughs were the focus of the London Legacy Development Corporation, the body responsible for overseeing the implementation of the Legacy commitments: Newham, Hackney, Tower Hamlets, and Waltham Forest (Bernstock 2014). The youth we worked with in London lived in the Host borough of Newham; it was in Newham that the majority of the Olympic-related facilities were built, as well as being the site of the related developments of the Westfield shopping mall and Stratford High Street.

Newham has the youngest age structure in England and Wales; around 30% of Newham's population are children and young people under the age of 20 (LBN 2011). It also has the second most diverse population in the UK, with 70% of residents being non-white (ibid.). The 2008 School Census recorded 144 distinct languages spoken at home, and Newham is thought to have the highest population of refugees and asylum seekers in London (ibid.). Before the Olympics, the employment rate stood at just 56.2%, the lowest of any London borough, and significantly below the London average rate of 62.7% (ibid.);[1] the unemployment rate for minority residents in the borough (14.5%) was more than double that of the white population (6.7%). As of May 2010, 21.3% of working-age residents were claiming out-of-work benefits, in contrast with a London average of 14.4% and a national average of 14.7% (ibid.). Not surprisingly, Newham has one of the highest rates of child poverty in London, and is one of the top ten most deprived boroughs in London and nationally (ibid.). In terms of housing, the rate of private ownership is lower than the national average, and reliance on social housing is high. In 2009, fully half (50%) of the social housing stock in Newham was designated as below Decent Homes Standard (ibid.; see also Kennelly and Watt 2012).

The high degree of deprivation in Newham, and in East London more broadly, drove The East London Communities Organisation (TELCO) to try to leverage stronger social justice commitments from the Olympic bid committee. A membership based organization made up of a diverse array of East London churches, mosques, colleges and schools, TELCO is part of a larger civil society umbrella organization called London Citizens. As in Vancouver, the bid committee was quite amenable to TELCO's social legacy suggestions, recognizing the benefit of integrating community-led concerns for enhancing the winnability of their portfolio. The London bid ultimately integrated seven key social responsibility commitments, arising as a result of their consultations with TELCO and London Citizens.[2] These commitments, which TELCO called the 'people's promises' and were also known as the 'Ethical Olympics Charter' (Timms 2012), were summarized in the "London 2012 Olympic Games Official Report Volume 1" (LOCOG no date, 54), as follows:

- Promoting fair employment policies and procurement strategies.
- Using tools such as local jobs brokerage schemes and local training courses to promote the use of local labour, and providing a pool of skilled workers from which to draw a workforce.
- Delivering affordable homes for Londoners.
- Staying in line with the Mayor's target that 50 per cent of new homes should be affordable as set out in the London Plan.
- Investigating the potential for a community land trust.
- Establishing the feasibility of a pilot project to deliver mutual home ownership through a community land trust.
- Developing training and skills programmes.

TELCO and the London Citizens were strategic in their efforts to get the bid committee to listen to their concerns and integrate their priority commitments into the bid. In an interview with Neil Jameson, the Executive Director of London Citizens, he notes that:

> The only reason we were taken seriously is that the IOC needed to see Londoners in favour of the games. We're the largest civil society organization in East London and therefore that was our power. We voted to not support the Games unless our proposals were taken seriously and we had a signed letter, publicly signed [by bid co-chair, Lord Coe]. Once we did that, we were very enthusiastic about the Games, we were delighted when London won because we had the deal.
>
> (Personal communication, 2011)

TELCO knew that the London bid required public support in order to win favour with the IOC. They used their substantial influence among their members to draw people out to support the bid, once their commitments were incorporated into it. Unlike the Impacts of the Olympics on Communities Coalition (IOCC) in Vancouver, London Citizens was also able to maintain strong relationships with the various agencies responsible for delivering the London legacy. This in itself was no small accomplishment; the bureaucracy responsible for implementing the London Olympics and their legacy commitments is complex. Managed by the Department of Culture, Media and Sport, the bodies responsible for both the Games and the legacies include the London Organizing Committee for the Olympic and Paralympic Games (LOCOG), the Olympic Delivery Authority (ODA), the London Development Agency (LDA), and the Olympic Park Legacy Company (OPLC), to name a few of the key players.

In our conversation in 2011, one year before the London Games, Jameson was pleased with the outcome of the living wage employment commitment that had been made, though less clear about whether the housing commitments would be kept:

> So we'll see on the housing but actually it is, as I say, a very good story. Living wages, it's outstanding, there's never been a living wage in the Olympics before, where all the jobs were guaranteed a higher wage than the state minimum. The Olympic Delivery Authority were able to use their purchasing power, which was substantial, to negotiate a better deal for workers. They would not have done that if local people hadn't organized. It wasn't that they were against it, they wouldn't have thought of it. So the message to the world is if you organize you can get things, if you don't organize you get very little and the more effectively you organize the more you can get.

Jameson's enthusiasm about the potential benefits to be gained by community organizing around the London Olympics is echoed in various academic articles (Wills 2013; Timms 2012), though others are wary of the limits to London Citizens' Olympic organizing capacity (Armstrong, Hobbs, and Lindsay 2011). Certainly the efforts of the London Citizens group were impressive; by 2014, the community land trust for which they had been advocating was confirmed to be set up in Bow, not far from the Olympic Park (Allen and Cochrane 2014). This model of housing was explained by Neil Jameson:

> Basically the land is given for free to a trust which we set up and in perpetuity the land remains in the ownership of that trust. We then contract with a developer to build houses there and the houses are sold without the price of the land being included in the house. In East London, because of the price of land being so high, [for] most houses at least a third, if not half, of their price is land. So if you take the price of the land out of the price of the house you can in fact construct a[n affordable] house, that would be our aim. These would be family housing, it's critically important that we have family housing, because all the housing being built at the moment is one and two bedroomed accommodation.

While the establishment of a land trust is an impressive achievement, and is no doubt due to the organizing acumen of London Citizens, the number of units that will follow the land trust model will be miniscule in comparison with the documented need. The development in Bow, which is in the Olympic borough of Tower Hamlets, will provide 252 new homes; however, only 23 of those will belong to the community land trust (Howard 2014). This is a far cry from what TELCO had been hoping to achieve when they initially supported the bid; as Neil Jameson told me in 2011, "We're fairly confident [the community land trust] will happen, we'd settle for a reasonable 200, 300, 500 houses." Thus, while the new urban community land trust won after many years of organizing by London Citizens is an important achievement, it is comparatively a drop in the bucket in terms of housing provision.

What the organizing of the London Citizens did achieve is the provision of legitimacy and popular support to the bid committee when they were working to convince the IOC to award them the Games. The integration of the 'people's promises,' alongside the commitment to regenerate multiple neighbourhoods in East London and provide a legacy for young people, were key to the surprising success of the bid over the perceived front runners Paris and Madrid (Poynter 2009). This was no doubt due at least in part to the shifting priorities of the IOC, with their emphasis on social responsibility and social legacy goals at the centre of their new Olympic modernizing efforts. But the housing goal established in the London bid, to "deliver affordable homes for London" – which was later given a number of between 30,000 and 40,000 homes, of which half would be 'affordable' (Bernstock 2014) – was ultimately significantly diluted courtesy of a number of policy shifts and the pressures of market-driven approaches to housing development.

The shifting terrain of housing policy: from 'social' to 'affordable' rents and cuts to housing benefit

One of the significant policy transformations that happened in the period between the bid and the 2012 Games was the replacement of the 'social rent' model with the 'affordable rent' model (Bernstock 2014). Under the former regime, social rents were typically set at 50% of market value, and sometimes less in more expensive areas (Wiles 2014). They allowed families to rent housing without relying on housing benefit (social assistance) to do so. Affordable rents, on the other hand, are set at 80% of market value, making a significant difference in the monthly cost of housing.

The slippery semantics of 'social rent' versus 'affordable rent' are a key part of the London Olympic housing legacy story. For those who are not familiar with the way in which the terms are used, it would appear that the London Olympics were able to do what previous host cities have not: provide affordable housing as a direct Olympic legacy. For instance, the report of the UN Rapporteur on Adequate Housing approvingly cites the IOC's information about the housing plans for London, noting that "half of the 2,800 units in the Olympic Village are to become affordable housing after the Games, while current plans for the Olympic Park site are for around 10,000 new homes, around 35 per cent to be affordable housing"

(Rolnik 2009, 5). Such numbers look impressive, when taken out of context about the difference between 'social rents' and 'affordable rents.' While affordable rents (at 80% of market value) are important, they are more likely to serve the needs of middle income earners who are also struggling to afford housing, particularly in London (Doward 2014). As the London Tenants Federation points out, "much of the housing defined by Government as affordable, isn't affordable for households that have below median income level in London" (London Tenants Federation 2012, 4).

For the youth we spoke to in London, the shift towards 'affordable rents' meant they could not expect to live in such housing, including the Athlete's Village.

Olu (2012):   Now when you talk about affordability, we can't afford anything so when they use the word affordable it's not affordable, it's for people that have a job and can pay rent. Live their lifestyle. They are nice buildings though, so I still kind of hope one day that I can [live there].

Leslie (2013):   They're saying that the new affordable is £30,000 [in annual income, to pay for affordable housing]. Now, that's a benchmark already, that half of Stratford is not on. That's a benchmark that I'm not on. I'm on £7 an hour, so right now, I don't think so. I really don't think so.

As Olu notes, the new buildings going up were very nice, and would have been attractive places to live. But Leslie's impression that people in his neighbourhood would not be able to afford so-called 'affordable' rents is borne out by the data. In 2009, the average income in Stratford was £24,435, and in Newham, the borough in which Stratford is located, it was £23,265 (LBN 2010). As noted, housing need is acute and wait lists for social housing are substantial. On the London Borough of Newham's housing information page, they warn potential home-seekers that "[d]emand for social housing is extremely high in Newham and there are currently thousands of households on our housing register" ("Newham" no date). In 2012 the Department of Communities and Local Government documented 34.9% of the Newham population as being on a housing waiting list, or more than one person for every three people living in the borough; this is the highest of any borough in the country (Bernstock 2014). Watt (2013) notes that the housing waiting lists across the Olympic host boroughs saw a 42% increase between 2005 (the year the London bid was won) and 2011 (the year before the Games), a much steeper rise than the nearly 19% average increase for London and England. On the Newham housing website is a table illustrating the average length of time on a waiting list for different forms of housing; the numbers range between 7 years and 1 month for a ground floor bedsit (a bachelor apartment) and 13 years and 11 months for a four bedroom house ("Newham" no date).

There is no question, then, that the need for social housing in the area is significant. It is also clear that the 2005 commitments to housing in the original Olympic bid were intended to address this need for *social* (as opposed to

Figure 3.1 An example of one of the many signs around Stratford prior to and during the Games, advertising 1 and 2 bedroom units available to purchase, in this case through a 'shared ownership' scheme (author photo, 2012).

affordable) rents. One of the 'people's promises' that helped London win the bid in the first place was a strong commitment to social housing: "Staying in line with the Mayor's target that 50 per cent of new homes should be affordable as set out in the London Plan." The London Plan to which this statement refers was first set out in 2004, and would have been the version the bid committee was referencing in 2005. This first London Plan, developed under the previous London mayor Ken Livingston, not only emphasized that 50% of the housing built would be affordable, it also stressed that 70% of this housing would be designated social (Bernstock 2014). This was in recognition of the substantial need for such housing, throughout London but particularly in East London, identified as a 'priority area' in the 2004 version of the London Plan (Mayor of London 2008). So the earlier commitment to housing, an integral part of London's successful bid, was initially about *social* rents, and meeting the housing needs of local populations. What later happened, as we have seen, was a shift towards 'affordable' rents, following larger nation-wide trends. As Hodkinson and Robbins (2013) argue, this was part of a wider assault on the social welfare safety net by the Conservative-dominated UK coalition government elected in 2010.

The story of the Athlete's Village is an important component of the 2012 Olympic housing legacy – and it is a very complex one. Prior to the Olympic bid, permission had already been granted for 5,000 homes to be built as part of the Westfield Stratford City development. It was anticipated that the building of the Athlete's Village, with plans to convert it to housing after the Games, would thus provide additional housing over and above the units already planned (Bernstock 2014). In 2007, plans were revised so that the Athlete's Village became integrated into the original Stratford City scheme, raising questions as to how much additional housing could actually be claimed as an Olympic legacy (Bernstock 2014). Original plans to create 4,200 housing units post-Games were down-sized ultimately to 2,800 units. Of these, approximately half, or 1,379, were designated 'affordable' (Bernstock 2014). Of these affordable units, about half would become 'social,' creating 675 units of social-rented housing, or 24% of the total units. Interest in the social housing units has been high, with 17,000 registering their desire to live there (Bernstock 2014). Since residents have the right to buy these properties, it is possible that over time some of these units will convert to market housing (Bernstock 2014).

If we consider these numbers in light of the formula set out in the 2004 London Plan, the number of social units ought to have been closer to 1,400: that is, the original number of proposed units in the Athlete's Village (4,200), divided in half (2,100), would be affordable. Of these, 70%, or approximately 1,400, would be social units. In other words, less than half of the original commitment to social housing was met within the Athlete's Village, now called East Village. And East Village was the good news story in terms of Olympic social housing development; of the other five neighbourhoods counted as part of the Olympic housing legacy, all still in the development stage, the percentage of affordable rents is set at 30% or less, with an even smaller proportion of that number being designated as social rents (Hill 2015).

One important factor in the low number of social housing units in East Village was the loopholes created by the original public-private partnership behind the Athlete's Village project. Just as occurred in Vancouver, the developer who had won the contract for building the Athlete's Village – in this case an international company called Lend Lease – was unable to access the necessary financing to capitalize the project after the economic crash in 2008. The UK government was responsible for ensuring that the project was completed, and ultimately did so by taking on the full financing of it, transforming Lend Lease into the contractor. Any risks associated with the Athlete's Village thus became public risks, rather than private (Bernstock 2014). Reports at the time suggested that the money for the shortfall might be pulled from the Mayor of London's annual budget for affordable housing, causing a public outcry (Bar-Hillel 2008). Other reports suggested that it would come from the Olympic contingency fund (Kelso 2008). Wherever the money ultimately came from, what had originally been conceived as a private–public partnership, with shared risks, became a publically funded project from which private developers were able to benefit. As Jules Boykoff (2014) points out, the shifting of private risks onto public shoulders is typical of the economics that accompany contemporary Olympic Games.

The shortage of social housing in East London had been a crisis for many years, and it had only gotten worse with the changes in housing policy from social to affordable rents. The 2004 London Plan, with its emphasis on building social housing, had not been meeting its targets since its inception; only 47% of the London Plan target for social-rented homes was met between 2007 and 2010 (London Tenants Federation 2012). By 2013, the effects of these wider policy contexts were being felt directly by the youth we were working with in Newham. While some had been able to secure council housing or housing association flats in the area (for a more detailed discussion of this, see Watt and Bernstock 2016), many spoke of the pressure they were under to accept housing in other parts of the city or even the country, moving them far from their social supports. This was due in part to changes to the housing rules, explained to us in 2013 by a support worker in the temporary housing where we were conducting our research. She told us that previously, people moving into government-supported housing (council or housing association) had some choices about where they could live; with the changes in the rules, "now, they can give you wherever they want. It could even be Birmingham, Manchester and if you turn it down you're taken off the list straightaway." In other words, refusing to move into available housing means you will lose your chance to get such housing. This puts pressure on people to accept housing even in other cities, far from their families, friends, and other supports. The youth were aware of these changes, which caused them a great deal of anxiety. As Angelica noted:

> There's no placement in Newham, not even Stratford. They only have housing outside of London, so they can move you to Birmingham and if you refuse the property for whatever reason then you're off the housing register.

Compounding the crisis of the lack of availability of local social housing, the government introduced the first of two housing benefit caps in 2013. A 'cap' on housing benefit essentially means that the cost of housing may rise, but the corresponding social assistance will not. Many of the youth we spoke to in 2013 were wondering what it would mean for them to try and find housing in Newham given these changes to social assistance, which most of them relied on to live. As Leslie told us:

> The changes are a bit slippery. Again it's deception because they haven't told you everything, but they expect us to just go on willy nilly and just, oh, okay. The transitional stage is here, then it starts and then everyone don't know what's going on and all of a sudden everyone gets sanctioned.

As housing became more scarce and benefit caps limited the options of the youth we spoke to, policy shifts towards awarding the 'deserving poor' with housing

were also having an effect on the likelihood that the youth would find housing – a shift that Penny Bernstock (2014, 130) notes has succeeded in "effectively wind[ing] back housing policy fifty years." The youth we spoke to were under pressure to perform appropriately in order to earn a space in housing. One of the support workers told us that a panel of external representatives make the decisions about which of the youth in the supportive housing structure she worked at would 'win' more permanent, and scarce, council housing spaces. Of the fifty youth who put forward their names each year from this one block of temporary housing, only fifteen spaces were allocated from Newham council to house them. Not surprisingly, competition is fierce for these spaces, and the youth are required to 'sell' themselves in order to demonstrate that they are 'deserving' of the housing. As described by the support worker with whom we spoke:

> The guy who wrote this [application for council housing] came to me yesterday and he had just a paragraph, and I said, "You're not selling yourself." Those were my words, "You're not selling yourself." Because it's an opportunity and so I know that that young person has done so well in a short period of time and I think that is important for him. . . . I mean you've got a lot of young people that really do engage and that's what this is all about. It isn't just about housing, you want them to engage and do well and a lot of them have really done well. They'll regularly attend breakfast club meetings, they'll get involved with research projects, and they're the people, sometimes, as long as their rent is paid and they're not engaging in anti-social behaviour, they'll be the ones who sometimes get [nominated for council housing].

The net effect of these policy shifts was that low income youth (and other low income populations) living in Newham were less and less likely to find suitable housing in their immediate area, exerting pressure on them to leave. There were four key policy shifts that formed the backdrop to these pressures, including: the conversion from a social rent to an affordable rent regime; the revision of housing rules such that people requiring social housing could be relocated to different parts of the country; housing benefit caps; and the incremental transformation of housing from an entitlement to something that must be 'earned' through good behaviour. While the housing policy landscape is bigger than the Olympics, the presence of the Olympics in East London exacerbated these pressures, for instance through the accumulation of additional debt due to the bailout of the Athlete's Village. Equally important is that the housing commitments to provide social housing in the area that would alleviate the dire housing need – which had formed a part of the initial London bid and helped London win the Games – were ultimately not met.

Rent increases and gentrification pressures: Old Stratford vs. New Stratford

Another important part of the London Olympic housing story is the effect on the immediate surrounding neighbourhood in terms of gentrification pressures and the rise in private rental prices. Gentrification of the area was apparent to the youth before the Games began (see also Kennelly and Watt 2012). The following excerpts are from focus groups conducted in 2011:

> *Focus group 1:* I think that's why the prices are going to go up even more so there's going to be lots of people living in the borough who aren't going to be able to afford the stuff, with the restaurants and stuff it's going to be too pricey to live around here.

> *Focus group 2:* The prices have already gone up and up, so there's no chance, we haven't got no hope really unless we get something really soon or get a really good job and buy our own place. I wouldn't like to live around Newham; I'd like to move out of Newham.

> *Focus group 3:* I think that the money they're spending on the Olympics is definitely going to change the area to a much higher-class area and all the people that don't have the money to stay in the area are going to be kicked out. After the Olympics has finished I don't think it's just going to be a dead area, I think it's going to be a giant tourist attraction that's going to generate millions for years to come . . . it's not for us, you know what I mean.

Watt (2013) draws on Peter Marcuse's work to discuss how gentrification can create displacement pressures, "'[W]hen a family sees its neighborhood changing dramatically, when all their friends are leaving, when stores are going out of business and new stores for other clientele are taking their place [. . .], when changes in public facilities, transportation patterns, support services, are all making the area less and less livable'" (as quoted in Watt 2013, 101). Gentrification experienced by the youth largely took the form of the closure of affordable shops and the transformation of existing businesses into higher-priced retailers. Michael illustrates the latter through the image in Figure 3.2, taken in 2011.

Another impact on the local community where the youth lived was the imposition of Olympic by-laws that prohibited the use of trademark protected terms such as 'Olympics', 'London 2012' or combinations of words such as 'medals,' 'gold', 'silver', 'bronze' etc. Such brand protection is required by the IOC of all host cities, though London organizers were particularly vigilant about potential incursions on the Olympic brand (Boykoff 2014). One local restaurant used by the youth was affected by this suite of laws; despite having been in the community for many years before the bid or the Games, 'Café Olympic' was forced to change its name to 'Café Lympic' (see Figure 3.3). During a walking interview in 2012, Isaac identified this café as a "wonderful, healthy eating" place that was "away from Westfield, away from the shopping mall." As he noted, "the only thing that has changed here is the sign and the price of the food. The price has gone up."

Also relevant to the youth we worked with was the rise in private rental prices in the area, which rose faster and more steeply than house purchase prices in Stratford in the years leading up to the Olympics (Bernstock 2014). This has important implications for low income and working class residents who rely on

this is a cafe that has been reformed
for the olympics this place used to be
affordable for people on a low budgit.
Just one of many shops that are
to expensive to go to.

Figure 3.2 Image from Michael's photo journal in 2011. His text reads: "This is a café that has been reformed for the Olympics. This place used to be affordable for people on a low budget. Just one of many shops that are too expensive to go to."

private renting as a means to house themselves and their families. As one support worker told us, "There are few options available for young people, apart from private renting. I mean realistically that is the only option they have. I think the homelessness problem is just going to grow."

The rise in private rental prices generated a great deal of investment from those interested in 'buy to let' schemes – in other words, people who bought up rental stock in the area in order to rent it out for short-term or holiday stays, particularly when the Olympics were taking place. Stratford High Street was the site of intense development of such high-end rental units, characterized by "high density, tower constructions, with relatively few family size housing units" (Bernstock 2014, 147). Between 2000 and 2012, there were 2,321 new units built along the Stratford High Street, and a further 2,126 planned (Bernstock 2014). Of these, 24% were designated affordable, including a mix of social, shared ownership and intermediate rent

Figure 3.3 Café Lympic (photo credit: Paul Watt, 2012).

and sale products (Bernstock 2014).[3] The numbers of units designated as 'social rent' in these buildings were well below a third of the new developments. Penny Bernstock notes that, while Stratford has benefitted from substantial infrastructure development, the "private sector is increasingly unwilling or unable to make any significant contribution to affordable housing development" (2014, 149).

These towers were the subject of scrutiny and skepticism by the youth, who saw them as beautiful new buildings that had been built for affluent others, rather than in order to meet their own housing needs. As noted by one participant during a 2011 focus group:

> There's going to be probably a lot of people coming over from other countries as well that are willing to pay all this money and can afford it, and they're going to be taking up all the spare places to rent for just the Olympics. Whereas there's people like us waiting, sitting there like [on the housing] list, waiting to be found somewhere and housed. Now we're being pushed aside and [being told] "hold on," even though [the government] got all this money, we're spending it on this [high end developments]. You lot are not important even though this is our country, we've got the Olympics.

The youth were understandably pessimistic about being able to access private rental housing in the neighbourhood, not only due to the high prices but also because of the logistical barriers in place. One significant issue for the young people in our study was finding a guarantor who would be responsible for the rent should they not be able to pay it. As one of the housing support workers told us:

> They're having lots of problems with [private renting] because they're going to landlords and the landlords want guarantors. Some of my residents haven't got family, they're here for a reason, so that's causing a headache as well. I've had one resident who's lived here for three years, she's ready to move on and she hasn't got a guarantor, she's got no parents in her life. She's found four properties so far and every landlord wants a guarantor.

The youth were also at a disadvantage with private rental units due to security of tenure issues. As the same support worker noted, "Private accommodation, you don't know how long you're going to be in there and the rent is very high." This sentiment was echoed by one of the youth during a 2011 focus group:

> I personally think the closer to the Olympics it comes the more people are scared of moving out [of their supportive housing structure] anyway because even if you were to get a place now, the time from now to when the Olympics starts your rent is going to [be] turned up so much that you're not even knowing what to expect. If you get a house, it might be affordable now, give it a couple of months and you can't afford it no more, you might be getting kicked out and starting at the beginning again and then there's nowhere for you to go because then you're going to be blacklisted and stuff [from the council housing list].

Bernstock (2014) conducted interviews with people living in the new buildings in Stratford High Street, and concluded that the 'new migrants' to the area were largely young professionals, in singles or couples and without children. They were intending to live in the area for no more than five years as part of building equity in order to 'move up the housing ladder.' They did not identify with the other residents who had lived in Stratford prior to the development of the Stratford High Street, instead seeing themselves as part of the 'new Stratford.' Bernstock notes that this view supported the division of Stratford into two segregated portions: "A new Stratford with parkland, Westfield shopping centre and lots of new apartments, and an old Stratford characterised by the old shopping centre, disinvested Local Authority run housing and deprivation" (Bernstock 2014, 179).

The notion of 'two Stratfords' matched the experience of the youth who lived in 'old Stratford.' As one participant commented in a 2011 focus group, "expensive housing in a shit area, it makes no sense." This was a sentiment shared by many of the youth we spoke to, who were bewildered by the speed of high end development happening in their neighbourhood, and wondered how it would fit in an area that they had long experienced as deprived and stigmatized. The division between the high density towers going up on Stratford High Street and their own straitened circumstances is clear in a series of images produced by Olu in his 2011 photo journal (see Figures 3.4a, b and c).

Figure 3.4a Image from Olu's photo journal in 2011. His text reads: "This image shows a few of the companies that will benefit from the regeneration."

Figure 3.4b Image from Olu's photo journal in 2011. His text reads: "This image shows a few luxury flats with various bedroom numbers available. Only a small percentage of this if any will go to people like myself. Only the people that can afford it will get it."

Figure 3.4c Image from Olu's photo journal in 2011. His text reads: "This image shows a contrast between the old and the new which is going up. Half of these properties are in a state of disrepair and yet there are new ones going up."

Noteworthy is that none of the other 12 youth who completed the photo project in 2011, nor the four youth who took us on walking interviews in 2012, included the section of Stratford High Street that had been developed as part of their everyday experiences of Stratford. The reason for this is apparent to anyone who walks around the area: 'old Stratford' is spatially divided from 'new Stratford' by both the Stratford mall and the new Westfield mall (which is confusingly referred to at times as 'Stratford City,' as its full name is 'Westfield Stratford City'). The original Stratford mall is the de facto entrance from the Stratford bus and train station to the older section of the neighbourhood, and is notable for its budget shops and market stalls that cater to the immigrant and working class populations that call the area home. Westfield mall is part of the Olympic regeneration project for the area and served for the duration of the Olympic Games as the entrance to the Olympic Park, in the exact opposite direction to the old Stratford mall. The old mall was additionally obscured in the period leading up to the Games by a large-scale sculpture of what appear to be swimming fish ('the Stratford Shoal' – see Figure 3.5), which caused a controversy when they were installed (see also Manley and Silk 2013). Intentionally designed to obscure the old mall, which was

Figure 3.5 'The Stratford Shoal' obscuring the entrance to the original
Stratford mall (author image, 2012).

considered less attractive than the new Westfield development, local people questioned why £3 million was being spent on this work of public art rather than on some of the more pressing social needs in the neighbourhood (Bloomfield and Rogers 2010).

While Stratford High Street appeared in only one of the photo journals created by the youth, the new Westfield Mall played a prominent role in many of the photo journals that the youth produced for us in 2011. Still under construction when these photo journals were completed, the captions accompanying the youths' photos of Westfield documented their bewilderment at the placement of this mall in their low-income neighbourhood. Figure 3.6, from Jessica, is characteristic of these sentiments:

Figure 3.6 Image from Jessica's photo journal in 2011. Her text reads: "Europe's largest shopping centre? How about Europe's largest [housing] estate? Sport fanatics or homeless?"

Youth in our study noted that the contrast between the 'new' Stratford with Westfield mall, and the 'old' Stratford with its high level of deprivation, carried the potential to exacerbate class conflicts, where the 'haves' would be the subject of intense resentment by the 'have-nots':

Leslie: My biggest fear was that [Westfield] Stratford City would be . . . well, it says it for itself, a city within a city, which then provides an invisible barrier, because you've got the people that go to Westfield with £1,000 and spend money and you've got, what my friend said earlier, he's a window shopper, he'll go there because he hasn't got no money, and that instantly, that will spark tension, potentially hatred because, 'you've got what I can't have.'

The development of the 'new Stratford,' including both the Westfield mall and Stratford High Street's high density towers, has ultimately become another element of gentrification and displacement in the area. Experienced by the youth we spoke with as a world that was quite separate from the Stratford they knew, the rental units built in the new towers were not typically within their reach financially. Even if the youth were to secure one of the scarce designated social-rented units that had been included in the Stratford High Street developments, they would have found themselves in a sea of higher income people and would likely face stigmatization and isolation, as documented by Bernstock (2014) in her study of the area. While the youth we worked with were increasingly under pressure to move towards private rentals in the face of decreasing availability of social housing, they could not expect realistically to secure such housing in Stratford, ultimately forcing them to move out of the area where many of them had spent their entire lives. Furthermore, the spatial and symbolic division between 'old' and 'new' Stratford represented for the youth further evidence of their exclusion from avenues of access and affluence, potentially breeding resentment and conflict.

Conclusions

London's original housing commitments were impressive, and the bureaucratic infrastructure they established in order to meet their legacy goals even more so. In 2011, before the Games happened, the collective view of the key workers at the supportive housing structure in which we were doing our research was that the legacy promises of regeneration and opportunities for the youth they worked with would be a real outcome of the Olympics. By 2013, however, high hopes had turned to bitter disappointment and a sense of betrayal:

You would have thought that in a place like Newham, where you've got the legacy of the Olympics, that you would see something positive to come out of it, especially for young people. And I'm not really seeing that, to be honest.

The majority of the youth, on the other hand, were fairly cynical about the like-lihood of a positive legacy throughout our research. While some reported that they had been excited about the Olympics coming to their city when the bid was first won, by the time we talked to them in 2011 they were already getting a sense that the Games were being used to improve the lives of others, not them. Indeed, the overwhelming feeling that emerged from the youth throughout our research was of an area being transformed such that it would be out of their reach, both in terms of pricing and also the types of services and facilities being built (Kennelly and Watt 2012; Watt 2013; Kennelly and Watt 2013). The promises made to regenerate the neighbourhood, providing much-needed social housing in the process, was ultimately transformed into housing for the middle classes and the creation of a 'new Stratford' that was spatially and economically distinct from the 'old Stratford' where the youth lived. Due to policy changes such as the shift from social rents to affordable rents and the implementation of a housing benefits cap, in combination with the rise in private rental prices and the erosion of commitments by private developers to provide social housing in their new buildings, both the youth and the youth support workers we spoke to expected that the youth would be forced to move out of the area.

It is important to note that these policy shifts were both bigger than, and also an integral aspect of, the Olympic housing story. The housing benefits cap and the policy shift towards awarding only the 'deserving poor' with housing were part of an ideological shift to the right, ushered in by a change in government. The housing policy context in 2005, when the London bid was won, was thus significantly different than it was in 2012, when the Games happened (Bernstock 2014). The shift in housing priorities and policies meant that the bodies responsible for Olympic-related development and legacy commitments were able to effectively move the focus away from using regeneration to address disadvantage and instead create regeneration that serves the needs of middle income earners. This is particularly significant when we consider that the initial success of the bid, as was also the case in Vancouver, was based on its social commitments to provide a housing legacy and ensure that marginalized populations were not displaced by the Games. What we see here is a clear instance of social legacy commitments being used to win the Olympic bid, then being discarded or radically transformed when policy and budgetary contexts shifted. The result is that a host city and its population, which largely embraced the bid and felt rightfully pleased that the Olympics would be used to generate opportunities and housing for those who resided in East London, were ultimately left with a legacy of gentrification and displacement, providing opportunities for middle income earners and developers at the expense of local impoverished populations.

Notes

1 After the Olympics, unemployment remained high; Newham had the second highest unemployment rate in London as of 2013 (Trust for London and New Policy Institute 2013). Olympic impacts on employment will be discussed in more detail in Chapter 4.
2 For more on this process, see www.citizensuk.org/campaigns/london-2012-olympics/ accessed October 15, 2014.

3 'Shared ownership' schemes consist of a renter buying a portion of the property, then gradually paying off more of the property price over time, ultimately becoming the owner. Intermediate housing is available for rent or sale above social rent levels, but below market levels.

Bibliography

All website URLs were accessed between September 2014 and December 2015.

Allen, John, and Allan Cochrane. 2014. "The Urban Unbound: London's Politics and the 2012 Olympic Games." *International Journal of Urban and Regional Research* 38 (5): 1609–24. doi:10.1111/1468-2427.12147.

Armstrong, Gary, Dick Hobbs, and Iain Lindsay. 2011. "Calling the Shots: The Pre-2012 London Olympic Contest." *Urban Studies* 48 (15): 3169–84. doi:10.1177/0042098 011422397.

Bar-Hillel, Mira. 2008. "Housing Cash 'Used for 2012': Money for Affordable London Housing Could Be Used to Make up a Shortfall in Funding for the Athletes' Village." *London Evening Standard*, August 13.

Bernstock, Penny. 2009. "London 2012 and the Regeneration Game." In *Olympic Cities: 2012 and the Remaking of London*, edited by Gavin Poynter and Iain MacRury. Burlington, VT: Ashgate Publishing Ltd.

Bernstock, Penny. 2014. *Olympic Housing: A Critical Review of London 2012's Legacy.* Farnham, UK: Ashgate.

Bloomfield, Ruth, and David Rogers. 2010. "£3 Million Sculpture to Hide Stratford Eyesore." *Building Design.* February 19. www.bdonline.co.uk/news/£3-million-sculpture-to-hide-stratford-eyesore/3158377.article.

Boykoff, Jules. 2014. *Celebration Capitalism and the Olympic Games.* London and New York: Routledge.

Davis, Juliet, and Andy Thornley. 2010. "Urban Regeneration for the London 2012 Olympics: Issues of Land Acquisition and Legacy." *City, Culture and Society* 1 (2): 89–98.

Doward, Jamie. 2014. "'Endies': Employed with No Disposable Income Are Struggling in London." *The Guardian*, September 13 (section: UK news). www.theguardian. com/uk-news/2014/sep/13/endies-employed-no-disposable-income-struggling-in-london.

Hill, Dave. 2015. "What's Happened to 'Affordable' Housing on London's Olympic Park?" *The Guardian.* July 8. www.theguardian.com/uk-news/davehillblog/2015/jul/08/whats-happened-to-affordable-housing-on-londons-olympic-park.

Hodkinson, Stuart, and Glyn Robbins. 2013. "The Return of Class War Conservatism? Housing under the UK Coalition Government." *Critical Social Policy* 33 (1): 57–77. doi:10.1177/0261018312457871.

Howard, Emma. 2014. "Affordable London Home Scheme Launched by Mayor Boris Johnson." *The Guardian*, March 20 (section: Global). www.theguardian.com/global/2014/mar/20/affordable-london-homes-scheme-mayor-boris-johnson.

Kelso, Paul. 2008. "Taxpayers to Bail out 2012 Games Village." *The Guardian*, June 20 (section: Sport). www.theguardian.com/uk/2008/jun/20/olympics2012.politicsand sport.

Kennelly, Jacqueline, and Paul Watt. 2012. "Seeing Olympic Effects through the Eyes of Marginally Housed Youth: Changing Places and the Gentrification of East London." *Visual Studies* 27 (2): 151–60. doi:10.1080/1472586X.2012.677496.

Kennelly, Jacqueline, and Paul Watt. 2013. "Restricting the Public in Public Space: The London 2012 Olympic Games, Hyper-Securitization and Marginalized Youth." *Sociological Research Online* 18 (2): 19.

LBN. 2010. "Stratford and West Ham Community Forum Profile." London Borough of Newham Community Leaders and Engagement. www.newham.info/research/CFProfiles/StratfordWestHam.pdf.

LBN. 2011. "Newham: Key Statistics." London: London Borough of Newham.

LOCOG. No date. "London 2012 Olympic Games Official Report Volume 1." London: London Organizing Committee of the Olympic Games and Paralympic Games.

London Tenants Federation. 2012. "The Affordable Housing Con." London. www.london tenants.org/publications/other/theafordablehousingconf.pdf.

Manley, Andrew, and Michael Silk. 2013. "Liquid London: Sporting Spectacle, Britishness and Ban-Optic Surveillance." *Surveillance & Society* 11 (4): 360–76.

Mayor of London. 2008. "The London Plan. Spatial Development Strategy for Greater London." www.london.gov.uk/thelondonplan/docs/londonplan08.pdf.

"Newham." no date. *East London Lettings Company.* https://www.ellcchoicehomes.org.uk/Data/ASPPages/1/1270.aspx.

Poynter, Gavin. 2009. "London: Preparing for 2012." In *Olympic Cities: 2012 and the Remaking of London*, edited by Gavin Poynter and Iain MacRury. Burlington, VT: Ashgate Publishing Ltd.

Rolnik, Raquel. 2009. "Special Rapporteur on Adequate Housing as a Component of the Right to an Adequate Standard of Living, and on the Right to Non-Discrimination in This Context." United Nations General Assembly. www.ohchr.org/en/issues/housing/pages/housingindex.aspx.

Timms, Jill. 2012. "The Olympics as a Platform for Protest: A Case Study of the London 2012 'ethical' Games and the Play Fair Campaign for Workers' Rights." *Leisure Studies* 31 (3): 355–72. doi:10.1080/02614367.2012.667821.

Trust for London and New Policy Institute. 2013. "London's Poverty Profile 2013 Newham Press Release." London. www.londonspovertyprofile.org.uk/press/lpp-2013-newham-press-release/.

Watt, Paul. 2013. "'It's Not for Us': Regeneration, the 2012 Olympics and the Gentrification of East London." *City* 17 (1): 99–118. doi:10.1080/13604813.2012.754190.

Watt, Paul, and Penny Bernstock. 2016. "Housing in Post-Olympics East London: Broken Promises or Sustainable Legacy?" In *London 2012 and the Post-Olympics City: A Hollow Legacy?*, edited by Phil Cohen and Paul Watt. Basingstoke: Palgrave Macmillan.

Wiles, Colin. 2014. "Affordable Housing Does Not Mean What You Think It Means." *The Guardian*, February 3. www.theguardian.com/housing-network/2014/feb/03/affordable-housing-meaning-rent-social-housing.

Wills, Jane. 2013. "London's Olympics in 2012: The Good, the Bad and an Organising Opportunity." *Political Geography* 34 (May): A1–3. doi:10.1016/j.polgeo.2012.12.003.

4 Olympic employment legacies in Vancouver and London

Precarious jobs, low wages, and gender inequality

The Olympics and Westfield is [supposed to be] giving so much opportunity to [local young people] but they're not [actually] giving it – it's almost like they're putting it on a plate in front of everyone and saying, "Look at this but don't touch it."

(Jessica, London youth participant, 2011)

They say we're going to have more jobs for the Olympics, [but then] you're going to get laid off once the Olympics are done.

(Annie, Vancouver youth participant, 2009)

One year before the Olympics took place in their respective cities, both Jessica and Annie had already realized that the promises made about employment opportunities for young people were not going to be realized. Neither Jessica, a white working class woman who grew up in Newham, nor Annie, an Aboriginal woman who moved to Vancouver as a girl, would ultimately attain any work or volunteer opportunities from the Games. This was the experience of most of the youth I spoke to in both cities, particularly the young women. Some of the men were able to secure low-paid and short-term work in construction or security, but they were the exception rather than the rule. In this chapter, I focus on the projected economic benefits for host cities – and, more specifically, commitments to increased employment – claimed by bid committees in an effort to win popular support for their bids. Claims about economic benefits are one of the major components to any successful Olympic bid, despite the fact that "the perennial claims that hosting the Olympics or the World Cup is an engine of economic development find little corroboration in independent studies" (Zimbalist 2015, 118).

The promise of an economic boom and its associated jobs intersects with commitments to social legacies, as the employment assurances made often hinge on providing work for the long-term unemployed, young people, and other marginalized local populations. This was the case in both Vancouver and London, where bid committees broadcast highly inflated economic predictions to the public, including astonishing numbers of jobs. In London, employment was supposed to be generated for local residents of working class East London as part of their regeneration strategy; in Vancouver, jobs were promised for inner-city residents, as part of the Inner City Inclusive Commitments Statement. In what follows, I discuss predictions made by the Vancouver and London bid committees for employment, volunteerism, and economic benefits more generally. Since the Games in each city are now complete, I offer comparisons between the predictions and the actual numbers generated, as well as looking at what Olympics boosters told the public. I then consider the initiatives that were targeted specifically towards assisting marginalized residents and youth into employment and volunteerism. Finally, I turn to the experiences of the young people, documenting the manner in which gendered and classed distinctions impacted their capacity to attain and keep the scarce jobs and volunteer positions that came available before and during the Olympic period.

Economic impact studies and their public framing: "The Olympic bid is all about jobs, jobs, and more jobs"

Finding, interpreting, and comparing economic impact studies and their spin-off products (press releases, bid committee promises, and follow-up evaluations to name a few) is a challenging task. The language of economic impact studies is often intentionally opaque, and multiple caveats are included in order to protect the authors from accusations of inaccuracy (Crompton 2006). The numbers that are used in the various documents are often unsourced, and the methodologies described in only the loosest terms. Claims to academic integrity are frequent, though the checks and balances of academic publications are notably missing, such as blind peer review and transparent citation of sources. Comparing across documents creates additional challenges, as there is no consistent format or methodology used in economic impact studies (Kirkup and Major 2006); even more confusing is that the numbers subsequently broadcast through the media rarely resemble the results of the economic impact studies themselves. Despite these challenges, I have sought to parse the numbers presented in the case of the Vancouver and London Olympics, focusing on the impact studies commissioned by the respective bid committees, claims made within the bid documents themselves, the media releases and editorial comments of key actors in the bid and organizing committees, and the official evaluations completed after each Games.

Both the London and Vancouver bid committees commissioned economic impact studies as part of their preparation for winning the Games. The original Vancouver economic impact study was prepared by the Capital Projects Branch of the BC Ministry of Competition, Science and Enterprise (Gray 2002) and focused exclusively on economic impacts. London's study assessed not only economic impact, but also social and environmental impacts of the Games (PwC 2005). Each of these studies contain flaws and exaggerations that John Crompton (2006) describes as common 'mischievous' problems of economic impact studies. These problematic claims were then multiplied through their misrepresentation in public media by bidding committees and Games promoters.

Crompton argues that, "most economic impact studies are commissioned to legitimize a political position rather than to search for economic truth" (2006, 67). He notes that "the purpose of economic impact analysis is to measure the broader economic benefits that accrue to a community" (2006, 67) in order to help that community make decisions about whether to support a proposal that will require the use of tax dollars. As such, they can play an important political role in decision-making processes, provided that they are conducted with integrity. Unfortunately, as Crompton notes, "because the motivation undergirding them usually is to prove the legitimacy of the sponsor's economic case, the temptation to engage in mischievous practices is substantial" (2006, 67).

One such 'mischievous practice' is the flaw of including local residents in economic impact numbers. Crompton describes the problem with this as follows:

> Expenditures by those who reside in the community do not contribute to an event's economic impact because these expenditures represent a recycling of money that already existed there. There is no new economic growth, only a transfer of resources between sectors of the local economy.
>
> (Crompton 2006, 70)

This distortion was particularly apparent in Vancouver's economic impact report. This report (Gray 2002) provides both a *gross* and *incremental* assessment of the projected economic impacts of the 2010 Games. The gross impacts, which include both residential and tourist spending, are rationalized by the author for inclusion in the report with the statement that "every dollar spent in preparing for and hosting the Games will have an economic impact, regardless of who spends the dollars" (Gray 2002, 6). This kind of reporting is extremely problematic, as it overlooks the probability that "if local residents had not spent their money at the tourism attraction, they would have disposed of it either now or later by purchasing other goods and services in the community" (Crompton 2006, 70). In other words, this is a matter of *displaced* spending, rather than *new* spending. Although such expenditures ought not to be included in an economic impact assessment, they often are "because when expenditures by local residents are omitted, the economic-impact numbers often become too small to be politically useful" (Crompton 2006, 70).

Although it is only the incremental numbers that represent new spending, the Vancouver economic impact report breaks out the numbers for both gross and incremental spending in separate tables, and provides an estimate of the tax revenue for each. Each of the tables is sub-divided into estimates for 'low effort/ low response,' 'average effort/average response,' 'better effort/better response,' and 'best effort/best response,' representing different possible economic scenarios that might ensue. In the 'best effort/best response' category, the total estimated tax revenue from gross spending is reported as CDN$1.131 billion, which includes federal, provincial, and local taxes (Gray 2002, 7). The total estimated tax revenue of incremental spending in the 'best effort/best response' category is reported as CDN$982 million for all levels of taxation combined. The projected period over which this revenue would be realized is between 2001 and 2020, thus making it a long-run projection (i.e. longer than the Games-time impact in 2010).

Including gross numbers in the economic impact report clearly provides a much more compelling estimate for tax revenues resulting from the 2010 Olympic Games. But apparently this number was not high enough. In an editorial published in the *Vancouver Sun* on October 25, 2002 by Jack Poole, the chairman and CEO of the Vancouver 2010 Bid Corp (Poole 2002), Poole argued that the 2010 Olympics could generate *$2.5 billion in incremental tax revenue*! This number is more than double the most optimistic forecast of the *gross* tax revenue projected by the economic impact study, which had been published earlier that same year. Poole does not state in the article where he gets his numbers from, but he is unequivocal about this revenue being incremental (i.e. new money brought by tourists) rather than gross revenue (i.e. money recirculated by local residents as well as brought in by tourists):

> "Net incremental taxes" means the present value of new taxes to the two senior governments, again, all provided by visitors to B.C. Taxes from local spending are not included. In other words, this [CDN]$2.5 billion is a brand new source of tax revenues that otherwise would not happen. That's $2.5 billion!
>
> (Poole 2002)

It is not clear whether Poole is speaking about the longer-run projection reflected in the economic impact report, from 2001 to 2020, or the short-run impact of tourist spending during the Games. We now know from the Olympic Games Impact Study (Vanwynsberghe and Kwan 2013, 96) that the actual tax revenue generated by visitors to Vancouver during the Games was somewhere between CDN$10 million and $19 million. This number is substantially lower than even the 'low effort/low response' estimate provided by the original economic impact statement for incremental tax revenue, at CDN$376 million (Gray 2002, 7) – which, if we divide by ten to account for the ten year period over which it is projected, gives us a tax revenue for one year of approximately CDN$38 million. Certainly the reality of tax revenue was nowhere near that trumpeted by Jack Poole in his 2002 editorial. Not coincidentally, Poole's hugely inflated numbers were published three months before a non-binding plebiscite in the City of Vancouver regarding residents' support for the Games.

A related issue in the 'mischievous procedure' of including local residents is the problem of the *substitution effect*, which is often not acknowledged in economic impact assessments (Crompton 2006). This refers to the phenomenon of providing employment estimates without noting that some, or perhaps all, of those jobs will be filled by people who would have been otherwise employed elsewhere. In other words, there is not a net increase in employment; rather, those who would have otherwise been employed in (for example) constructing housing or security for banks instead get employment in constructing stadiums or security for Opening Ceremonies. Related to this is the 'mischievous use of employment multipliers'

(Crompton 2006), where the employment estimates do not distinguish between full-time, part-time, and seasonal jobs, nor between the likelihood that those already in employment will simply be given more hours, rather than new jobs being created (in the service sector, for instance). Mischievous use of employment multipliers is also an issue when employment estimates imply that all jobs will be filled by local residents from within the community.

The London Olympic Games Impact Study (PwC 2005) reported on potential employment in the 'social impacts' section of their report, rather than in the 'economic impacts' section. They begin the section on 'Employment' by stating that "[s]taging the Olympic Games in the Lower Lea Valley [which encompasses the Olympic boroughs of Hackney, Newham, Tower Hamlets and Waltham Forest] will stimulate a vital economic regeneration programme in London's poorest and most disadvantaged area. The Olympic Park will provide local people with significant improvements in job opportunities, education and skills and training" (11). This was typical of the pro-Olympic rhetoric and was a significant component of the bid committee's efforts to win popular support and woo the IOC. The Olympic Games Impact Study reports that "the number of full time equivalent ('fte') jobs likely to be created or supported by the anticipated increases in expenditures and investment between 2005 and 2016 ranges from 38,000 ftes in London and 8,000 ftes in the UK as a whole" (PwC 2005, 11). Of these, they predicted that 7,966 ftes would go to North East London residents.

In the 'economic impact' section of the report, the authors note that "a significant proportion" of employment in London is held by those who live outside of the city and commute in (PwC 2005, 5); despite this, distinctions between the potential employment opportunities and who is likely to hold them are not made in the section titled 'Employment.' The notion of 'full-time equivalent' jobs is also misleading, as it suggests that the jobs created will be full-time employment rather than the more likely reality of new jobs being part-time, short-term, and insecure labour. Finally, the report makes no mention of the substitution effect of the jobs created, suggesting instead that they will be added to already pre-existing jobs rather than potentially replacing jobs that would have been created through other stimulus projects. This is particularly true of large-scale projects such as the Olympics which rely on substantial government funding. As both Delpy and Li (1998) and Crompton (2006) argue, government investment needs to be viewed with caution when generating economic impact numbers, as any government spending in one area means less government spending in another.

One of the strengths of the London economic impact study is that it used a model for its economic predictions called the Computable General Equilibrium (CGE) model which is "more likely to give realistic economic impact estimates" (Kirkup and Major 2006, 281). This is in opposition to the more commonly used Input-Output model which accounts for the positive impacts of an event but is "incapable of modelling most of the negative impacts" (ibid.). According to Charney and Vest (2003), neither model is particularly good for forecasting, though both are commonly used for this purpose. The CGE model used in London's economic impact assessment produced relatively accurate and even modest employment numbers: the report predicted 8,000 ftes for North and East London; after the Games, it was estimated that 9,700 Olympic jobs went to residents of the Olympic boroughs (Abbott 2013).[1] This fairly accurate prediction, however, was not high enough for the purposes of promoting the event. Disregarding the numbers from its own impact study, the London Olympic bid committee promised 20,000 jobs for the Olympic boroughs, as part of its emphasis on urban regeneration (Ali 2013; Abbott 2013). The number of jobs promised is even higher if the post-Games legacy commitments are included; as Diane Abbott, Member of Parliament for Hackney North and Stoke Newington notes in her comments to Parliament on November 8, 2013, "[W]e were told that the Olympics would transform prospects, help 20,000 workless Londoners from the five host boroughs into permanent employment by 2012 and create 12,000 job opportunities in the area of the park post-games" (Abbott 2013). As Abbott points out, the actual numbers were less than half of those promised; it is also unclear how many of these jobs in the Olympic boroughs went to people who were previously unemployed, and how many of the jobs were part-time or contract positions versus full-time work.

In a study of employment created by the London Olympic Games up to and including 2011, the year before the Games and arguably the peak moment of Olympic-related employment due to venue construction, Dan Brown and Stefan Szymanski (2012, 563) found that "the direct employment effects of the Olympics are small." They note that this was true across London but particularly striking in the host boroughs, which were promised "wider employment opportunities and improvements in the education, skills and knowledge of the local labour force in an area of very high unemployment" (London's candidate file, as cited in Brown and Szymanski 2012, 546). Of particular import in their study is that the host boroughs of Hackney, Newham and Tower Hamlets *did* experience an improvement in employment outcomes between 2004 and 2011 – however, the bulk of these jobs came from banking, finance and insurance (BFI) and public administration, education, and health (PAEH). The construction sector, on the other hand, experienced a net *decrease* in three of the five host boroughs (Greenwich, Hackney and Tower Hamlets), even though it was increasing across non-Olympic boroughs in the city. As the authors point out:

> It is intuitively difficult to believe that a large proportion of the PAEH and BFI employment increases were the direct effect of the construction activities taking place on the Olympic site, and so the importance of direct Olympic employment effects seems questionable.
>
> (Brown and Szymanski 2012, 563)

Of the construction jobs generated by the building of Olympic infrastructure, Brown and Szymanski (2012, 550) highlight that "on average, less than a quarter of those employed on the Olympic site are resident within the five boroughs, and, indeed, it is possible that even many of these have migrated into the area at least temporarily to take advantage of the temporary employment opportunities."

This confirms the legitimacy of the concerns raised by local MP Diane Abbott, about the level of employment provided for local residents and the long-term unemployed on the Olympic site (Abbott 2013).

The Vancouver economic impact study, using an Input-Output model, makes a range of predictions regarding employment. In Appendix A of the report, the author describes in careful language that the 'jobs' summarized in the tables are in fact 'person years' of employment, but this distinction is not apparent in the tables which are in the main section of the report. In a critical assessment of the economic impact numbers, David Green, a Professor of Economics at the University of British Columbia, clarifies that 'person years' "correspond[s] to one year of full-time employment – approximately 1,800 hours of work in a year" (Green 2003, 5). As Green notes, conflating 'person years' with 'jobs' is misleading, as one person may hold the same 'job' for more than one year, meaning that multiple 'person years' are accounted for within that single 'job.' The tables included in the main body of the report simply use 'jobs' as their descriptive category. As in the rest of the study, the tables report on a range of scenarios, from 'conservative growth' to 'aggressive growth.' The report's author also breaks out the 'job' numbers according to two related, but separate, infrastructure projects: the development of the Vancouver Convention and Exhibition Centre and the infrastructure for the 2010 Olympic Games. The final table reports on these two numbers combined, predicting a range from 118,000 'jobs' (actually, person years) at the conservative end to 228,000 'jobs' (person years) at the optimistic end (Gray 2002, 33).

In a press release dated November 22, 2002, the British Columbia government drew on this highest estimate to report that BC could anticipate "more than 220,000 total jobs." Though they note earlier that this number is generated when "combined with an expanded convention centre," they conclude by stating that, "The Olympic bid is all about jobs, jobs, and more jobs" (as cited in Shaffer 2014). Thus the number of 'jobs' projected through the media to be a result of the Olympics is at the very highest end of the economic impact statement's estimate; the media report also does not make the distinction between 'jobs' and 'person years' of employment.

In the post-Games Impact Study for Vancouver 2010 (Vanwynsberghe and Kwan 2013, 43), the number of jobs estimated to have been created in BC from January 2003 to December 2010 was between 38,530 and 51,510. These numbers are substantially smaller than the 220,000 jobs projected by the government through its 2002 media release. It is also not clear what the authors of the post-Games Impact Study mean by 'jobs' here. Their numbers are drawn from an analysis undertaken by PriceWaterhouseCoopers (PwC 2011), which produced a series of seven reports calculating economic impacts at different stages of Olympic preparation, during the Games and afterwards. In Report 6 of their series (PwC 2010), PriceWaterhouseCoopers note that they compare their pre-Games estimates to those generated by a report that drew on the methodology used by the original Economic Impact Study conducted by the BC Ministry of Competition, Science and Enterprise, described above (Gray 2002). It is therefore reasonable to assume that the numbers PwC are reporting on as 'jobs' are also 'person years' of employment. They also note that their numbers do not include 'jobs' created by the building of the Convention Centre and Sea-to-Sky highway. This makes it difficult to compare to the numbers that were promoted by the BC government in their press release, but if we look back at the original economic impact study, we see that it predicted between 37,000 and 83,000 'jobs' if the building of the Convention Centre is removed. It would seem, then, that the original estimates, as in the London case, are not too far off the mark, with the caveat that it has never been clear whether the 'jobs' predicted or reported were full-time, part-time, or contract labour, nor how well these 'jobs' paid. Notably, these were not the numbers used to promote the Games; instead, the largest possible estimate was broadcast as the likely outcome of the Games. With a gap of 183,000 between the public claim of 220,000 jobs and the modest (and ultimately more accurate) projection of 37,000 jobs, employment estimates were clearly exaggerated to persuade the local population to support the Olympics.

The numbers generated by both the economic impact study and the post-Games evaluation in Vancouver are still missing vital information. First of all, they do not provide any sense of how many of these jobs went to local residents, never mind how many of them, if any, went to inner-city residents. Secondly, none of the reports address the question of whether these 'person years of employment' represent new jobs or the displacement of employment from one sector of the economy to another. The closest answer to this question comes from the Olympic Games Impact Study (Vanwynsberghe and Kwan 2013), which notes that the unemployment rate in Vancouver dropped faster than in the comparable metropolitan area of Toronto, and drew close to the competing metropolitan areas of Calgary and Edmonton in the neighbouring province of Alberta. As the authors note, "the comparatively faster rate at which the unemployment rate decreased in Vancouver and the narrowing gap with the Albertan CMAs (Census Metropolitan Areas) between 2003 and 2009 suggest that Vancouver may have enjoyed an Olympic advantage with respect to unemployment rate between 2003 and 2009" (37). However, the authors note that any such advantage evaporates during the event year and post-Games, belying the promises of a long-term stimulus to the economy in terms of job growth. It appears that at least some new jobs were created by the Olympics, judging by the comparative advantage Vancouver enjoyed in the pre-Olympic years. But the numbers are vague and lacking in specificity.

Through a careful comparison between the numbers generated by the Vancouver and London economic impact studies, those that were promoted by Olympics boosters, and the actual outcomes, one trend is glaringly apparent: Olympics promoters consistently misled the public about the projected economic benefits of hosting the Games. They did so by publicizing far larger employment numbers than were merited, either ignoring the results of their own studies, or using the largest possible estimates from them. They were also vague about the type, length, and income of the jobs that were to be generated. Although Vancouver and London made commitments to employment for marginalized residents living in the poorest parts of their cities, the economic estimates tell us little about how these commitments would be met. At least one study in London (Brown and Szymanski 2012) suggests that these promises did not bear fruit. In the next section, I examine in detail the initiatives that were designed to meet the social legacy commitments to support inner-city, unemployed, and young people into work in each city.

Olympic opportunities for marginalized residents

The need for employment in both of the neighbourhoods that were identified by VANOC and LOCOG as their target – the Downtown Eastside of Vancouver, and East London – is certainly pressing. In Vancouver, 67% of residents of the Downtown Eastside are low-income and 22% are unemployed, about three times the national unemployment rate in Canada; at least 40% of residents rely on government support in the form of welfare or disability payments (Linden et al. 2013). Prior to the Olympics, Newham carried an unemployment rate that was double the national average, and almost a quarter of the population had no qualifications (Ryan-Collins and Sander-Jackson, 2008). In both areas, youth unemployment is particularly high, and even more so for Aboriginal (in Vancouver) and Black and Minority Ethnic (in London) youth (OECD 2008; Gunter and Watt 2009).

One of the promises made by the Vancouver bid committee via the Inner City Inclusive Commitments Statement was to create "training and short- and long-term employment opportunities for inner-city residents to encourage a net increase in employment" (VANOC 2009, 11). The Vancouver Organizing Committee for the 2010 Olympic and Paralympic Games (VANOC) supported the Building Opportunities with Business Inner City Society (BOB) as the major component of this commitment. BOB is the project that was showcased by VANOC as their most prominent demonstration of social inclusion (Vanwynsberghe, Surborg and Wyly 2013). However, BOB pre-existed the Olympics, established by the Vancouver Agreement with CDN$7 million of funding between 2002 and 2010 (Western Economic Diversification Canada 2010). This funding was supplemented by CDN$1.5 million from the Canadian Olympic sponsor Bell Canada (Vanwynsberghe, Surborg, and Wyly 2013).[2] To claim the results of BOB as a direct legacy of the Games is somewhat misleading; while the infusion of Olympic sponsorship money presumably allowed it to expand its efforts, BOB would have existed with or without the Vancouver Olympics.

With its Olympic partnership, BOB's focus shifted towards Olympic-related projects. At least three initiatives under BOB were related to the Olympics: the RONA Fabrication shop,[3] the Bladerunners program, and a Community Benefits Agreement (CBA) with Millennium Southeast False Creek Properties as part of its bid to win the building of the Olympic stadium. This CBA promised CDN$750,000 for a 'Legacy Fund' that would "support pre-employment and skills development training, and to aid in the transition from training to employment through 100 construction jobs on the Olympic Village site reserved for inner-city residents" (Vanwynsberghe, Surborg, and Wyly 2013, 2084). The RONA

Fabrication (or Fab) shop provided training for urban youth and Aboriginal peoples "who have had difficulty entering and staying in the workforce" (RONA 2008); RONA is a Canadian home renovation superstore similar to Home Depot. The program provided them with carpentry training to create items for use in the Olympic Games, such as podiums, street barricades, hockey stick racks, and picnic tables. Four groups of trainees, composed of approximately 17 people each, were meant to go through the program (RONA 2008). The commitment of the program was to create 64 jobs, of which 32 were filled by 2007–08 (Vanwynsberghe, Surborg and Wyly 2013). The Bladerunners program has existed since 1994, and is a widely recognized and very successful employment program for Aboriginal and otherwise marginalized youth in Vancouver (Greater Vancouver Regional Steering Committee on Homelessness 2010). They partnered with BOB in the lead-up to the Vancouver Olympics to train youth to work on the Athlete's Village, as part of the Community Benefits Agreement with Millennium, described above. According to Vanwynsberghe, Surborg and Wyly (2013), 114 inner-city residents were employed as a result of the CBA, including 11 young people from Bladerunners.

An additional inner-city initiative that did not fall under BOB was a partnership with United We Can, "a social enterprise that operates a recycling depot for those who retrieve bottles and cans with monetary value because of a provincially imposed deposit" (Edelson 2011, 813). The people who collect the cans and bottles are collectively referred to as 'binners' and are generally low-income and sometimes homeless individuals. The term 'binners' comes from the fact that often in order to retrieve the cans and bottles, individuals must jump into the large garbage bins located outside of apartments, restaurants and hotels. The City of Vancouver allocated funds to pay "more than 70" individuals from the Downtown Eastside to collect cans and bottles during the Olympic Games; the funds came from the Olympic and Paralympic Legacy Reserve Fund (CBC 2009). The binners were paid CDN$10 an hour for four-hour shifts.

Taken together, the four initiatives described above would have optimistically generated a total of 248 jobs for inner-city youth and residents (assuming that RONA met its goal of creating 64 jobs). This was out of a total number of Olympic jobs of between 38,530 and 51,510 (Vanwynsberghe and Kwan 2013); in other words, an infinitesimally small percentage of the total Olympic jobs are known to have gone to inner city residents, including inner city youth. It is likely that some of the employment generated prior to and during the Games also went to inner-city residents, though the barriers to attaining such work were significant (discussed in more detail in the final section of the chapter). While moving previously unemployed and unskilled young people into work is not an easy task, what is noteworthy for the purposes of this book are the exaggerated promises made as part of the bidding process, without requisite systems in place to ensure that such commitments could be met – or even measured.

In London, efforts to employ previously workless Londoners and residents of East London were more developed, though their ultimate success is unclear. Mayor Boris Johnson introduced two schemes to move the long-term unemployed into Olympics-related employment: the 2012 Employment Legacy project, and the Host Borough Employment project. The former was designed to support people throughout London into employment for at least 12 months, while the latter focused specifically on the Olympic boroughs, including Newham. Both were part of the London Employment and Skills Taskforce for 2012, which was a body established in 2006 "to bring together the main organizations and agencies responsible for employment and skills provision in London with the specific aim of maximising the employment and skills benefits of the 2012 Games for workless Londoners" (SQW 2013, 44). The Taskforce's overall goal was to move 70,000 workless Londoners into Olympic-related employment, including 20,000 from within the Host Boroughs. The Employment Legacy project and the Host Borough Employment project were supposed to begin in 2010; when their implementation was delayed until 2011, concerns were raised that the majority of Olympic-related

Figure 4.1 Image from Freddie's photo journal in 2011. His text reads: "Where's the help? They say they're hiring now but several people in our focus group haven't heard a reply from them, is it a joke or something to look good with?"

employment opportunities had already been filled (Donovan 2012). Both projects also downgraded their 12 month employment plan to 6 months for participants, in recognition of the short-term nature of much Olympic-related employment (Donovan 2012; Vanderhoven 2012). While a final evaluation report concluded that the overall goal set by the London Employment and Skills Taskforce for 2012 to move 70,000 workless Londoners into Olympic-related employment was achieved, the findings of the evaluation suggest that efforts to move the long-term unemployed and Host Borough residents into Olympic-related employment were less successful (SQW 2013). The report, which was funded by the Mayor of London, does not give details on these findings.

It proved to be quite challenging to find a consistent estimate on the number of previously workless Host Borough residents who attained employment through the Olympics. One estimate suggests that 9,700 residents of the Olympic boroughs were employed by the Olympics (Abbott 2013; Ali 2013), though this number does not account for how many of these were previously unemployed. In an unsourced document posted to the London Growth Boroughs[4] website, a briefing paper intended for senior officials and politicians in the six Host Boroughs claims the numbers are much higher. Specifically, the document states that 1,951 Host Borough residents were directly employed by LOCOG; of these, they claim that 1,064 were previously workless. They further state that 22,381 people employed by Olympics contractors were Host Borough residents, of whom 7,609 were previously workless (Conneely and Rahman 2012). The report claims that these numbers were measured at 'the peak' of Olympic-related employment; yet evidence from the Olympic Delivery Authority's own numbers suggest otherwise. Brown and Szymanski (2012) drew on the ODA's Employment and Skills Update to provide a table that breaks down the number of people employed at both the Olympic Park and the Olympic Village from Host Boroughs, Other London Boroughs, and Outside London between September 2008 and April 2011. They argue that the 'peak' period of Olympic employment was in 2011, when the construction phase was at its most active. At that time, only 3,110 Host Borough residents were employed by Olympics contractors.

When I went searching for the Olympic Delivery Authority's information in order to confirm which of these numbers were more accurate, I found a report on Employment and Skills Training dated July 2011 that is much more closely aligned with Brown and Szymanski's numbers than those reported to the six Host Boroughs. In the source I found, as part of the web archive of the ODA, they reported 1,196 Host Borough residents working on the Olympic Park, and 1,529 working on the Athlete's Village, for a total of 2,725 as of July 2011 (Olympic Delivery Authority 2011). Of these, 13% and 11% on each project respectively reported themselves as 'previously unemployed' – though this designation does not tell us whether they were long-term unemployed, or simply did not have a job prior to landing the contract with the Olympic Park or Athlete's Village. Certainly, it appears that the numbers being presented to the Host Boroughs after the Olympics were completed are misleading at best, or fabricated at worst. The stats that are available suggest that the goal of moving 20,000 unemployed Host

Borough residents into Olympic-related employment was not met, and indeed perhaps only one-tenth of this number was achieved.

There was significant concern among London residents, and East London residents in particular, that 'foreigners' were coming in to scoop up Olympic employment, effectively displacing long-term local residents from such opportunities (Lindsay 2014). This concern was expressed by participants in my research, who identified Eastern European workers as those most likely to 'take' their jobs. The truth of this claim is difficult to verify; such concerns were certainly evident in right-wing media outlets, who commonly propagate the notion that 'outsiders' are stealing jobs from hard-working Londoners as part of a wider xenophobic and racist politics (Lindsay 2014). On the other hand, it is equally likely that employers extended more hours or additional contracts to their pre-existing workers, rather than hiring new workers from East London or elsewhere, particularly given the recession conditions in which the post-2008 Olympic work took place (Druker and White 2013).

London Olympic employment opportunities were often framed in terms such as employing an 'inclusive and diverse workforce,' phrases that were broad enough to be used in a number of different ways. In a qualitative study of the policy-implementation process around London Olympics employment, Lynn Minnaert (2013) found that the different actors in the system (for example the London

Figure 4.2 Photo taken by Isaac in 2011. In debriefing this image, Isaac said: "It's a Job Centre. The Job Centre now, they've never offered a job. And they should do more things for Westfield, as I'm saying. More advertising. Do you know what I'm saying? Advertise this. Let me see a sign, or let me see something."

Organizing Committee of the Olympic Games (LOCOG), the Olympic Delivery Authority (ODA), and Host Boroughs) prioritized different elements of 'inclusivity' and 'diversity' in their practice. For instance, where the Host Boroughs and local Job Centres were more focused on employing local people, LOCOG placed an emphasis on diversity and inclusion by employing people with disabilities. The net effect was an uneven application of policies designed to bring local and previously workless people into employment.

One of the commitments that the advocacy organization London Citizens was able to elicit from the bid committee through their 'people's promises' was a living wage for all employed in Olympic-related jobs (LOCOG no date; see also Chapter 3). The London Living Wage campaign, which pre-existed the Olympic bid, advocates for wages to be set according to the cost of living in London (Living Wage Foundation 2015); the living wage is typically set above the minimum wage, which is the government-established lowest level at which employees can be paid. The London Living Wage was positive for the lowest-paid workers, such as security and logistics workers, but did not have much impact on construction workers, who were already paid above this level (Druker and White 2013). The construction industry was governed by a Memorandum of Agreement (MoA) signed by the Olympic Delivery Authority and representative trade unions that set, among other policies, an agreement that all construction workers on the Olympic Park would be directly employed – in other words, employees would be paid directly by the companies rather than being self-employed. This was a significant shift, as about 40 per cent of the UK construction workforce "is not 'employed' in the conventional sense but rather is engaged through subcontractors, agencies or payroll companies on the basis of 'self-employment,' which, in many cases, provides a thin disguise for an ongoing employment relationship" (Druker and White 2013, 569). This shift provided an advantage to workers, as those who are nominally 'self-employed' are likely to be at the bottom of the wage structure. The MoA applied to the Olympic Park but not the Athlete's Village or the nearby Westfield shopping mall (Druker and White 2013).

In addition to employment, both Vancouver and London made commitments to volunteerism, particularly for young people and socially marginalized residents. The Vancouver organizing committee emphasized their commitment to volunteerism through the claim that, "The Games will help create an enhanced talent pool with new skills – in particular for people in the inner-city and Aboriginal communities" (as cited in Benson et al. 2013, 211). LOCOG prioritized the employment and skills development of young people in their 'Employment and Skills Strategy' document, produced in 2010. The document outlines six initiatives designed to help "young people to gain valuable work experience and to enable them to move into sustainable future employment" (LOCOG 2012, 6). These initiatives included training, some employment, and many volunteer opportunities – the latter as a stepping stone towards future employment. Their target was to engage 339 young people in a range of paid and unpaid opportunities, including one-week placements; as of 2011/12, they had reached 80 young people (LOCOG 2012, 19). Many of their initiatives were specifically aimed at disadvantaged youth in the Host Boroughs. The UK Department for Culture, Media, and Sport made the following case in 2007 for the benefits of Olympic volunteering to local young people:

> Community volunteering, arts centres and sports clubs all provide activities for young people to make new friends, learn new skills and bolster self-confidence. Getting young people engaged in community activities benefits us all, regardless of age. 2012 will generate a host of these kinds of opportunities. We want to use the London Games to inspire more young people to get involved, to reap these benefits, and to engage more with the communities in which they live. Our plans . . . [are to create] an active generation through an unprecedented range of volunteering opportunities for everyone around the UK, including young people before, during and after the 2012 Games.
>
> (Cited in Lindsay 2014, 88)

Despite such rosy rhetoric, research suggests that the types of people who tend to be recruited to Olympic volunteerism are those who already have the skills and capacities to fulfil the required roles, tending towards experienced service and white-collar workers rather than those who require extensive training (Minnaert 2013; Benson et al. 2013). Mega-events also draw 'volunteer tourists' who travel between large-scale sporting and other events in order to experience them first-hand through short-term volunteer positions (Brown, Hixson, and McCabe 2013); such individuals have a degree of mobility that comes with a form of class privilege not available to the participants in my research. Finally, it is extremely questionable whether moving impoverished young people who are otherwise seeking employment into volunteer opportunities is actually of benefit to them; making volunteerism a part of employment strategies is akin to exploiting young workers who have no other options available to them.

Marginalized youth seeking work in the Olympic city: Class and gender barriers to employment

When I first spoke to youth in Vancouver and London the year before their respective Olympic Games happened, many expressed cautious optimism about the number of jobs that they anticipated becoming available to them. They had clearly been receptive to the 'jobs, jobs, jobs' rhetoric that had been circulated by their respective bid committees. As one participant noted in a London focus group in 2011, "There's going to be lots of jobs. Advertisements are all over the road about taking part in the Olympics, playing your part, remembering over the next few years that you assisted." But alongside this optimism was the dawning realization that the promised employment boom was not taking place. As Erin noted in Vancouver in 2009, "I thought at first it would be good because there'd be lots of jobs. But I don't really see that happening. I still see people struggling, searching for jobs every day." As we now know, the promise of 'jobs, jobs, jobs' was not borne out in either city. But another piece of the story of Olympic employment has to do with the mechanisms that prevent some people from attaining what work is available, particularly youth without education or training, and those who are homeless or marginally housed.

The Economy, Culture, and Sport Committee of the Greater London Assembly, made up of members of parliament from the three major political parties, set out to investigate how accessible employment opportunities would be "to those the Games were intended to help: long-term unemployed Londoners and those with few or no skills" (Economy, Culture, and Sport Committee Members 2011, 8). They concluded that "there are a number of hurdles which may limit how accessible the Games-time roles will be" to disadvantaged Londoners, including youth. Among these hurdles they included the effects of the recession, barriers created by the benefits system, and cuts to public-sector funding (ibid.). I would add to this list two further hurdles: one relates to the cultural expectations surrounding work and volunteerism among poor and working class young people, and the other to the institutional and structural barriers in place that inhibit young people from either pursuing or retaining work, which are powerfully structured by factors such as gender and class. These elements in combination played a role in both Vancouver and London.

The barriers facing the young people in my study when trying to capitalize on Olympic-related employment opportunities can be understood in part with the help of Pierre Bourdieu's concepts of *habitus, doxa, field* and *cultural capital*. These concepts highlight the manner in which individuals are socially located within a matrix of dispositions, opportunities and obstacles, structured in relation to their social class but not fixed as such. An individual develops their *habitus* in relation to the *field* in which they are located, with its own specific set of *doxic* norms. The *doxa* of a field describes the common sense beliefs and customs that are endemic to that field; when someone is in the *field* with which they are accustomed, typically the *field* in which they grew up, their *doxa* is like that of a 'fish in water' – they feel in place, in other words. On the other hand, if they are attempting to navigate a *field* with which they are not familiar, they can feel like a 'fish out of water', or distinctly out of place. The *habitus*, which Bourdieu has defined as a "socialized subjectivity" (Bourdieu and Wacquant 1992, 126), is shaped by the set of social relations to which the subject is exposed, which are often inextricable from his or her class location in a stratified society. An individual accrues *cultural capital*, among other forms of capital, through his or her exposure to ideas, institutions, and credentials that accumulate to indicate his or her social position within his or her specific *field*. While *cultural capital* has been used by Bourdieu and others to imply a hierarchy whereby a somewhat linear system of accumulation can locate one in terms of his or her position in the wider social realm, others have made use of the notion of *subcultural capital* to indicate that differing forms of *capital* can have value in different types of *fields* (Thornton 1996; Kennelly 2011). This concept has been applied with particular vigour in relation to young people, who arguably form their own sets of cultural norms that are internally referent to the local youth subcultures, cut through by specificities of class, gender, and racialization shaped by their attendant 'parent cultures' (Dillabough and Kennelly 2010; Hall and Jefferson 2006).

We can use Bourdieu's concepts here to delineate the overlapping but separate *fields* that the youth in my study needed to navigate in order to access Olympic employment and volunteer opportunities. The youth in both Vancouver and London came from poor and working class histories; many of them had experienced family breakdown, most had left secondary school early, and very few had any higher education credentials. The *field* in which they had grown up was thus largely shaped by poverty, which meant that they did not have access to the extra-curricular skills-building and volunteer opportunities that are common for middle class youth. Many of them also had a hostile relationship to schooling and other institutional structures, having experienced these as sites of failure rather than support. Although almost all of our participants reported work experience in the past or present, all of the jobs were low-income and insecure. For the women, typical jobs included cleaning, waitressing, or telemarketing; for the men, unskilled labour in the construction industry, warehouse work, or other forms of physical labour (moving assistant, landscaping) were reported.

Iain Lindsay uses Bourdieu's concepts to account for the experiences of informants in his ethnography of Newham in the years leading up to the 2012 Olympics. He recounts the stories of Newham residents who declined the opportunities that were supposed to be available from the Olympics, citing a resigned 'what's the point' attitude that reflected their previous experiences of institutional failure and the likelihood that their efforts would be for nought. As Lindsay (2014, 95–96) notes, "In reality many lacked the *habitus* to understand the *doxa* required to benefit from Olympic opportunities during the short time-frame in which they were made available ... The situation experienced throughout this research indicated that many of those who lived in Newham felt segregated and excluded from Olympic delivery benefit and from the regenerated Olympic locales."

The experiences recounted by Lindsay's informants were similar to those of many of the youth who participated in my study, particularly in the feeling of being left behind by Olympic opportunities. Many expressed a 'what's the point' attitude to applying for Olympic job and volunteer opportunities, particularly related to the short-term nature of the positions. As one London participant noted in a 2012 interview, "When the Olympics has gone, all those companies are going to duck out, they aren't going to be in London no more so what else are they [employees] going to do?" A similar sentiment was expressed by some of the youth in Vancouver; Colvin reported in 2011, "I had opportunities to work in the Olympics but at the time I had a job where I was there for a year, and to leave that job to maybe make a dollar an hour or more for two weeks, it was stupid." Others were unable to discern how to attain Olympic jobs or voluntary positions; in an interview with Mary in London in 2012, she stated that she wanted to try for Olympics catering work, but did not know how to go about finding such jobs.

Olympic volunteer positions were particularly mysterious for some of the youth, who could not see the value in giving their labour for free when they needed an income in order to survive. Unless the volunteer labour were to translate directly into paid employment, it simply did not make sense to the youth to take it on. As Freddie remarked in London in 2011:

> I don't think that's me really innit, I just want to get straight hands in and start working. If it was volunteering on a construction site now, I wouldn't mind for a little while because it's very hands on work, innit. So I wouldn't mind doing that, two, three weeks experience volunteering, or even for a month, just so they can see how I do all round and then yeah, if they like me, I'll gladly work, as long as I enjoyed the experience.

This particular attitude about the value of volunteer labour is a working class, as opposed to middle class, approach to employment. Whereas middle class youth are educated, through parental figures, institutions and peers, into the value of volunteering for the sake of CV building and expanding one's professional networks, working class youth are less likely to have received this form of cultural education. This made the Olympic volunteer opportunities unappealing to them: why would one volunteer to direct tourists around the Olympic Park, for instance, if it were not going to lead directly to employment?

Unlike in Lindsay's study, many of my research participants were quite active in trying to secure the job and volunteer positions that they had been assured would be available to them. This was more the case in London than in Vancouver, which may be in part due to the nature of the supportive housing situation in which the London-based youth lived, with key workers encouraging them (or requiring them) to apply for work or volunteer positions. However, the youth in the Vancouver portion of our study also sought, and in some cases, obtained, Olympic-related employment. The youth in London reported trying to attain paid or volunteer positions in catering, bar work, security, construction, as a London Olympic 'Gamesmaker', and working retail at the Westfield's shopping mall. The male youth in Vancouver reported trying to find work mostly in security and construction; the female youth in Vancouver did not report seeking work or volunteer opportunities with the Games. The barriers that prevented them from attaining such employment were certainly partly due to the lack of fit between the *habitus* of the youth, and the *field* of Olympics employment, as well as their lack of appropriate *cultural capital*. But often the barriers were institutional in nature, as opposed to cultural, making it difficult or impossible for the youth to proceed with their quest for employment.

Scott, who was one of the few of our London participants to ultimately secure Olympics-related employment, told us in 2012 of the job experience that had preceded his success. He had been called up by the Job Centre to work as a 'cherry picker driver' (operating a hydraulic crane used on construction sites) on one of the Olympic sites; upon applying for the job, he was required to take part in what he described as "a long process" of interviews: "It was like a month, two months of interviews and that, it started in February and we didn't start work 'til March." During this time, he was not receiving any pay, and then he was required to do a period of training for which he also did not receive pay:

> So I had to stop signing on, I won't get no money for a month and that, they won't give me no money to look after me, do you know what I'm saying? So for that month I was sort of struggling. I couldn't really do much, you know what I'm saying? And it didn't seem to bother them geezers who was employing me, because they'd already been paid, they'd got their money.

Although Scott ultimately was able to secure work doing construction on the Olympic Park, he reported that he was unable to continue his work there once the Olympic site was passed on from "the construction side of it" over to the "entertainment industry." At that point, his criminal record meant that he was no longer permitted to work on the site, despite the fact that he had been working there for months already.

The institutional and systemic barriers for the Vancouver-based youth were largely to do with their status as homeless or street-involved. In a focus group in 2009, the following conversation ensued:

Woman 1: Once you're homeless, it's like nearly impossible to get a job. I'm sorry. How are you supposed to have a job when you have nowhere to sleep? How are you supposed to have a job when you can't find food? You know? Your whole day is dedicated to like getting food and like getting warm.
Man 1: And you get depressed.
Woman 1: That's right.
Man 1: There's like a lot of times when you're not sleeping or you're not–
Man 2: Like I had a job for a while and I got kicked out of [the short-term youth shelter] so then I had nowhere to sleep.
Man 1: Yeah. Yeah. A lot of that happens.
Man 2: I worked till 11 every night and if I worked there then, like where was I going to go afterwards? I had to like, basically ditch work to figure out where I was going to sleep that night.
Man 1: So that's it. It's basically really hard to find a job.

One of the issues that makes finding work challenging for youth who are homeless or marginally housed is the difficulty of keeping track of paperwork. Homeless and marginally housed youth often lack the proper identification, and it can be difficult to obtain without the help of youth workers or social service providers. In 2010, a young man in Vancouver told us that he had been hoping to apply for Olympic-related work but missed the recruitment period because he did not have the proper ID. In 2012, Todd in London told us that he had been offered a job as a driver for the Olympics. He was sent a letter with the information about where and when to start, but he lost it. Upon calling them back, he was told that they could not help him unless he found the letter. This meant that he lost out on the opportunity that he had thought was already secured.

Given the barriers already outlined, very few of the youth with whom we spoke in Vancouver and London found Olympic-related work. Of those who did, all except one was a male employed in either construction or security. The one exception was a young woman in London who obtained a catering position (from which she was fired when the Olympics ended). Another exception was a young woman in Vancouver who disclosed that she was a sex worker and anticipated getting more clients during the Games. These disparities highlight an important issue that is not part of the populist discourse surrounding the 'jobs, jobs, jobs' promises of Olympics boosters: the gendered nature of the jobs that are created. While potentially some of the white-collar work and volunteer positions were more equitably distributed between women and men, the work that was going to those at the lower rungs of the social opportunity ladder were distinctly skewed towards men. In a Vancouver-based interview in 2010, Sandy reflects on the sexism she encountered in relation to the binning opportunities created by the partnership between United We Can and the City of Vancouver:

> I wonder how do people get onto these programs? Because I've been in every situation where people have been offered that kind of [opportunity] and I've been like ten times more capable than most of the people [who were] offered anything and I'm still not receiving any attention from any of the people that are offering that. Which is really bullshit. You know, like, I'm standing right beside the guy that gets offered the job. It kind of seems like they're sexist. Because I'm a woman, they don't think that I know where to go or how to bin properly. Which is complete bullshit. I've been in many bins in my day.

The disparity in opportunities for homeless and marginally housed young men and women is consistent with other research that has found young women to be at a distinct disadvantage when it comes to employment opportunities (Klodawsky, Aubry, and Farrell 2006; O'Grady and Gaetz 2004). The feel-good rhetoric of the 'jobs, jobs, jobs' promises of Olympics proponents conceals this reality, particularly in relation to those at the lower end of the economic spectrum.

This is not to suggest that the employment secured by the young men in this research was particularly stable, well paid or secure. I will illustrate some of the major issues through an extended discussion of the experience of Isaac, a participant in the London portion of my research. Isaac was one of the few participants throughout this research project with whom we were able to speak over three consecutive years. He was a participant in the 2011 focus groups, interviews, and photo journals in London; he returned to participate in a focus group, interview, and walking tour in 2012; and then came back again for a 2013 focus group and interview. Over the course of this time, we learned of Isaac's efforts to secure a position as a security guard, either with the Olympic Games or at the Westfield mall.

Isaac was a Black man of slender build with short dreadlocks and a West Indian accent. He reported being repeatedly stopped and searched by police, and was troubled by the racism that he perceived in these interactions. He was also a father, and did his best to provide support to his 'baby mother' and child. As was common among our participants, he and his child's mother were not in a partner-type relationship, though Isaac reported that they were on amicable terms. In 2011, Isaac had just completed the SIA (Security Industry Authority) training that would permit him to attain the badge required to do security work in the UK. He had already completed the training previously, but it had expired by the time the Olympics security opportunities were coming available. He had not attained employment with that training the first time around. Each round of training cost £250 (US$380); Isaac managed to pay for the first course himself, and then received funding from his local housing association for his second attempt. Although he had aspirations to work in performance, particularly in music or drama, he was hopeful about his prospects of finding security work, and optimistic that it would be work he would enjoy. As he said:

> It don't make sense to do a job you don't love, that's me really. I'm not saying "oh I won't work in McDonald's," we all have to start from somewhere, but I don't see the sense in that because if I don't love it I'm not going to show the good work. But it's good to have a job that you love, and as I say I'd like to do security, I'd like to do a lot of things, I'd like to do my drama, but it's just open doors really, some doors need to be opened.

Isaac had previously worked in a range of low-income positions, including as a cleaner and a cashier; he had also completed a variety of training courses for different types of work, including customer service in order to attain retail work. But the prospect of gaining a position in security was at the forefront for him, as he anticipated it would be a longer-term and better-paid form of work than he had previously held. This was a view that was commonly held by participants in both Vancouver and London. The following focus group exchange in London in 2011 illustrates this; the participants are discussing the SIA course and what is involved in being a security guard:

Man 1:	It's not easy, though, it's a serious job, yes. You know?
Man 2:	You [must] be passionate.
Interviewer:	What do these jobs pay if you get one?
Man 1:	They pay good, lovely. As far as I know, lovely.
Man 2:	If you've got a [SIA] badge, you can work anywhere.
Man 1:	They have a lot of jobs.

While it was true that there were 'a lot of jobs' working security during the Olympics in both Vancouver and London, they were not long term and they were not well paid. In a media interview with the CEO of one of three firms supplying security workers for the Vancouver Olympics, it was reported that while the company might be "interested in retaining some of these employees after the Olympics, most will have no job security. Their contracts will range anywhere from a few weeks to three months" (McLean 2009). The article characterized the search for security guards as a task of "recruiting and training 5,000 temporary security workers." In London, a "secret security guard" wrote missives for *The Guardian* as an insider to the security training and job experience with G4S, the massive security firm contracted to provide security for the London Olympics. G4S had encountered a great deal of scrutiny and controversy just prior to the Games due to the shortage of security workers they had managed to recruit, leaving the British army to fill the shortfall (Boykoff and Fussey 2014). The "secret security guard" reported that she expected to be paid minimum wage (£6.08/hour; US$9/hour) for her G4S training (separate from the SIA certification), and then £8.50 per hour (US$13) for subsequent 12 hour shifts (The secret security guard 2012).

When we saw Isaac again in 2012, he was proudly wearing his Olympic security badge around his neck, giving him access to the park and a discount on transit when travelling to and from his shifts. When we spoke to him throughout the first week of the 2012 Games, he was waiting to be called for his first shift with G4S:

> At the moment I have not been called but you know I am sure I will get a call one day. But it is a shame, you have something not being used at the moment, knowing that you are a neighbour, you are just literally a two minute walk away and there is nothing for you.

Isaac's comment foreshadowed his experience to come: as he noted, his labour, though ready for use, was not being taken up, despite the fact that he lived right around the corner from the site and despite the reported shortage of G4S security workers. In our interview with him that year, he noted that he had been waiting for this opportunity for five years, from when he took his first security training course: "I mean five years is a long time, it pays off [though], got my accreditation done so I'm just waiting for a phone call now, well I hear they need people now so." Although he had not yet received a shift, Isaac was optimistic that he would soon get one, and also feeling positive about finding ongoing security work after the Olympics either with G4S or through another company, by virtue of the job experience he would gain at the Olympics.

When we followed up with Isaac in 2013, we discovered that his five years of waiting had not, in fact, paid off. Despite working a few hours during the Games, Isaac was not paid for his time, and never received further shifts. As he reported:

> I think you heard it on the news, they had a little fight with the company. You know money, financial problems and such forth and I don't know the full thing but . . . they had to stop and it affected my Jobseeker's [benefit]. But yeah, I just had to get back on my feet and just try from a different [angle] you know.

The "little fight with the company" that Isaac references here is the controversy-wracked deployment of security workers by G4S, which was condemned by many including various Labour Members of Parliament (BBC News 2012). Isaac tried to be philosophical about the set-back, claiming he was happy to have had the experience:

> Yeah I didn't get paid. As I say it was just experience, just being there and just being for the public and that. I wasn't really thinking about the money to tell you at the time. I wasn't sure if I would get paid . . . as I say a lot of these jobs, that's what they're for, like voluntary. I just put my [experience] to use or whatever I can, you know, and that was it.

Isaac's forced voluntary experience, which in previous years he had been anticipating as the doorway to a future career, had resulted in economic hardship not only because of the lost wages but because his social assistance benefits were cut as a direct result. Registered with G4S to work, the portion of his benefits that were intended for helping unemployed individuals get back into work was scaled back, a situation that took him weeks to resolve.

As Isaac's experience illustrates, even young people who took all of the appropriate steps in order to gain the (poorly paid and insecure) employment available through the Olympics were not necessarily able to benefit. Even though G4S had a shortage of staff, and even though Isaac had his certification, his training, and his badge, he still was not given the opportunity to work. Furthermore, his efforts were ultimately rewarded with an administrative mix-up that meant he lost his Jobseekers allowance for a period of time, leaving him to scramble to pay his bills. The year after the Olympics ended, Isaac was in the same position he'd been in before the Games; having paid (twice) for expensive security training, he still did not have either work experience or job prospects. Isaac's experience illustrates some of the "hurdles" which limited "how accessible the Games-time roles" (Economy, Culture, and Sport Committee Members 2011, 8) were for those who were supposed to benefit from Olympic employment. His case was neither unique nor unusual; various other youth reported similar barriers and challenges to securing Olympic employment, even when they were ultimately successful. More often, the youth I spoke with in Vancouver and London either felt that the Olympic employment opportunities were completely out of reach, and not worth going for, or they couldn't figure out how they might go about obtaining them.

Conclusions

The Olympic promises of 'jobs, jobs, jobs' in both cities were used to generate public support for winning the bids. Linked to these promises were commitments that jobs would be targeted towards the long-term unemployed, young people, and residents of Vancouver's and London's East sides. The more modest, and accurate, economic impact predictions were ignored by bid committees and Olympics boosters, in favour of exaggerated claims about both the numbers of jobs that would be created and the overall economic impact of the Games. Such numbers occluded the possibility of substitution effects (i.e. that those who would otherwise be employed would simply be displaced to Olympic jobs) and provided no details on issues such as wages, stability, and gender disparity for the available opportunities. Employment promises focused on 'inner-city employment' (Vancouver) and jobs for 'previously workless residents of the Olympic boroughs' (London). While each city had initiatives directed at these populations, evidence suggests that the results ranged from meagre to unclear. Volunteer opportunities were also trumpeted as a benefit for marginalized residents of their respective host cities, including young people.

In considering the experiences of homeless and marginally housed youth in both cities, we see that the issues impacting on their capacity to attain Olympic-related employment or volunteer opportunities are quite complex. While both groups expressed hopefulness about gaining jobs and volunteer positions prior to the Games, it did not take long for them to realize that they were going to be largely left out of the Olympic opportunities. Through a combination of systemic barriers, including the lack of match between the youths' *habitus* and the *field* of Olympic opportunities, very few of the young people in our study attained Olympic jobs. Those who did were almost all men employed in construction and security, reproducing the gender inequality already faced by young impoverished women in both cities. And as Isaac's story illustrates, following all of the correct steps in no way guaranteed Olympic employment. Even apparently straightforward efforts to attain insecure and poorly paid jobs were stymied. While we can only guess as to the story on the side of G4S, presumably institutionalized racism and classism played a role in Isaac's lack of success in attaining security shifts.

Collectively, the analysis of the economic impact numbers, the unfulfilled promises of employment for marginalized residents, and the stories of the young people in my study demonstrate again that Olympic proponents build their bids on claims to help marginalized host city residents and young people, without the requisite structures in place to ensure that such commitments are fulfilled. The economic promises made by Olympic bid committees are important in winning the support of their host city populations, support that is necessary for the IOC to award the bid committee the prize of the Olympics. Yet, just as with housing promises, commitments to support marginalized populations through jobs, volunteer opportunities and training turned out to be largely empty. While some economic benefits were enjoyed by each city (though not nearly on the scale that was promised by the bid committees), these benefits were generally not shared with the marginalized residents who had been an integral aspect of bidding efforts to win the Games. While the youth in my study were not generally *worse* off for employment as a result of the Olympics, neither were they noticeably *better* off. From my vantage point at the time of writing in 2015, a few years after the Games ended in each city, employment statistics for young people have worsened: in London, young people between the ages of 16 and 24 are nearly three times more likely to be unemployed than older people, the starkest disparity in 20 years (Boffey 2015); the numbers are even more disparate for Black and Minority Ethnic youth (Hughes and Crowley 2014).

In Vancouver, the youth unemployment rate has steadily grown since the Olympics, also part of a nation-wide trend (Chisholm 2014; Kolm 2013; Government of Canada 2013). The promise of long-term economic benefits for host city residents and young people has clearly not been met.

Even if some jobs were created by the Games – and some of the youth in my study did attain such jobs – the question remains whether this is an appropriate use of substantial government funds and the energy of thousands of civil servants. As Andrew Zimbalist (2015, 121) asks, "If instead of building an Olympic park in East London, London had provided rental subsidies and tax credits to artisanal industry and retail businesses or additional funding for, say, technical education, what enduring effect on employment in the surrounding boroughs might that have wrought?" Likewise, if the Building Opportunities with Business (BOB) project in Vancouver had taken its Vancouver Agreement funding and used that to develop job opportunities with local businesses that have a long history in Vancouver, rather than focusing on Olympic-related infrastructure projects, what longer-term benefits might have accrued to its participants and the local economy? While speculation can be endless, the point is that the Olympics skews everything towards it, and comes with significant opportunity costs (Zimbalist 2015; Am Johal, personal communication). As Andrew Zimabalist (2015, 32) concludes in his extensive study of the economics of hosting mega-events like the Olympics, "In both the short and the long run, hosting a mega-sports event is likely to prove a present and future burden rather than a benefit to the host country's economy."

Notes

1 It is unclear how many of these jobs were full-time versus part-time and contract labour. Thus the estimate of 8,000 full-time equivalent positions may have been quite accurate.
2 Vanwynsberghe, Surborg and Wyly (2013) state that BOB was created in collaboration with VANOC. This contradicts the claim made in the final report on the Vancouver Agreement, which states that "The VA funded the establishment of BOB and has provided over [CDN]$7 million from 2002–2010 for BOB activities" (Western Economic Diversification Canada 2010, 23).
3 Vanwysberghe, Surborg and Wyly (2013) put the RONA fabrication shop under the auspices of BOB, though it is not clear from other sources whether it fell under the BOB purview or was a separate initiative. For example, the press release by RONA makes no mention of BOB (www.rona.ca/corporate/Rona-vancouver-2010-fabrication-shop-providing-trainees-with-tools-for-life). The BOB website is no longer active, and so I was not able to confirm the status of the RONA fab shop there.
4 The Olympic Host Boroughs have been re-dubbed the London Growth Boroughs since the Olympics ended; they are seeking to maximize the legacy of the Games through a strategy called 'Convergence.' Their goal is that "Within 20 years the communities who host the 2012 Games will have the same social and economic chances as their neighbours across London" (growthboroughs.com).

Bibliography

All website URLs were accessed between September 2014 and December 2015.
Abbott, Diane. 2013. "The Olympic Legacy in East London." November 8. www.dianeabbott.org.uk/news/speeches/news.aspx?p=102956.

Ali, Rushanara. 2013. "The Olympic Legacy Has Failed to Bring Jobs to London's East End." *The Guardian*, January 27 (section: Comment is free). www.theguardian.com/commentisfree/2013/jan/27/olympic-legacy-failed-jobs-london.

BBC News. 2012. "Games Security 'Not Compromised.'" *BBC News*. July 12. www.bbc.co.uk/news/uk-18813729.

Benson, Angela M., Tracey J. Dickson, F. Anne Terwiel, and Deborah A. Blackman. 2013. "Training of Vancouver 2010 Volunteers: A Legacy Opportunity?" *Contemporary Social Science* 9 (2): 210–26. doi:10.1080/21582041.2013.838296.

Boffey, Daniel. 2015. "Youth Unemployment Rate Is Worst for 20 Years, Compared with Overall Figure." *The Guardian*, February 22. www.theguardian.com/society/2015/feb/22/youth-unemployment-jobless-figure.

Bourdieu, Pierre, and Loïc J. D. Wacquant. 1992. *An Invitation to Reflexive Sociology*. 1st edition. Chicago: University of Chicago Press.

Boykoff, Jules, and Pete Fussey. 2014. "London's Shadow Legacies: Security and Activism at the 2012 Olympics." *Contemporary Social Science* 9 (2): 253–70. doi:10.1080/21582041.2013.838292.

Brown, Dan, and Stefan Szymanski. 2012. "The Employment Effects of London 2012: An Assessment in Mid-2011." In *International Handbook on the Economics of Mega Sporting Events*, edited by Wolfgang Maennig and Andrew Zimbalist. Northampton, MA: Edward Elgar Publishing Ltd.

Brown, Graham Paul, Eliza Hixson, and Vivienne McCabe. 2013. "Privileged Mobility: Employment and Experience at the Olympic Games." *Sport and Tourism* 18 (4): 265–86.

CBC. 2009. "Vancouver Hires Binners to Recycle Olympic Cans." December 18. www.cbc.ca/1.832857.

Charney, Alberta, and Marshall Vest. 2003. "Modeling Practices and Their Ability to Assess Tax/expenditure Economic Impacts." Paper presented at the AUBER conference, New Orleans.

Chisholm, Mike. 2014. "Young, Unemployed and Losing Hope in BC's Boom Economy." *The Vancouver Observer*, January 9. www.vancouverobserver.com/life/young-unemployed-and-losing-hope-bcs-boom-economy.

Conneely, Mary, and Oliur Rahman. 2012. "6 Host Boroughs – Skills and Employment Update Special Edition. London 2012 Games Time Jobs Final Update – November 2012." https://static1.squarespace.com/static/50b4ab77e4b0214dc1f631e9/t/5135c6ece4b055d8b6194676/1362478828641/HB+Skills+and+Employment+Update+-+London+2012+Games+Time+Jobs+%28Nov+12%29.pdf.

Crompton, John L. 2006. "Economic Impact Studies: Instruments for Political Shenanigans?" *Journal of Travel Research* 45 (1): 67–82. doi:10.1177/0047287506288870.

Delpy, Lisa, and Ming Li. 1998. "The Art and Science of Conducting Economic Impact Studies." *Journal of Vacation Marketing* 4 (3): 230–54. doi:10.1177/135676679800400303.

Dillabough, Jo-Anne, and Jacqueline Kennelly. 2010. *Lost Youth in the Global City: Class, Culture, and the Urban Imaginary*. 1st edition. New York: Routledge.

Donovan, Tim. 2012. "London 2012: Olympics Jobs Legacy 'Falls Short.'" *BBC News*. August 9. www.bbc.com/news/uk-england-london-19184807.

Druker, Janet, and Geoffrey White. 2013. "Employment Relations on Major Construction Projects: The London 2012 Olympic Construction Site." *Industrial Relations Journal* 44 (5/6): 566–83. doi:10.1111/irj.12038.

Economy, Culture, and Sport Committee Members. 2011. "Review into the Employment and Skills Opportunities of the 2012 Games-Time Period." Greater London Assembly.

www.london.gov.uk/moderngov/documents/s6358/06b%20Appendix%201%20-%20 Review%20of%20employment%20and%20skills%20opportunities%20of%20the%20 2012%20Games%20time%20period.pdf.

Edelson, Nathan. 2011. "Inclusivity as an Olympic Event at the 2010 Vancouver Winter Games." *Urban Geography* 32 (6): 804–22. doi:10.2747/0272-3638.32.6.804.

Government of Canada, Human Resources and Skills Development Canada. 2013. "Labour Market Bulletin – British Columbia: April 2013 (Quarterly Edition)." March 8. www. esdc.gc.ca/eng/jobs/lmi/publications/bulletins/bc/apr2013.shtml.

Gray, John B. 2002. "The Economic Impact of The Winter Olympic and Paralympic Games." British Columbia: Capital Projects Branch, Ministry of Competition, Science and Enterprise.

Greater Vancouver Regional Steering Committee on Homelessness. 2010. "3 Ways to Home News Bulletin." 16. Vancouver. http://metrovancouver.org/planning/homelessness/ Homlessness%20Docs/Bulletin16.pdf.

Green, David A. 2003. "Olympic Impacts: Should We Expect An Employment Boom?" Vancouver: Canadian Centre for Policy Alternatives BC Office.

Gunter, Anthony, and Paul Watt. 2009. "Grafting, Going to College and Working on Road: Youth Transitions and Cultures in an East London Neighbourhood." *Journal of Youth Studies* 12 (5): 515–29. doi:10.1080/13676260903083364.

Hall, Stuart, and Tony Jefferson, eds. 2006. *Resistance Through Rituals: Youth Subcultures in Post-War Britain*. 2nd edition. London; New York: Routledge.

Hughes, Ceri, and Lizzie Crowley. 2014. "London: A Tale of Two Cities. Addressing the Youth Employment Challenge." London: The Work Foundation. www.thework foundation.com/DownloadPublication/Report/361_London%20-%20Tale%20of%20 Two%20Cities%20-%20FINALweb.pdf.

Kennelly, Jacqueline. 2011. *Citizen Youth: Culture, Activism, and Agency in a Neoliberal Era*. New York: Palgrave Macmillan.

Kirkup, Naomi, and Bridget Major. 2006. "Doctoral Foundation Paper: The Reliability of Economic Impact Studies of the Olympic Games: A Post-Games Study of Sydney 2000 and Considerations for London 2012." *Journal of Sport & Tourism* 11 (3): 275–96. doi:10.1080/14775080701400943.

Klodawsky, Fran, Tim Aubry, and Susan Farrell. 2006. "Care and the Lives of Homeless Youth in Neoliberal Times in Canada." *Gender, Place, and Culture* 13 (4): 419–36.

Kolm, Josh. 2013. "Why Are so Many of Canada's Young People out of Work?" *CBC News, Canada*, June 21. www.cbc.ca/1.1370260.

Linden, Isabelle Aube, Marissa Y. Mar, Gregory R. Werker, Kerry Jang, and Michael Krausz. 2013. "Research on a Vulnerable Neighborhood – The Vancouver Downtown Eastside from 2001 to 2011." *Journal of Urban Health: Bulletin of the New York Academy of Medicine* 90 (3): 559–73. doi:10.1007/s11524-012-9771-x.

Lindsay, Iain. 2014. *Living with London's Olympics: An Ethnography*. New York: Palgrave Macmillan.

Living Wage Foundation. 2015. "What Is the Living Wage?" Accessed January 28. www. livingwage.org.uk/what-living-wage.

LOCOG. No date. "London 2012 Olympic Games Official Report Volume 1." London: London Organizing Committee of the Olympic Games and Paralympic Games.

LOCOG. 2012. "Learning Legacy: Lessons Learned from Planning and Staging the London 2012 Games." London: London Organizing Committee of the Olympic Games and Paralympic Games. http://learninglegacy.independent.gov.uk/documents/pdfs/equality- inclusion-employment-and-skills/cp-locog-employment-and-skills-strategy.pdf.

McLean, Catherine. 2009. "EMPLOYMENT: Security Firms Crank up Olympic Hiring Machine Can They Recruit and Train 5,000 Temporary Workers in Just a Few Months? Reputations – and Future Contracts – Are at Stake." *The Globe and Mail (1936–Current)*, October 14 (section: Report on Business). http://search.proquest.com.proxy.library. carleton.ca/docview/1400817154/abstract?accountid=9894.

Minnaert, Lynn. 2013. "Making the Olympics Work: Interpreting Diversity and Inclusivity in Employment and Skills Development Pre-London 2012." *Contemporary Social Science* 9 (2): 196–209. doi:10.1080/21582041.2013.838290.

OECD. 2008. *Jobs for Youth/Des Emplois Pour Les Jeunes: Canada 2008*. Canada: OECD Publishing.

O'Grady, Bill, and Stephen Gaetz. 2004. "Homelessness, Gender and Subsistence: The Case of Toronto Street Youth." *Journal of Youth Studies* 7 (4): 397–416. doi:http:// dx.doi.org.proxy.library.carleton.ca/10.1080/1367626042000315194.

Olympic Delivery Authority. 2011. "Employment and Skills Update." London. http:// webarchive.nationalarchives.gov.uk/20120403073945/www.london2012.com/documents/ oda-publications/jobs-skills-futures/jsf-bulletin-july-11-stats.pdf.

Poole, Jack. 2002. "Olympics Investments Make Bid Worthwhile: [Final Edition]." *The Vancouver Sun*, October 25 (section: Editorial).

PwC. 2005. "Olympic Games Impact Study: Final Report." London: PriceWaterhouse Coopers.

PwC. 2010. "The Games Effect. Report 6: Preliminary Economic Impact of the 2010 Olympic and Paralympic Winter Games on British Columbia and Canada to March 31 2010." Vancouver: PriceWaterhouseCoopers.

PwC. 2011. "The Games Effect. Report 7: Global Summary of the Impact of the 2010 Olympic and Paralympic Winter Games on British Columbia and Canada 2003 to 2010." Vancouver: PriceWaterhouseCoopers.

RONA. 2008. "RONA Vancouver 2010 Fabrication Shop Providing Trainees with Tools For Life." August 14. www.rona.ca/corporate/Rona-vancouver-2010-fabrication-shop-providing-trainees-with-tools-for-life.

Ryan-Collins, Josh, and Paul Sander-Jackson. 2008. "Fools Gold: How the 2012 Olympics is Selling East London Short, and a 10 Point Plan for a More Positive Local Legacy." London: Community Links.

Shaffer, Marvin. 2014. "Looking Back on the Vancouver-Whistler Winter Games | CCPA Policy Note." February 6. www.policynote.ca/looking-back-on-the-vancouver-whistler-winter-games/.

SQW. 2013. "Olympic Jobs Evaluation Final Report." London. https://www.london.gov. uk/sites/default/files/GLA%20Olympic%20Jobs%20Final%20report.pdf.

The secret security guard. 2012. "G4S Trainee: 'Most People Failed the Initial X-Ray Exam. But Not for Long.'" *The Guardian*. July 23. www.theguardian.com/business/2012/ jul/23/g4s-trainee-x-ray-exam.

Thornton, Sarah. 1996. *Club Cultures: Music, Media, and Subcultural Capital*. Hanover: Wesleyan.

Vanderhoven, Ellen. 2012. "London 2012: A Social Legacy for East London?" London: Community Links.

VANOC. 2009. "Vancouver 2010 Bid Report." Vancouver: Vancouver Organizing Committee of the Olympic and Paralympic Games.

Vanwynsberghe, Robert, and Brenda Kwan. 2013. "Olympic Games Impact (OGI) Study for the 2010 Olympic and Paralympic Winter Games: Post-Games Report," October. http://circle.ubc.ca/handle/2429/45295.

Vanwynsberghe, Robert, Björn Surborg, and Elvin Wyly. 2013. "When the Games Come to Town: Neoliberalism, Mega-Events and Social Inclusion in the Vancouver 2010 Winter Olympic Games." *International Journal of Urban and Regional Research* 37 (6): 2074–93. doi:10.1111/j.1468-2427.2012.01105.x.

Western Economic Diversification Canada. 2010. "Evaluation of the Vancouver Agreement." www.wd.gc.ca/images/cont/12531_eng.pdf.

Zimbalist, Andrew. 2015. *Circus Maximus: The Economic Gamble Behind Hosting the Olympics and the World Cup*. Washington, DC: Brookings Institution Press.

5 Policing and security in Vancouver

Making the city look good when the world is watching[1]

[W]hen they did the Olympics they needed so many different police that they grabbed different police from all over BC, and all over other provinces, to fill in the spots that were needed. And because of that there's a lot more police officer activity, and there's a lot more newer police officers. It's changed everything. . . . I thought [the Olympics] was going to be good. But I didn't really understand how it was going to affect the people living on the street, it really did affect us big time. No busking. Too many police, couldn't stay on the street, [they] really moved us.

(Mike, Vancouver, 2011)

When Mike thought back to what happened during the Olympics the year before, what remained with him most clearly was the police presence and the overwhelming crowds. He had done his best to steer clear of the events, opting to stay inside and avoid as much as he could. Living on and off the streets of Vancouver and California since he was 17, at age 20 Mike was clear that the police were not there to protect him and his friends. He relayed a story of calling the police to help him out one time, and having them treat him as the suspect instead of the victim. As a white working-class youth who resembled the stereotype of a street kid, with ripped clothing, tattoos, and a mohawk, Mike found the escalating numbers of police on the streets of Vancouver during the Games to be extremely intimidating. He was well aware that police had been seconded from elsewhere in the country, and was directly impacted by their presence when, for example, he was told not to panhandle on Granville Street during the Olympics. As he noted in retrospect, "It's changed everything."

Policing before, during, and after the Games had an enormous impact on homeless and street-involved youth in Vancouver, and each stage looked different than the others. In the year leading up to the Games, homeless youth were 'moved' through pressure tactics, short-term housing, and criminalization, so that they would not be physically visible when the Olympics took place. During the Games, there were far more police officers on the streets, many of whom had been seconded from police forces across the country. After the Games, the police presence remained highly visible, though the social issues that had not been addressed through the intensification of the security state (such as drug use and homelessness) slowly re-emerged on Vancouver's streets.

Policing and security practices in Olympic cities are a significant aspect of the packaging of the host city as a modern, competitive, and desirable locale (Bernhard and Martin 2011). By providing a city that is 'safe and secure,' event organizers can "elevate a city's 'brand', [and] its competitive edge in the global marketplace of urban centres" (Molnar and Snider 2011, 161). Boyle and Haggerty (2009) have termed this particular manifestation of the security complex 'spectacular security.' Developing this concept in relation to the Olympic Games, Boyle and Haggerty suggest that this version of spectacle, "involves ongoing processes whereby social life is processed and packaged for mass visual consumption in a society increasingly oriented to appearances in the service of capitalism" (2009: 259). Yet it is not commitments to policing or amplified security that populate bid books when cities are trying to win the Games. Unlike social legacy promises, such as urban regeneration or the employment of inner-city residents, policing and security form part of what Boykoff and Fussey (2013) call 'shadow legacies.' Shadow legacies are not incorporated into Olympic legacy commitments or speculation about the outcome of the Games by Olympics boosters. Instead, these are the flip side of social legacy promises, unstated Olympic outcomes that are not part of the self-promotion efforts of Olympic committees trying to win popular and IOC support for their bids. While Vancouver did provide an indirect reference to the potential negative effects of Olympic policing and security practices via its Inner City Inclusive Commitments Statement – through a claim that civil liberties, the right to democratic protest, and access to public spaces would be protected – the London legacy and bid documents contain no reference to the impacts of policing or security measures on local populations. This is particularly remarkable given the enormous public expense represented by security spending in each city. An early low-ball estimate of CDN$175 million for Vancouver security ballooned to just under CDN$1 billion by the time the 2010 Games occurred (Boyle and Haggerty 2012). London's security costs ultimately ended up at over £1 billion (Hopkins and Gibson 2012), almost four times higher than the original security budget of £282 million (*BBC News London* 2012). The staggering amounts of public money spent on Olympic security alone merits intense scrutiny about the use of these funds and their impact on local residents; when twinned with the pre-existing social scientific evidence documenting that Olympic security practices disproportionately affect marginalized residents in host cities (Boyle and Haggerty 2009; Small et al. 2012; Lenskyj 2002), it is appalling that disclosure of the potential impacts of policing are not an integral requirement of Olympic bids.

Olympics security scholars Pete Fussey and Jon Coaffee (2012) outline some of the major trends that are shared across diverse Olympic cities with respect to their strategies for Olympic security. Of the five themes they outline, four were of particular relevance to the youths' experiences in Vancouver before, during, and after the Games: the expansion of urban militarism, the use of private security forces, the reconfiguration of space, and the prescription of behaviour through targeted policing (Fussey and Coaffee 2012). The only theme that did not have a major impact on the youths' lives, at least that they commented on, was that of 'observing the spectacle', referring to the degree to which electronic surveillance is introduced and normalized through Olympic security practices. CCTV monitoring was an issue in Vancouver, and the implications and consequences are discussed by Hier and Walby (2014) and Vonn (2010), among others. But the youth did not notice the introduction of CCTV cameras as a major impediment to their lives and movement in the city, and thus I do not devote space to the topic here.

Before the Games: Producing a 'civil city' through policing and security

The reconfiguration of space, the use of private security, and the prescription of behaviour through targeted policing were all significantly at play for the youth in the year before the Olympics began. According to Fussey and Coaffee's (2012) characterization, the reconfiguration of space refers both to efforts to 'design-in' counter-terrorism features into the built environment, and also the "broader regeneration of host neighbourhoods or even regions" (2012, 278). It is the latter that was particularly felt by the youth in my study. The prescription of behaviour refers to "the extensive use of 'zero-tolerance' style policing approaches and exclusion orders" (2012, 278). These two forces combined in the year prior to the 2010 Olympics, manifesting for homeless and street-involved youth as intensified police pressure to not be visibly present in the downtown core or the more affluent West side of the city.

During my 2009 fieldwork, the most prominent item of discussion in the focus groups and interviews was the degree to which the youth felt they were being specifically targeted by the police for minor infractions, and being pressured to 'move east' and away from the downtown core. As Richard stated, "[The police] try and move you out to the East side a lot." When I asked him what they do to move people to the East side, he told me that the police would harass him, saying things like, "'I'll come here in this area and keep on trying [to get you to leave]'. They're really like, 'homeless people aren't even supposed to be around these areas.' And they treat people just really crappy and a lot of people are, you know, just trying to survive. But it's just the way of the city, with the Olympics and that. Sweeping everything under the table." When I asked him what areas the police were moving people out of, he told me, "I've seen it's mostly this area [West end]. Mostly the downtown area and this rich area."

A similar conversation ensued in a focus group that year:

Man 1:	Maybe the police presence itself wouldn't matter but there's also more pressure to not be on the streets.
Man 2:	Like, it's harder now than it was a few years ago to be outside. Like, there's a few parks that I used to go to and a few roofs that I used to climb on and I can't go there any more. It's harder.
Interviewer:	*[Picking up on a comment made earlier]* Because of the police?

Man 1:   Yeah, the police. It's not that having more police. That doesn't
                bother me. But it's that they're doing more, too.

Woman: They're getting into certain neighbourhoods. There are certain
                neighbourhoods they won't let you in, but in the West end, if they
                find you in one place? They'll be checking it every night after that
                for about a month.

Group: [General murmurs of agreement.]

Interviewer: What neighbourhoods do they not bother you in?

Man 1:   East Van.

Woman: East side.

Man 1:   They don't care if you're down there. They'll come up to me while
                I've been using drugs and they're like, we don't care that you're
                using. Just [stay out of sight].

Based on their descriptions, I have created a map of the areas from which the youth felt that they were being excluded in the year prior to the Olympics. Streets that the youth named as sites of targeted policing included Granville Street, Burrard Street, Robson Street, Nelson Street, Seymour Street and Cordova Ave. They also described being moved on if they were sleeping under the Burrard Street Bridge, and they commented on the virtual emptying out of Pigeon Park, an inner-city park in the Downtown Eastside. The dotted rectangles denote approximate areas of exclusion; the dashed rectangle denotes the area in the Downtown Eastside into which they felt they were being pressured. The arrow indicates the location of Robson Square, which was the heart of the non-sporting Olympic festivities in downtown Vancouver. The areas of Granville Street and Robson Street that are within the dotted rectangles are prominent tourist areas; Robson Street is a shopping district with numerous middle- and high-end shops such as the Gap, Banana Republic, and Roots. Granville Street is a pedestrian and busses-only walkway that underwent a series of renovations in the years prior to the Games, in an effort to make it more attractive (Smith 2011). The small strip of West Cordova delineated with a dotted line is the tourist-oriented and affluent Gastown area, directly adjacent to the Downtown Eastside, though extending farther west. The small X is the location of Pigeon Park, which became part of a new walking corridor built between Chinatown and Gastown called the 'Carrall Street Greenway,' designed to allow tourists to access these two popular neighbourhoods without encountering the grittier section of the Downtown Eastside (Small et al. 2012). As the map illustrates, the youth felt that they were being pressured to not be in areas where tourists would see them, and instead to move east into the impoverished section of the city known as the Downtown Eastside. This can be understood as part of efforts to reconfigure the downtown core in order to more closely align it with the clean and affluent image that Vancouver was hoping to convey to Olympic tourists.

There were two specific initiatives implemented in Vancouver in the years leading up to the Olympics that were largely responsible for the reconfiguration of space and amplified zero-tolerance policing experienced by the youth, as well as

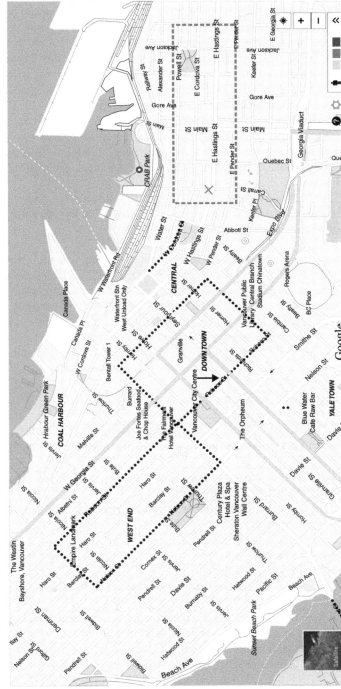

Figure 5.1 Areas of exclusion for homeless youth in downtown Vancouver before the Olympics. The dotted rectangles denote areas of exclusion; the dashed rectangle denotes the section of the Downtown Eastside into which they felt they were being pressured. The arrow indicates Robson Square. The X is the location of Pigeon Park. One dotted line indicates Gastown, the other indicates the Burrard Street Bridge.

their experiences with private security forces: 'Project Civil City' and the Vancouver Police Department's 2009 Business Plan. The first was introduced by then-mayor Sam Sullivan in 2006 and had an explicit focus on ensuring that the city was ready for the arrival of the Olympics in 2010 (Sullivan 2006). Part of the Civil City initiative was the Downtown Ambassadors program; unlike other Ambassador programs in major Canadian cities, which draw on local residents as their 'Ambassadors', this one made use of trained security guards to patrol city streets (Sleiman and Lippert 2010; Boyle and Haggerty 2011). Run by Genesis Security and the Downtown Vancouver Business Improvement Association (DVBIA), Ambassadors were "trained to provide hospitality assistance and crime prevention services" with a focus on what they term "quality of life" issues "such as panhandling, litter, theft, illegal vending, and graffiti" (Genesis Security no date).

The youth I spoke to in 2009 had many negative reports of interactions with the Ambassadors. Marianne, whose story I described in more detail at the beginning of Chapter 2, described the following encounter:

> I remember when [the Ambassadors] first came out I was pregnant and I was sitting down on Granville Street. I wasn't panhandling. I wasn't asking people for money and they were like, "you need to move." And I was like, "what? . . . I'm eight and a half months pregnant." They're like, "We don't care. It's not our job, we're trying to make our city look more nice." They told me, "It doesn't help to have homeless people kicking around on the streets. . . . You're making our city look bad. Don't you know? We have the Olympics coming."

And in a 2009 focus group, the following conversation ensued:

Man:	It's almost as if you're in a fascist place because [security] guards are walking around and kicking homeless people in the head.
Woman:	Because they're overstepping their bounds.
Man:	Yeah. They try to get in your face.
Woman:	They move you at 2:30 in the morning, okay? If you're sleeping outside.
Another woman:	And they're not allowed to do that.
Group:	No. No. I know.
Woman:	Yeah, they're not allowed.
Woman 2:	And they'll kick you when you're sleeping. Just, wake up.

The youth I spoke to were not alone in experiencing the Downtown Ambassadors as extremely problematic. In 2009, Pivot Legal Society and the Vancouver Area Network of Drug Users (VANDU) launched a complaint against the Ambassadors, which was heard by the BC Human Rights Tribunal (CBC News British Columbia 2009). Pivot and VANDU alleged that the group "discriminates against the homeless and drug users in the city," stating that they "'act very much like home-less police' because they tell people who sit, sleep or panhandle on sidewalks to move along, and that they are not welcome" (Canadian Press 2012). Although the suit was dismissed in 2012 because the tribunal did not feel they could establish a definitive connection between the alleged adverse treatment and a prohibited ground of discrimination, Tribunal Member Tonie Beharrell offered the following important caveat:

> [It] should not be taken . . . that I accept the DVBIA's [Downtown Vancouver Business Improvement Association's] assertion in this regard. In particular, I note that the evidence . . . raises the potential that the Ambassadors were not acting solely on the basis of illegal behaviour, but were also targeting certain types of individuals. I also note that the removal of individuals . . . is, intuitively, much more likely to occur with respect to individuals who are or appear to be members of the Class than with other members of the public.
>
> (Pivot Legal Society 2012)

Project Civil City and its accompanying Downtown Ambassadors program was shut down near the end of 2008 with the election of Mayor Gregor Robertson under the left-centrist party Vision Vancouver. But when the Vancouver Police Department introduced their business plan in 2009, it was critiqued as "an unwanted remnant of the previous city council's controversial Project Civil City program" (CBC News 2009). The VPD plan included additional numbers of police patrolling the Downtown Eastside, more street spot checks (whereby a person can be stopped and asked for identification or other questions), and more by-law violation tickets issued (Pablo 2009). The plan suggested that "with more officers being dedicated to the area, and more of their shift spent enforcing the law on the street, the disorder and offending associated with this area will decrease, increasing the quality of life and safety for all residents and visitors in the area" (as cited in Pablo 2009). In order to implement the plan, the Vancouver Police Department's 'Beat Enforcement Teams' (BETs) were increased by 200% in the period prior to the Olympics (Molnar and Snider 2011).

Not surprisingly, the youth reported the year prior to the Games as a time of more frequent and more intense interactions with police officers. As Josh said in a 2009 interview, "The cops are much more tightly wound because of this Olympics thinking. 'Fuck, the Olympics are coming. We're going to have tourists. It's going to be a big boom for us.'" Several of the youth had experiences with being ticketed or arrested for loitering, panhandling, or one of the other myriad 'crimes' that are part of the constellation of 'safe street' strategies that police can draw on in order to punish the poor (Wacquant 2009). If they did not have first-hand experience, they knew someone else who had. Richard describes being arrested for sleeping on Granville Street – at least, that is what he understood his crime to be. He recounts that he was not told what he was arrested for or charged with until the following day, after spending a night in jail. Malz was frequently asked to move by police when panhandling in the downtown area; although he

Figure 5.2 Trot's photo journal images capturing the 'cleaning out' of the alleys,
which he attributes to the increase in tickets issued by police prior to the
Games.

had not been ticketed for panhandling, he knew several others who had received
such tickets. Allison pointed out the intensified policing focus on Pigeon Park,
noting that the police presence there was forcing people to move their drug deals
into the alleys or the hotels, because "the police aren't going down the alleys."
Allison documented her dismay at the clearing out of Pigeon Park through her
photo journal (see Figure 5.3).

The common theme running through the majority of stories such as these was
the focus on moving visibly homeless or drug-using people out of prominent areas
and into parts of the city where they would not be seen by visiting tourists. While
the additional threat of a terrorist attack was sometimes referenced by the youth
as a justification for the increased policing, they felt that the tactics used by the
police were ineffective at stopping such threats, and instead increased their own

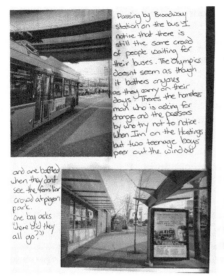

Figures 5.3a and 5.3b Excerpt from Allison's photo journal, discussing the clearing out of Pigeon Park. Her text reads: "Passing by Broadway station on the bus I notice that there is still the same crowd of people waiting for their buses. The Olympics doesn't seem as though it bothers anyone as they carry on their days. There's the homeless man who is asking for change and the passers-by who try not to notice. When I'm on the Hastings bus two teenage boys peer out the window and are baffled when they don't see the familiar crowd at Pigeon Park. One boy asks, 'where did they all go?' I ask, 'where did they put them?' They both look at me in surprise. I see policemen, only following the orders of those in power, give tickets to those on the streets. I wonder about the mental state and history of those people. Why they wouldn't go to the bug-infested scary emergency shelters put up? I think about why I couldn't leave my house for a month – not by choice but I just couldn't. I think about my history my abuse and neglect my homeless drug-infested past. Now I remember my new life, my condo, my job . . ."

marginalization. In a 2010 interview, Barry reported being regularly stopped by police in the period leading up to the Games. When asked about his thoughts on this experience, he remarked:

Barry: It's a waste of time and it's a violation of my civil rights. And I can't do anything about it because the Olympics are on and there's a terrorist [drive], which trumps everything . . . I can't blame them for being wary with all the bullshit. If I was a terrorist I'd want to hit the Olympics. I can't blame them but it's as annoying as all hell.

Interviewer: For the legitimate concerns of security that you alluded to, do you think that those are being addressed by these searches in your neighbourhood?

Barry: Hell, no. . . . They're just doing it to try and bust people. Get them off the street so the tourists don't see them.

The reconfiguration of space that was facilitated by focused policing in visible tourist areas was supplemented by literal 'cleansing' of the belongings of homeless people from city streets. Joanna reported witnessing such an incident one night near Pigeon Park, the same park that Allison had described with dismay as being cleared out, and which many of the youth had remarked upon as a formerly bustling site that had since been emptied of inhabitants.

Joanna: Oh yeah. I've seen them do the cleaning sweeps on the streets and stuff like that. Like, I read about them at first and then I seen some. It was these people with a truck. They just said that they had to move their [homeless people's] stuff because they were clean-sweeping the street. And then after that they were going around telling everyone, "oh, you have to move your stuff. You have to move right now or else we're going to move it." And then they came in with this dumpster truck thing, and they started tossing people's stuff if they didn't get rid of it. And then they just came along and sprayed down the [streets]. Someone came along and picked up all the garbage first. And then whatever stuff was out they just tossed in the garbage. There was people who came after to pick up all the little pieces of paper. And then they sprayed all along the street with two big trucks.

Joanna witnessed this street cleaning incident in the middle of the night when she was waiting for the bus to get home from work. She thought the trucks doing the cleaning were City of Vancouver trucks, due to the markings and the lights. She was outraged at seeing people's belongings tossed away in this manner, though helpless to do anything about it.

In 2009, the province introduced new legislation that gave the police even more powers to move homeless people off the streets. Officially titled the "Assistance to Shelter Act," activists dubbed it the "Olympic Kidnapping Law," in light of the authorization it granted to police to forcibly move a person from the street to a shelter. Ostensibly limited by police assessment as to whether the person in question is considered to be 'at risk' due to inclement weather, the BC Civil Liberties Association decried the law, stating that "This bill would have police arrest citizens who are not guilty of any crime, and detain them without any charge, simply because they are homeless" (Paulsen 2009). Taken in combination with the Civil City initiative and the 2009 business plan of the VPD, it is perhaps not at all surprising that the youth experienced an intensification of policing and security in the year prior to the 2010 Olympics. This was in keeping with the expectations of Olympic critics and watchdogs, who knew that an Olympic Games typically heralded more police scrutiny of vulnerable populations. What is typically assumed, however, is that the policing will be at its most intense *during* the Games. This was not the case. From the reports of the youth I worked with, it was *prior* to the Olympics that the most focused and egregious interactions with police and private security took place. During the Games, it was another story altogether.

During the Games: Police restraint when 'the world is watching'

The general consensus of the youth during the Games (2010) and particularly thinking back on them (2011) was that the police had acted with considerable restraint during the Vancouver Olympics. This finding was supported by at least one other study, which found that policing during the Olympics was 'responsible' and that "the VPD were not attempting to clear marginalized individuals from public spaces" (Small et al. 2012, 130). This was surprising to everyone (myself included), as we had all been anticipating an overzealous police force attempting to keep the city safe and manageable for tourists. There was so much community concern about the potential for abusive or overzealous policing during the Games that the BC Civil Liberties Association and Pivot Legal Society ran a legal observer training course designed to train local citizens to become "the watchful eyes that will be focused on police, military and private security conduct to ensure accountability" (Eby and Price 2010, 5). At least one anti-Olympic activist I spoke with attributed the restraint of the police to the oversight of bodies like this one, and this may well be part of the story. But I think another important explanation has to do with the desire of the city's elites that Vancouver 'look its best' when the 'world is watching' – and looking its best does *not* include looking like a repressive police state that tramples on the rights of marginalized peoples.

Policing and security for the 2010 Olympics was governed by the 2010 Vancouver Integrated Security Unit (VISU), which included the RCMP (Royal Canadian Mounted Police, a federal policing body), the Canadian Armed Forces, and seconded police from across Canada. The goal of this body was to have police 'on every corner' during the Games themselves (Anonymous 2010); this was achieved through the secondment of approximately 6,000 additional police officers from 119 agencies across Canada, approximately 5,000 Canadian Forces troops, and approximately 4800 additional private security (not including the private security that were already on hand through individual businesses and property owners) (Lawson 2011). This was in addition to the 1,327 Vancouver Police Department officers available as of January 2010 (Vancouver Police Department, retrieved May 9, 2011), a number that had grown from 1,124 in 2004 (Demers and Griffiths 2007). Combined, this became the "largest peacetime security operation in Canadian history" (Molnar and Snider 2011, 153).[2]

Given the swell of security officials within the city, it is somewhat remarkable that the youth reported a *drop* in police interactions: surely the behaviour of the youth did not change so much during the Games that less police intervention was warranted? And surely the presence of approximately *15 times* the normal number of security personnel would imply that *more* rather than *less* interactions would be likely? That this did not manifest gives weight to the theory of security spectacle advanced by Boyle and Haggerty (2009); the *appearance* of security was important, but equally important was the *appearance* of the city as liberal, tolerant, and welcoming. As John Rennie Short notes in his study of the Summer Olympic Games, the efforts of Olympic host cities to secure global city status relies on creating an image "of modernity and multiculturalism, part of the shared global discourse of democracy and liberalism while also adding a touch of the uniquely global" (Short 2004, 106). Given the intense focus on Vancouver by global media during the Games, any incident that might suggest that the police were engaging in targeted enforcement that infringed on the human rights or civil liberties of marginalized peoples within the city would not have enhanced the image that Vancouver elites were hoping to convey.

Some of the youth were cognizant of this aspect of the dynamic playing into their experiences with policing. As Colvin noted in 2011, reflecting back on his experiences with police during the Olympics:

> They were using very good discretion. And they didn't stick their nose where they didn't need to kinda thing. If they saw a situation that needed to be dealt with they dealt with it, but other than that they just let people enjoy themselves and enjoy the Games. I think they did a good job actually. I don't normally say that about the police (laughing). I think they were quite on the ball for that . . . It's amazing how calm they were.

Despite his praise of the police and their restraint, Colvin was quick to note the role played by global media attention in creating such behaviour: "They had the whole world watching them and they were on TV and like you can only do so much when you're being filmed, right?"

The global media spectacle was experienced by other youth as one of the mitigating factors for the lessening of negative police interactions during the Games. This occurred not only through the presence of international journalists, but also because the entire city had become a spectacle, and the people in it were expected to be spectators. This meant that the forms of behaviour considered acceptable shifted during the Games. For instance, Sandy conveyed being harassed by police, with escalating degrees of violence, in the weeks and months leading up to the Games, particularly when she and her friends were sitting on the steps of the Vancouver Art Gallery. The Art Gallery is located adjacent to Robson Square, the centre of Olympic celebrations within Vancouver. However, once the Games began, she reported the following:

Sandy: Oh, that [being moved on by the police] doesn't usually happen anymore, with that big TV screen there [near the steps of the Vancouver Art Gallery].

Interviewer: OK. Why?

Sandy: Because the TV screen's there. . . . It's a big fucking TV screen, have you seen it?

Interviewer: Yeah, but why does that matter?

Sandy: Because now we're not loitering [laughs]. Now we're not loitering *because* we're watching TV. Isn't that awesome?

Captured in this vignette is the malleable nature of so-called criminal behaviour; what had been intensely surveilled and punished in the weeks preceding the Games had now become banal or innocent in light of the media spectacle of the Olympic Games (see also Kennelly and Watt 2011). Thus the spectacle of security at Olympic mega-events did not produce monolithically negative interactions for homeless youth with police; indeed it appeared to have a mitigating effect and permit youth, temporarily, greater mobility and freedom from surveillance than they typically experienced within Vancouver.

While some of the youth enjoyed this reprieve from intensive policing, others found it puzzling. As Vanessa said in 2011,

> Because everybody was breaking the law, having a good time after the events and stuff, they [the police] would just say, "OK, spill it [beer] out and you can go on your way." Or, "OK, don't jaywalk. If I see you next time I'll charge you." So, it was kinda like they were sidestepping what they had to do as well. They're saying little things, which are not little things in regular days, are all right. In front of people that came from different cities.

The general mood of permissiveness seemed to be towards behaviours that were connected to celebrating the Olympics. Loitering on the Art Gallery steps, drinking beer as part of an Olympic street party, or jaywalking in order to get to Olympic celebrations were all tolerated within this context. But other behaviours were not exempt from police attention during the Games. Out of view of media cameras or tourists, youth reported being harassed by police during the Games for what I would call 'image breaking' – actions that would otherwise be tolerated but were seen as inappropriate in the context of an Olympic Games, unless they were occurring in the midst of a large crowd celebrating on Granville Street. These grouped around such petty crimes as public intoxication, skateboarding, and jaywalking. Several of the youth reported being arrested for public drunkenness, or for smoking marijuana in public, both infractions which are typically tolerated in the context of weekend nights out in Vancouver. One participant recounted his friend's skateboard being confiscated by the police, who claimed it was dangerous to others despite the skateboarding happening early in the morning when there were no other people around. Another reported being given two tickets for jaywalking during the Olympics. Each of these incidents were considered by participants to be atypically policed during the Games, identifying them as actions they or their friends had taken outside of the context of the Olympic Games without problem.

Just as it was clear to the youth that the focus of the police and security forces was to maintain a positive image of the city for the sake of the visiting tourists and media cameras, so also was it clear that their own needs and concerns were not at the centre of police actions and decision-making during the Games. As Angela remarked in 2010, the police were "not watching out for us. They're watching out for the people who are here for the Olympics. You know? It's just so frustrating." For youth who did not match the expected characteristics of visiting tourists or even of affluent residents, they found themselves stopped and questioned as to whether they were 'in place.' Justine described being stopped by police in the affluent West end neighbourhood where she lived in temporary housing:

> "You don't look like you're from around here," that's what they'll [the police] say. And it's like, I just live down the street actually. And they're like, "Are you sure? What's your name? What's the address," and then like interrogating you for nothing when you walk down the street. Just because you don't look like you belong in the area.

Many of the youth also reported on the ongoing pressure they experienced to not be visible in tourist areas, a continuation of the reconfiguration of space that had begun in the period before the Games. This took the form of being forced into shelters, or, barring that, being held in jail for the duration of the Games. In a 2011 focus group, the following comments were made:

Man: I remember, during the Olympics they just shoved everyone into shelters. Just like, temporary shelters. It was just a temporary solution. Once the Olympics were over they just got pushed right the fuck out.

Woman: The ones that didn't find an SRO [single residence occupancy] hotel to stay in, and refused to go to a shelter, they were just put in jail. They were put in jail. And they were held to the end of the Olympics.

During an interview in 2010, Andy said, "I myself haven't been moved but I woke up with people who the cops have forced into shelters. Well, not forced, but they forced them into it: it's your choice. Go to the shelter or go to jail." In the same year, Stephanie noted that she had heard about police trying to intimidate people into shelters: "If you're not going to willingly go to a shelter I will force you to go to a shelter. Which is ridiculous."

The youth also relayed stories of others they knew being given bus tickets out of the city; others reported knowing people who had been given money to leave Vancouver and move to nearby cities such as Chilliwack. Although it is impossible to verify or negate these stories within the context of this research project – my efforts to find formal documentation of such practices came up empty – it is clear that homeless youth were feeling immense pressure to absent themselves from visible tourist areas of the city, as well as potentially leave the city altogether. Despite the slight alleviation of policing pressure during the Games under the glare of global media attention, homeless and street-involved youth in Vancouver knew themselves to be an unwelcome part of the global Olympic spectacle. As one woman reported in a focus group in 2011, "I just felt like I was being pushed away, out of the scene. Like, 'We don't want to see you during the Olympics. Just go hide during the Olympics.'"

After the Games: Back to 'policing as usual'

The most frequent comment I heard from the youth about policing after the Games was that there seemed to be more police around, but also that their behaviour had returned back to 'normal.' Colvin saw the police as "still the same old," while Janey said that the police "seem to be everywhere." Ajax reported seeing more police around, but did not find himself having more encounters with them. The following excerpt from Vanessa in 2011 captures the broad shift in policing described by many of the youth from before the Olympics until afterwards:

> I know when I first came down here and I saw Main and Hastings [in the heart of the Downtown Eastside], it was like swarms of people. Like I'd see people shooting up, doing crack, like right on the side of the road, not even caring. And then I remember, right before the Olympics, that the homeless people had those tents set up or whatever, and then right after that the area was like, cleared for the Olympics. So I definitely think that now, the big influence of why Main and Hastings and that area has changed is because of the Olympics, for sure. But now that the Olympics are done and over with, a couple weeks ago I saw some people shooting up on the side.

Vanessa's description touches on many different elements: on the one hand, the significant degree of open drug use and the sheer mass of people on the streets of the Downtown Eastside prior to the Games, followed by the social and physical cleansing that happened in preparation for the Olympics. But also important here is the fact of the slow creep of 'normalcy' back to the Downtown Eastside, which in the case of this neighbourhood means the re-emergence of open drug use. What this suggests is that the crackdown on that neighbourhood, and others in the downtown core, was not a long-term or effective strategy for meaningfully shifting the social relations of deprivation, drug use, and poverty in the area. Instead, it was exactly what the Vancouver police claimed it was not: namely, city cleansing in preparation for the Olympic Games.

With the resignation that comes from repeated experiences of disappointment and neglect from the powers-that-be, the youth were matter of fact about the return to 'normalcy' that signalled the end of the Olympic era. At the least they were no longer being expressly targeted, as they had been before the Games; nor were they now being tolerated in public spaces for the sake of global media attention. Instead, their lives returned much to how they had been before the Olympics came to the city: facing ongoing police harassment (though not more so than usual), doing their best to scrape together an existence with very few opportunities, and trying to find viable shelter and employment in a city with very little housing and very few jobs.

Conclusions

In their discussion of the 'security-development' nexus at the Vancouver 2010 Olympics, Adam Molnar and Laureen Snider (2011, 151) write that "Mega-events . . . uphold the status quo of a neoliberal and *neoliberalizing* political economic order, intensifying and revealing the displacement of insecurity (such as social inequality and environmental externalities) onto marginalized populations" (emphasis theirs). The data from my study supports this assertion. Rather than policing and security practices being designed to support the well-being and safety of local marginalized residents, the implementation of new legislation, policies, and practices prior to the Games had the effect (and, at times, the explicit intention) of 'cleaning the streets' of those homeless or marginalized residents who would tarnish the reputation of Vancouver as a liberal and cosmopolitan city. Intensified with the excuse of the Olympic Games as a convenient deadline to work towards, the youth in my study experienced policing and private security (most notably the Downtown Ambassadors) as targeted towards moving them out of visible tourist areas and into the Downtown Eastside in the year prior to the Games. Interestingly, and against common understandings, they found policing during the Games to generally be more relaxed, particularly when it took place in the context of Olympic events and celebrations. This was not true across the board, however, as some of the youth experienced policing that seemed to be about policing the image of the city even during the Games, though notably not in view of media or other tourists. They also continued to experience pressure to not be a visible part of the Olympic city, relaying stories of people similar to themselves being locked up for the duration of the Olympics, or bussed out of the city altogether. After the Games were over, they noted that more police were now present on city streets, but they felt their interactions with them dropped back to 'normal,' or rather back to how it had been prior to the city cleansing that took place in preparation for the Olympics.

One implication of these findings is what it tells us about *when* those concerned about the policing of mega-events ought to be watching for negative impacts. The youth in my study experienced the most intense policing *prior* to the Games, rather than during. This flies in the face of common assumptions about how policing plays out during a mega-event, where it is assumed that crackdowns on marginalized residents will happen in the context of the Games-time period. This means that civil society and research initiatives designed to address or monitor policing activities are mistakenly focused on the Olympic period, rather than the time prior to the Games. One such example is the joint BC Civil Liberties Association and Pivot Legal Society legal observer training, which sent residents onto the streets of Vancouver during the Olympics to ensure that policing and security practices were not abusive; another is a study of research into the effects of street-level policing in the Downtown Eastside of Vancouver during the

Olympics, "to assess the potential impact on access to harm reduction services and injection-related risk behaviour" (Small et al. 2012, 128). While evidence from my study suggests that policing during the Games still may have problematic elements of targeting and enforcement, particularly outside the focus of media or tourist events, my data suggests that the period of greater concern is prior to the Games, when the majority of efforts are being put in place to ensure that the city is 'ready' for the moment when the 'world is watching.' While some of this may be specific to Vancouver and its context of extreme and visible poverty in the Downtown Eastside, it is almost certainly going to be part of the formula for policing and security practices in other Olympic cities.

Notes

1 This chapter draws partially on material from two previous publications: Kennelly, Jacqueline (2015). "You're Making Our City Look bad": Olympic Security, Neoliberal Urbanization, and Homeless Youth. *Ethnography* 16 (1): 3–24; and Kennelly, Jacqueline (2015). "Promoting 'Civility': City Marketing and Exclusion of the Young and the Poor (Vancouver 2010)", in Vida Bacj (ed.). *Securing and Surveilling the Olympics: From Tokyo 1964 to London 2012 and Beyond*. New York: PalgraveMacMillan.
2 It also became the progenitor for the intensive and aggressive policing against G20 protesters later that same year in Toronto. The integrated security model that had been developed in Vancouver was exported to Toronto in June, under the same security firm, Contemporary Security Canada. The policing of G20 protesters resulted in "allegations of police brutality, unlawful detention, and other breaches of civil liberties" (Kitchen and Rygiel 2014, 201).

Bibliography

All website URLs were accessed between September 2014 and December 2015.
Anonymous. 2010. "Police to Be 'on Every Corner.'" *Victoria Times-Colonist*, February 12.
BBC News London. 2012. "London 2012: Olympic Security Cost Raises Concern among MPs," March 8. www.bbc.com/news/uk-england-london-17302068.
Bernhard, Daniel, and Aaron K. Martin. 2011. "Rethinking Security at the Olympics." In *Security Games: Surveillance and Control at Mega-Events*, edited by Colin J. Bennett and Kevin Haggerty. New York: Routledge.
Boykoff, Jules, and Pete Fussey. 2014. "London's Shadow Legacies: Security and Activism at the 2012 Olympics." *Contemporary Social Science* 9 (2): 253–70. doi:10.1080/21582041.2013.838292.
Boyle, Philip, and Kevin Haggerty. 2009. "Spectacular Security: Mega-Events and the Security Complex." *International Political Sociology* 3 (3): 257–74. doi:10.1111/j.1749-5687.2009.00075.x.
Boyle, Philip, and Kevin Haggerty. 2011. "Civil Cities and Urban Governance: Regulating Disorder for the Vancouver Winter Olympics." *Urban Studies* 48 (15): 3185–3201.
Boyle, Philip, and Kevin Haggerty. 2012. "Planning for the Worst: Risk, Uncertainty and the Olympic Games." *The British Journal of Sociology* 63 (2): 241–59. doi:10.1111/j.1468-4446.2012.01408.x.
Canadian Press. 2012. "Human Rights Case against Vancouver's Downtown Ambassadors Dismissed." February 7. www.cbc.ca/1.1268586.

CBC News. 2009. "Downtown Eastside Advocates Vow to Fight Police Crackdown." *CBC News, British Columbia*, February 16. www.cbc.ca/news/canada/british-columbia/downtown-eastside-advocates-vow-to-fight-police-crackdown-1.833862.

CBC News British Columbia. 2009. "Downtown Ambassadors to Face B.C. Human Rights Tribunal." July 7. www.cbc.ca/1.796567.

Demers, Simon, Adam Palmer, and Curt Taylor Griffiths. 2007. "Vancouver Police Department Patrol Deployment Study, Vancouver Police Department." Vancouver: City of Vancouver. http://vancouver.ca/police/assets/pdf/studies/vpd-study-patrol-deployment.pdf.

Eby, David, and Caroline Price. 2010. "Olympic Legal Observer Information and Training Guide." Vancouver: BC Civil Liberties Association and Pivot Legal Society.

Fussey, Pete, and Jon Coaffee. 2012. "Balancing Local and Global Security Leitmotifs: Counter-Terrorism and the Spectacle of Sporting Mega-Events." *International Review for the Sociology of Sport* 47 (3): 268–85.

Genesis Security. no date. "Downtown Ambassadors Program." www.genesissecurity.com/content.php?section=23.

Hier, Sean P., and Kevin Walby. 2014. "Policy Mutations, Compliance Myths, and Redeployable Special Event Public Camera Surveillance in Canada." *Sociology* 48 (1): 150–66. doi:10.1177/0038038513477755.

Hopkins, Nick, and Owen Gibson. 2012. "Olympics Security Bill: How It Soared to More than £1bn." *The Guardian*. March 9. www.theguardian.com/sport/2012/mar/09/olympics-security-bill-how-it-soared.

Kennelly, Jacqueline. 2015a. "Promoting 'civility:' City Marketing and Exclusion of the Poor (Vancouver 2010)." In *Surveilling and Securing the Olympics: From Tokyo 1964 to London 2012 and Beyond*, edited by Vida Bajc. New York: Palgrave Macmillan.

Kennelly, Jacqueline. 2015b. "'You're Making Our City Look Bad': Olympic Security, Neoliberal Urbanization, and Homeless Youth." *Ethnography* 16 (1): 3–24. doi:10.1177/1466138113513526.

Kennelly, Jacqueline, and Paul Watt. 2011. "Sanitizing Public Space in Olympic Host Cities: The Spatial Experiences of Marginalized Youth in 2010 Vancouver and 2012 London." *Sociology* 45 (5): 765–81.

Kitchen, Veronica, and Kim Rygiel. 2014. "Privatizing Security, Securitizing Policing: The Case of the G20 in Toronto, Canada." *International Political Sociology* 8 (2): 201–17. doi:10.1111/ips.12052.

Lawson, Dix. 2011. "Project Management and the RCMP Security Mission for the Vancouver 2010 Olympic Games: Safe and Secure Games through an Integrated Security Model." Four Seasons Hotel. http://static1.1.sqspcdn.com/static/f/616450/10952500/1298754931057/CWCC+PMI+Presentation+16+Feb+2011.pdf?token=ouyD6bbJckJQEoCdKHhOGnXwlFE%3D.

Lenskyj, Helen Jefferson. 2002. *The Best Olympics Ever?: Social Impacts of Sydney 2000.* Albany: State University of New York Press.

Molnar, Adam, and Laureen Snider. 2011. "Mega-Events, Mega-Profits: Unpacking the Vancouver 2010 Security Development Nexus." In *Security Games: Surveillance and Control at Mega-Events*, edited by Colin J. Bennett and Kevin Haggerty. New York: Routledge.

Pablo, Carlito. 2009. "Vancouver Police Plan Downtown Eastside Crackdown Ahead of Olympics." *The Georgia Straight*, January 21. www.straight.com/article-197388/vancouver-police-plan-downtown-eastside-crackdown-ahead-olympics.

Paulsen, Monte. 2009. "BC Preparing New Law to Apprehend Homeless." *The Tyee.* September 21. http://thetyee.ca/News/2009/09/21/HomelessLaw/.

Pivot Legal Society. 2012. "Tribunal Member Qualifies 'Downtown Ambassadors' Decision." *Pivot Points.* February 7. www.pivotlegal.org/pivot-points/blog/tribunal-member-qualifies-downtown-ambassadors-decision.

Short, John R. 2004. *Global Metropolitan: Globalizing Cities in a Capitalist World.* London; New York: Routledge.

Sleiman, Mark, and Randy Lippert. 2010. "Downtown Ambassadors, Police Relations and 'Clean and Safe' Security." *Policing and Society: An International Journal of Research and Policy* 20 (3): 316–35.

Small, Will, Andrea Krusi, Evan Wood, Julio Montaner, and Thomas Kerr. 2012. "Street-Level Policing in the Downtown Eastside of Vancouver, Canada, during the 2010 Winter Olympics." *International Journal of Drug Policy* 23: 128–33.

Smith, Charlie. 2011. "Granville Street's New Beat." *The Georgia Straight*, November 2. www.straight.com/news/granville-streets-new-beat.

Sullivan, Sam. 2006. "Project Civil City Tackles Crime, Public Disorder and Social Issues in Vancouver." *Sam Sullivan.* November 27. www.samsullivan.ca.

Vancouver Police Department. 2011. "Vancouver Police Department Organization." *The Vancouver Police Department: Beyond the Call.* http://vancouver.ca/police/organization/index.html.

Vonn, Michael. 2010. "CCTV and the 2010 Vancouver Games: Spatial Tactics and Political Strategies." *Case Western Reserve Journal of International Law* 42: 595–605.

Wacquant, Loïc. 2009. *Punishing the Poor: The Neoliberal Government of Social Insecurity.* First edition, paperback issue edition. Durham NC: Duke University Press Books.

6 Policing and security in London

Dispersal orders, racial profiling, and protecting tourists

There's a lot changing here as well. A lot. It looks clean and tidy. And a lot of police around.

(Todd, walking interview, London 2012)

What struck me most on first meeting Todd was his height – a lanky Black man well over six feet tall, Todd stood out in a crowd. His height contrasted with his voice, which was soft and subdued – except when relaying to us his frustration over being the frequent target of police attention. Todd opened up gradually to us through his interviews in 2012, one a standard face-to-face and the second a walking interview of Stratford a few days after the Olympics began. He also participated in a focus group. Through our time with him, we learned that he had moved to the UK from the Congo when he was 15, joining his father there, who he barely knew. He moved in with an aunt at age 18 to study Finance at a local college, but he dropped out when she kicked him out of her house. He did not tell us why she kicked him out. Now 23, he had been living in the supportive housing unit for a year, and was looking for full-time, permanent employment (what he called a 'proper job') so that he could move out and into his own place. He paid £40 a month out of his meagre social assistance to the mother of his 3-year-old daughter, and was expecting another baby in a few months. As he walked us around Stratford, he pointed out places where youth used to hang out, before the Olympic police presence drove them away. He also showed us locations of food shops he used to frequent, since closed and replaced with more expensive stores. On our request, he took us to the location near Westfield mall where he had recently been approached by the police, wrestled to the ground, stuffed into a van, then released without charges. He also showed us where his friend, Jonathan, had been knifed to death just outside of the mall, in full view of security cameras.

Todd's comment, which opens the chapter, precisely captures the dynamics of neighbourhood change in the area. "It looks clean and tidy," he noted, in stark contrast to the derelict state that had characterized the area prior to the Games' arrival; "And a lot of police around." I noticed this contrast as well on my first day back in London for my 2012 fieldwork, capturing it in a photo of

Figure 6.1 Police walking along Stratford High Street a few days prior to the Opening Ceremonies (author photo, 2012).

strolling Bobbies alongside overflowing pots of flowers on the Stratford High Street (see Figure 6.1).

As was the case in Vancouver, the story of security at the London Olympics has two facets: one has to do with the massive implementation of security infrastructure and personnel and their costs, while the other relates to the everyday experiences for local residents of targeted policing practices before and during the Games. Much has already been written about the former (MacDonald and Hunter 2013; Coaffee, Fussey, and Moore 2011; Fussey, Coaffee, Armstrong and Hobbs 2012; Fussey and Coaffee 2012; Boykoff and Fussey 2013; Raine 2015; Manley and Silk 2013; Whelan 2013); my focus in this chapter will be largely on the latter.

Although I have separated them here, these two facets of the London security story are in many ways inseparable. The rhetoric surrounding the need for Olympic security shaped the perceptions of the youth, generating forms of 'security thinking' that functioned to normalize the incursion of security and policing on their everyday lives (MacDonald and Hunter 2013; Manley and Silk 2013); this is the focus of the first part of the chapter. 'Security thinking' was much more marked in London than in Vancouver, likely reflecting the differing national experiences with terrorism. Such normalization was also resisted and refuted however, based on the young people's lived experiences with policing in London before the Olympics began – particularly for young Black men. As with housing commitments and employment promises, the history of what came before in each city shaped what happened during the Games for policing. The second section of the chapter describes a decade's long incursion on the civil liberties of UK youth, in the shape of 'anti-social behaviour orders' and associated 'dispersal orders,' which then became part of the arsenal of tools used by police to subdue local youth populations during the Olympics. Also fresh in the minds and experiences of the youth in 2012 were the 2011 riots, which began in response to the police killing of a Black man in Tottenham; the riots and their impact on the youth in my study in the lead-up to the Games are discussed in the third section of the chapter. The final section illuminates the constantly reiterated sense that the police were there for others, not for them, amplified in the wake of the murder of their friend at Westfield a few weeks before the Olympics began.

Legitimizing surveillance through security thinking

During a walking interview with three of our male participants in 2012, we ran into two female friends of theirs who also lived in the supportive housing unit where we had been doing our research. The men playfully directed the audio recorder towards the women and asked them a few questions related to our research:

Isaac: How does it look? As a resident young lady with a beautiful day and scenery, what do you think of Stratford right now?

Female respondent: I think it's all about to explode.

Scott: Okay so basically you are a sitting duck without no bread.

Female respondent: I am just a sitting duck on a target waiting to be pumped.

This exchange was typical of conversations that also took place during our focus groups, where the young women, in particular, referenced fears of terrorist attacks and the strong sense that hosting the Olympics had made London, and specifically their community of Stratford, a terrorist target. As colourfully described by the young woman we ran into that day, many of the women (and some of the men) felt themselves and their community to be 'sitting ducks' just waiting to be bombed or attacked by undefined terrorist outsiders. Manley and Silk (2013) suggest this is one of the troubling legacies of hosting an Olympic Games, as such mega-events serve "to reinforce the normalisation of surveillance" through "escalating attention towards the 'othering' of a minority population against a normalised majority" (361).

MacDonald and Hunter (2013) conducted a discourse analysis of texts available in the public sphere that were related to security operations for the London 2012

Olympic Games. Their analysis reveals that "a range of linguistic devices was deployed to give the impression that London 2012 constituted an exceptional set of circumstances" (82) which were then used "to justify the scale and extent of the security operations for London 2012" (83). They conclude that:

> The rolling juggernaut of the modern Summer Olympics appears to provide a quadrennial platform for the *talking into being* of a hypostatized "terrorist threat" in order to create a pretext for the implementation of periodic massive security operations in major cities around the world.
>
> (MacDonald and Hunter 2013, 84, emphasis theirs)

Such 'talking into being' that occurred within public documents was reproduced through comments made by the youth the year before and the year of the Olympics, as in the 'sitting duck' exchange above. But there was a distinct and noticeable gendering of these comments, also reflected in the exchange from our walking interview. Women were much more likely to say that they felt safer with more police around, due to the threat of terrorism and their perception that Stratford was now a target thanks to the Olympics. Most of the men, on the other hand, were suspicious of the police, and felt that an increase in policing in the area made them *less* safe. The following discussion from a 2012 focus group captures this dynamic:

Woman: So if anything was to go wrong, it will go wrong, but another side it's like yeah, there's loads of security. I've seen a lot of police patrolling the area. Not like how they normally do, but they've done it more, and I feel kind of safer on that side.

Man: If you're talking about being harassed by police, it's probably not safer. Because we'll get harassed more by the police.

These gender differences – which were marked though not universal – reflect the differing experiences between young men and women of histories of police harassment due in part to the introduction of 'zero tolerance' policing models in London in the late 1990s (Fekete 2013). The young Black men in our study almost universally had experienced being stopped and searched by police, which happened, as far as they could see, for no reason other than that they were Black and living in a poor neighbourhood. They were thus understandably wary about the introduction of more, and more intensive, policing in Stratford. It also meant that feelings ran high when one of the men expressed a sense of relief about there being more police around:

Man 1: They're overdoing it right now. There's more police than athletes.

Man 2: I'm happy there's police arriving.

Man 1: I'm not happy. What do you mean, you're happy? They're doing what? Walking like they're bad and doing what (shouting)? Nothing mate. Nothing, bro.

The expansion of policing in the area – which was amplified after the 2011 riots (Ginsberg 2011) – was just one aspect of the securitization of East London in preparation for the Olympics. Jules Boykoff and Pete Fussey (2013) argue that the Olympics introduced "extensive and intensive militarisation of the public sphere" (261), including surface-to-air missiles attached to residential buildings, the deployment of the Royal Navy's largest warship to the River Thames for the duration of the Games, the use of Typhoon jets and Lynx helicopters, and the purchase of more than 10,000 plastic bullets by the Metropolitan Police. London was already home to extensive security and surveillance infrastructure, which helped strengthen their original bid to host the Games (Coaffee, Fussey and Moore 2011). The introduction of further security and surveillance measures for the Olympics was thus "laminated over extant security infrastructures" (Coaffee, Fussey and Moore 2011, 3323).

One aspect of securitization that had a direct impact on the young people in my study has been identified by MacDonald and Hunter (2013) as "a process of systemic mimesis, [whereby] Olympic sites are being modelled to reproduce the mechanisms of exclusion found at national borders" (76). This took the form of a "protected perimeter with everyone and everything that comes in being searched and screened, airport style" (Raine 2015, 6). Originally developed for the Olympic venues themselves, this "airport style" screening was extended to other 'live sites', such as "fanzones with big screens in parks" (Raine 2015, 7). One such 'live site' was located at Stratford Park, a small urban park with a children's playground a few blocks away from the supportive housing where the youth lived. Many of the youth reported viewing the Opening Ceremonies on the screen at Stratford Park, since none could afford the prohibitively expensive ticket price of the event that was happening a few blocks in the other direction at the Olympic stadium. Indeed, this park was the primary point of access for the youth to Olympic events, besides their own television sets. Despite the fact that it was a public park, the logic of Olympic security had made the screening of local residents who wished to use the park – either for watching the Games or for letting their children play in the playground – part of the 'new normal' of East London during the Olympics.

We had a direct encounter with the screening process at Stratford Park during our walking interview with Isaac, Scott, and Chibali, only a few minutes after the exchange about 'sitting ducks.' As we approached the park, Isaac, who was wearing his Olympic security badge because of his work as a security guard, was talking:

Isaac: So this is the big, great park and as you can see before I enter, I have to put on my security badge. [Pauses to put on badge.] Yeah you get your normal routine checks and yeah. So as you can see the park is [lovely], it's a lovely day, lovely view. [Directed at security screener:] Just have a quick search that is alright. Yeah thank you.

Our walk took place in the middle of the afternoon, six days after the Games had begun. There were no major events taking place, though the screen was showing some live events as we walked through. There were a few small groups

Figure 6.2 The front gate of Stratford park in 2011, without the security screening in place. The image was taken by Isaac as part of his photo journal. His comment on this image at the time was: "Stratford Park is just right here. It needs more greenery. Nice park. You can make more things for the kids as well, the little toddlers as well. Do something more constructive with the park."

of people in the park, mostly families, most of whom did not seem to be watching the screen. The presence of the security screening was, in many ways, unremarkable, and we passed through without incident, stopping to have our bags searched. In its very ease lies that which is most disturbing about it: a public park in a democratic nation *ought not* to be a place where security screening happens. The public park, representative of the commons, paid for by public money, is by very definition a site that ought to be freely and easily accessible to all. Yet the logic of Olympic security trumps the rights of access of local residents to their park and playground, free from scrutiny and bag searches. As Manley and Silk argue (2013, 371–2):

> This may well be our post-Olympic reality: the 'legacies' and longer-term liberty costs of hosting the Games may well resemble lockdown London as opposed to Landmark London, where a range of new punitive measures and potentially invasive laws legitimise the use of force, new surveillance technologies, methods of dealing with protest, and joint army, municipal and private security action become 'normalised'. This brings with it a quiet accretion of restriction that will likely have a harsher and longer lasting

Figure 6.3 The inside of Stratford Park, taken during our walking interview with Isaac,
Scott and Chibali. In the background is the screen showing the Olympic
events; next to the screen is a security guard. In the foreground is the mostly
empty park. The security screening through which we passed in order to
access the park is not visible in this photo (photo credit: Paul Watt, 2012).

legacy on minorities and the poor, involving a massive police presence for
Black and Asian youth in the surrounding communities, new policing
techniques such as stop and search, the further stigmatisation of working-
class communities in policy discourse, and the familiar security architecture
of airports and international borders characterized by scanners, checkpoints,
ID cards, cordons, [and] security zones that have been rolled out in the heart
of the city.

Manley and Silk paint a dire picture of post-Olympic London, but the evidence
from my study suggests they may not be far off with their predictions. One
negative legacy they do not mention is the effect of such incursions on the
subjective sense of well-being and safety of local residents. One outcome of
Olympic securitization was a feeling among the youth participants in our study
that their rights had been eroded, and that they were less entitled to protections
from legal incursions than before the Olympics. This left them feeling more
vulnerable and less capable of asserting their rights, even a year after the Olympics
had ended. As discussed during a focus group in 2013:

One thing I noticed as well, they've passed certain laws which are still in place now, although they're not necessarily active, but then it confuses people about their actual rights. So we were given leaflets saying that we have to [give our names] when in the past we could withhold our name because we don't have to give it. Now we have to, apparently. It's just confused the issue now. And where they've not necessarily come down hard on us now but they might do in the future, if it does happen then they've got all these loopholes and laws that are [there] to say they can have their own way with us.

The results of 'security thinking', introduced by both the public production of security documentation as well as the massive security infrastructure that came with the Olympics, is a troubling mix of concession to the inevitability of being surveilled and confusion about one's rights in a post-Olympic security world. The fear of terrorist outsiders structured a cautious welcoming of securitization by the youth in our study, particularly from the women. But this was substantially tempered by a long history of hostile relations between police and local residents, particularly for young Black men. The outcome was a pronounced ambivalence – mixed with outright hostility – towards the introduction of expanded policing and security infrastructure in their neighbourhood.

Policing the young and the poor in East London: Anti-Social Behaviour and Dispersal Orders

Stratford Park, with its airport-style screening, was the site of another Olympic-related security incident for the three young men who were taking us on a walking tour that day. When they had attended the Opening Ceremonies at Stratford park six days prior, they had been approached by the police and asked to leave the park. It was at that moment that they learned that a 'Dispersal Order' had been put in place for their neighbourhood:

Interviewer: How did you find out about the dispersal order?
Chibali: I found out about it from a police officer: "Sorry mate like can we talk to you?" "What about officer? I am just sitting listening to some music in the park." We are already in the park but yeah you are still going to make an issue arise once we have gotten into the park. So why don't you use your initiative and ask me this when we was entering [through the security screening], because we did come in together.
Interviewer: Is this when you were watching the Olympics?
Isaac: Yes we were watching the Olympics Opening Ceremony.
Interviewer: What did they say?
Isaac: Basically they said you need a dispersal order, three of you need to go. It was only us three.

Dispersal orders are one of the powers authorized by the 2003 Anti-Social Behaviour Act. Part 4, sections 30–36 of the Act give the police in England and Wales the power "to disperse groups of two or more people from designated areas where there is believed to be significant and persistent anti-social behaviour and a problem with groups causing intimidation" (Crawford 2008, 756). A few days before the Opening Ceremonies of the Games, signs appeared around Stratford designating it as a dispersal zone. "All Stratford Park" was specifically listed among the range of streets that delineated the area (see Figure 6.4). The dispersal order was in place from 9:00 am on July 27, 2012 to midnight of October 26, 2012. The Olympics ran from July 27 to August 12 and the Paralympics ran from August 30 to September 10. The dispersal order thus coincided exactly with the start of the Games, and extended beyond them by about six weeks.

Figure 6.4 Dispersal notice, attached to a lamp post (photo credit: Paul Watt, 2012).

The dispersal orders that were introduced as part of the 2003 Act were immediately critiqued by scholars concerned that they "evidence a lack of respect for the rights of children and young people" (Walsh 2003, 105). Coming out of the then-Labour government's focus on reducing "anti-social behaviour and disorder," the emphasis was on reducing the incidents of "teenagers 'hanging around'; vandalism; graffiti and other deliberate damage to property or vehicles; attacks or harassment due to a person's skin colour, ethnic origin or religion; people using or dealing drugs; and, people being drunk or rowdy in public places" (Walsh 2003, 104). The 'anti-social behaviour' approach to policing youth has been identified as part of a larger neoliberal shift towards emphasizing personal responsibility in the context of simultaneous retrenchment of social supports such as education, public health care, social security and social housing (Jamieson 2012; Squires 2008). In other words, dispersal orders are one of a range of tactics designed to 'responsibilize' young people, assigning blame to them as individuals rather than looking to the social context that create the conditions whereby such 'anti-social behaviour' occurs.

From their inception, dispersal orders have been "associated with the anxieties generated by young people congregating in public places" (Crawford 2008, 759). The legal definition of anti-social behaviour introduces a strong component of subjectivity, being "that which causes or is likely to cause harassment, alarm or distress to others" (Crawford 2008, 758). Within a designated dispersal zone, a police constable or community support officer (CSO) can disperse groups of two or more "where their presence or behaviour has resulted, or is likely to result, in a member of the public being harassed, intimidated, alarmed or distressed" (Crawford 2008, 760). The dispersal law is not intended to ban groups from gathering, although police officers in previous studies have "found it very difficult to answer specific questions about what behaviour or whose presence might trigger dispersal" (Crawford 2008, 770). Being told to disperse does not con-stitute an offence, but resisting the dispersal order given by the police constable or CSO could result in an offence, punishable by up to three months imprisonment and/or a fine of up to £5,000 (Crawford 2008).

Dispersal zones are authorized on the basis of a senior police officer (Superintendent or above) having "reasonable grounds for believing that members of the public have been intimidated, harassed, alarmed or distressed in a particular locality as a result of the presence or behaviour of groups of two or more people" (Crawford 2008, 759). The reputation of Stratford as a 'rough' locale, attested to by many of the youth in all years of our research, as well as the presence of the riots the previous year, was likely deemed reason enough to implement a dispersal zone in the area. What is significant, however, is the timing of the order: the exact coincidence of the dispersal notice with the onset of the Summer Olympics suggests that these measures were not being put in place as the result of a set of recent events, but rather as a peremptory effort to reduce potential disruption to the Olympic Games. Security thinking justifies such incursions on the civil liberties of local young people. Dispersal orders, despite being on the books since 2003, were not in common use (Crawford 2008); their use during the Olympics is thus even more striking.

The rarity of dispersal orders goes some way to explaining the surprise with which they were met by the youth in our study. Familiar more generally with the language of the anti-social behaviour legislation (colloquially called ASBOs, for anti-social behaviour orders), the dispersal orders on the other hand were not known to the youth in our study, prior to the Olympics. This led them to misconstrue their introduction into law as being a recent occurrence and due entirely to the Olympics:

Chibali: Do you know what, there was no such thing as a dispersal order until the Olympics. How the hell did the government make up the laws like this? I don't understand. There should be some law against how you can just make up a law, do you get what I am trying to say? You can't just chuck a law out there like that and say dispersal order. What is dispersal order? I never heard this in my life.

During a 2012 focus group, one participant suggested that the dispersal orders had been introduced as part of the suite of efforts to fight terrorism in light of the Olympics:

When the Olympics came round there was something that was put in place stating that anybody seen walking with more than two people would get sent home, put on a curfew and whatnot, and that was put in place because of the terrorism act.

Also of concern is that when I returned in 2013, long after the dispersal order had ended, some of the youth thought it was still in place:

You can't sit outside here because there's ASBOs, no more groups of two and whatever. We're living [in] a block community, there's more than two people living in this area, so what do you want to do, you go to that park and you still can't go in the park ... [police] make it that way, they make people scared because the way they approach you and make it look threatening and dangerous.

The result was, yet again, an undermining of the youths' understanding of their legal rights and entitlements in post-Olympic Stratford. In her 2012 study of the experiences of youth with dispersal orders in the UK, Janet Jamieson found that youth generally had "a lack of clarity with regard to imposition, implementation and termination of dispersal powers" (455). This was certainly the case in Stratford, where the youth had not heard of dispersal orders, and once they did assumed that they were part of the suite of legislation put in place to address the threat of terrorism. They also did not know when it ended, and assumed it was still in place a year later.

The gendering of police-youth interactions was also at play with the dispersal orders. This is captured by the following story relayed to us in 2013 by a male participant during a focus group. He was reflecting back on an incident that happened during the Olympics:

The difference with girls, it's very unlikely that the police are going to be attracted to girls and trouble them. Me and my two cousins were walking through Stratford and a [police officer] told me "no gangs allowed," and I said to him, "what is a gang?" I said, "these are my family, you don't call family a gang, if there was a woman with 12 kids are you going to stop and say she's a gang?" And he said no, and I said why, "because she's a family" and I said, "these are my cousins, we're going to shop, we're allowed to shop in Westfield right?" And they [the police] don't say nothing.

From the accounts of our youth participants, it seems that the dispersal orders were disproportionately applied to the young Black men during the Olympic period, further reinforcing for them a sense of distrust of, and hostility towards, the police. This is consistent with previous research arguing that dispersal orders ultimately "undermine police-community relations and leave young people feeling resentful and unfairly stigmatised" (Crawford 2008, 756), and that young people feel "unnecessarily persecuted by the police in relation to dispersal" (Jamieson 2012, 455).

Rather than being a response to terrorism, dispersal orders are a tool with a long history of use for quelling threats, real or imagined, from young people living in impoverished neighbourhoods (Squires 2008; Jamieson 2012; Crawford 2008). The timing of the order, directly aligned with the beginning of the Olympics, suggests that the amplified policing of young, poor people in Stratford was a direct result of the Games themselves. When Lord Coe gestured to the 30 East London youth he had brought to Singapore to support London's bid and claimed, "more than ever, these Olympic Games are for you," it is unlikely he meant that "more than ever, you will be policed more intensely and with less regard for your civil liberties thanks to hosting the Olympics."

Reading the riots: Racial tensions and policing in Stratford

Most striking in the interviews with the youth in every year of the research was the degree to which the young Black men in our study had experienced targeted policing, perceived by them to be largely due to their skin colour in combination with their apparel (particularly if they were wearing a hooded sweatshirt, colloquially referred to as a 'hoody'). In a discussion of the history of policing of Black and Minority Ethnic (BME) communities in the UK, Liz Fekete (2013, 73) argues that "violence is now structured into the criminal justice system, as individuals from 'suspect communities' are no longer innocent till proven guilty." This statement is corroborated by the experiences of the youth in our study. Some illustrative excerpts from each year are below:

2011:

Jack: The problem with police, there are more policemen, but the problem is stereotyping. They see a Black guy with a hoody and maybe a jacket and they stop you. Now I've got a jacket this morning because it was cold, so I wore a jacket, but I was looking around. The police could stop you at any time, you're rushing for something and they're going to stop you, they're going to search you, they're going to hold your hand up. They're going to want to touch you and it's like, "What the hell?" Stereotyping is a very big problem.

2012:

Patrick: They used to stop me, stop and searching. Sometime when I used to go to school. A group of us coming from school, they all feel like yeah people they come from school, sometimes they are trouble, they stop and search us but they will find nothing.
Interviewer: How many times have you been stopped that way?
Patrick: About five, six, seven times something like that. But they never find anything on me.

2013:

Todd: I was walking past Stratford fire station and I saw some police and they stopped me and asked "what are you doing there," and I said "I am just walking home" and they said to me "have you heard about what happened here," and they said "we're going to have to search you because of what happened." And it's like, "why just me because there are people here, you're not searching everybody you just picked on me and searched me." And he said to me, "oh it's probably the way you are," and it was like "what do you mean the way I am?" And I started to get really upset, they just stopped me because of the way I am. And seven of them just attacked me, and it was just literally out there, kicking me . . . And then they took me out, and threw me out and they searched me and found nothing and they just said to me you can go . . .

The women in our study had a more mixed response to the police; as discussed above, many expressed feeling safer with more police around, reflecting a legitimate fear of sexualized violence and the possibility of victimization. The women in our study also reported being less likely to be stopped randomly by police than did the men. But some of the women were also frustrated by and suspicious of the police, in part because of what they had witnessed happening to their male friends:

Jessica: The other day I was going to go to the gym for the first time with my boyfriend and his friend, they're both Black. We walked around the corner, we were wearing tracksuits because we were going to the gym, and a van, a police van, pulled up, slid their doors open, while they were still driving, three of them jumped out, grabbed the two boys that I was with, put them up against the wall and everything. I'm standing there thinking "okay, what have you lot done that you haven't told me about" and in the end it was just a normal routine check. They did all of that, they didn't find nothing on them and then afterwards the police were laughing in their faces, they were being rude about it and saying "yeah, there was a fight around the corner." You know they're lying, it's just an excuse. If we were to react to that, all that would end up happening is all three of us would be sitting in a cell, because we can't fight back.

Jessica's thought to herself – "I'm standing there thinking 'okay, what have you lot done that you haven't told me about'" – is another significant component of the frustration experienced by the young Black men in our study with respect to policing. The stigma associated with being approached by the police was felt keenly, and was part of the overall experience of injustice. The negative effects of being stopped by police was thus not only pragmatic, as it might make the youth late for work or an appointment, but also reputational.

Louis: When you see someone get stopped you don't even think what it's for, you think it's something bad.

Chibali: That time I was stopped about my phone, I was on my way to a job placement, so I ended up getting there late, I had to explain. And your credibility is already down and you can't tell them, "I was stopped by the police." So you've got to say something else like, "the bus got stuck in a traffic jam, it was a headache," and a lot of them are going to be like um hm [skeptical sound].

Isaac: People are looking at you, it does look awkward and it looks embarrassing so you look like a criminal.

Some of the women and many of the men believed that the police were not from their neighbourhood, and were not looking out for the interests of their community. They also suspected the police of corruption. Both of these elements lessened their legitimacy, in the eyes of the youth:

Dumaka: I think there's a lot more crooked police than genuine police that are here to help the community. That's where the community gets let down because a lot of the time crimes happen, police get called and they're not there, do you know what I mean? Half an hour later they're still not there and then when little things [happen] they're right around the corner waiting and they will spend all their time, even though they've got other better things to do. There's a lot of discrimination, there's a lot of wrong treating going on and it's been going on for years. It will continue to go on.

Lucy: Of course they have their good sides, but I just think that they overuse their power sort of thing. Like of course they have high status,

> they're police and they have sort of control over us, but they think that just because they're the police they can do whatever they want.

These feelings of frustration and distrust of police were expressed even more ardently in 2012, after the 2011 riots which occurred the previous August. Originating in Tottenham, London in response to the "suspicious nature of the police shooting of Mark Duggan, and lack of communication with his family and the community about his death" (Lightowlers 2015, 90), riots and other public disturbances later spread to 66 locations across England, involving an estimated 15,000 people (Bridges 2012). Taking place over four days, it was the most widespread rioting in England since 1981 (Cavanagh and Dennis 2012). Tottenham had also been the site of the 1985 Broadwater Farm estate riot, which had occurred after a police operation resulted in the death of a resident (Bridges 2012). Although the media reporting quickly lost sight of the origins of the riots as being anger about police brutality (Fekete 2013; Cavanagh and Denis 2012), the youth in my study were largely unanimous in recognizing this as the spark for the riots, even if some expressed disapproval about the looting that later occurred.

Sara: But when you think about what the government did, yeah they scrap everything that happened before the riot, which was the policeman shooting the guy from North London. And they've just covered it up with young kids doing riot, young people rioting, rioting this, rioting that, but they don't know why it all started.

Scott: Yeah, man, I witnessed loads of it [the riot]. It's just the tolerance of the police, innit, everyone had enough of them and they just wanted to fight back, and the police realized they was under siege and they couldn't really do much about it.

Many of the youth in our study reported staying far clear of the riots, recognizing the likelihood of arrest were they to become involved. But one of the youth in our study was less circumspect, or perhaps less lucky, in avoiding the riots and the swell of police that marked the majority of government response to the crisis. Antoine was held for almost six months after being picked up by police on suspicion of involvement with the riots. After spending months in prison, he was released without charge. He felt the whole experience was ultimately related to efforts to make London look better for visiting tourists in light of the pending Olympic Games:

Antoine: [The police] want the youth off the road and anything specific they will just try and take you for. Obviously they try and put me in there for something I didn't do, which wasted my time, it made me miss my last birthday and Christmas and New Year, because I came out in January.

Interviewer: So they put you in right after the riots, like in August?

Antoine: Yeah, basically they were just trying to get all the young youths, just for the Olympics basically, they were trying to make everything better for the Olympics so they take anyone. I tried to claim charges [against the police] but they just try and say because it was during the riots everyone got mistaken [for other people].

Lee Bridges notes that "these riots were marked by a very different form of policing and pattern of arrest than have previously been the case" (2012, 7). There were 884 arrests made during the three main days of rioting, and nearly 1000 more were completed within the first week following the riot (Bridges 2012). But the bulk of arrests happened weeks after the riots; by February of 2012, over 4,000 riot-related arrests had been carried out in London, as a result of a major post-riot operation (Bridges 2012). Much was made in the popular media about the effects of the riots on perceptions of London prior to and during the Olympics (Hill 2011; Beckford 2012), suggesting that Antoine's assessment of the reason for the police crackdown may not have been too far off the mark.

Policing to protect tourists

One legacy of the intensive policing during and after the riots is that "the threat of arrest and being brought before the criminal justice system, with all the implications this might have for renewed conflict with the affected communities, will be more long-lasting than in previous riots" (Bridges 2012, 7). In other words, the harsh police crackdown on affected communities further eroded the trust between residents and police, particularly for young Black men. The sentiment expressed by Antoine, that the harsh policing after the riots was in large part to get youth out of sight and off the street in preparation for the Olympics, was reiterated in respect to other issues in the neighbourhood. Of particular impact for the youth in our study was the murder of their friend Jonathan at Westfield mall a few weeks before the Olympics began. Jonathan (a pseudonym) had participated in one of our focus groups in 2011. When we returned in 2012, we were shocked to learn that he had been the victim of a knifing at Westfield; the youth were still reeling from the news. His death came up many times over the course of our fieldwork that year and in 2013, and particularly in relation to the youths' feelings about the police response and what it indicated. They expressed a sense of betrayal that, with all of the extra policing and security in place in the lead-up to the Olympics, somehow their friend had not been better protected when he was in danger. They also felt cynical about the police response immediately after his death, attributing it to an effort to make Stratford *appear* safe rather than to actually protect young people.

Leslie: The riot was out of control. But whereas this Olympics thing, they're going on about how they've got snipers on the roof, yeah, long before the Olympics starts. To protect their foreign guests. But then Jonathan lives in Stratford, you know? He goes to Westfield which is, what, ten minutes [from the Olympic site] to Westfield. There's no protection for the people who live in London until after something bad happens.

Woman 1:   In terms of security, it didn't beef up until after Jonathan got stabbed, I didn't see no beef up of security. I think the beefing up of security, it's trying to hide what happened to Jonathan under the carpet. Because obviously, everyone in the world [knew] because it's Westfield and Westfield just opened. My friend Alisha told me that she heard someone got stabbed in Westfield.

Man 1:   It was the first time Westfield opened. That's going to be in history, first time for the biggest shopping centre in London, Europe.

Woman 1:   Opened, and something happened. And they're like, oh, crap, Olympics is gonna start. We can't have them thinking that London is dangerous, for people not to come. So they have, literally, you'd blink your eyes and there was police everywhere. It pissed me off. I was like, come on, why has this got to happen for police to come?

Sara: Because, obviously, they wanted to cover that fact because of the Olympics coming up, they don't want people to know that [Jonathan] died, 'cause Westfield is a big shopping centre and they don't want people to have bad thoughts about that so the people won't come to visit.

The riots had provided plenty of evidence for the youth in our study that the police were not interested in protecting them and their well-being; Jonathan's death cemented that feeling. To add insult to injury, the Olympic dispersal order combined with the targeted policing in their neighbourhood made it difficult for the youth to gather publicly in order to support one another after his death.

Jessica: It's so sad, like you see the police arresting people outside here and recently with our friend that did pass away, obviously it draws a lot of mates closer together, a lot of people want to be with their mates at a time like that. So because there's a lot of rules here [at the supportive housing unit] about how many people you can have in and how long they can be there, visitor's cars etc. etc., that's the main reason why I think people end up hanging round outside, because they come here and then there's one reason or another someone can't come in and no one wants to leave someone behind. So then people do end up going outside, never causing trouble, just chilling, talking, communicating. They'll kick a football in the car park when it's empty and that, they might just stand around and have a drink, they might stand around and smoke cigarettes. But you don't see them standing outside smashing windows and robbing people or fighting, they're keeping themselves to themselves and they're not doing any harm to anyone. So being harassed when they can't even be out there is not fair because if they're out there they're harassed, they come in just chatting and chilling away from everything, they're still being harassed, so all we can do is go and sit at home. Is that fair in our own neighbourhood?

Some of the youth also suggested that during the Olympics, the demeanour of the police had changed in response to the presence of tourists. This is similar to the experience of youth in Vancouver, who found the policing much less overt, at least in public spaces, for the course of the Games. Suhail, who had been stopped and searched many times prior to the Olympics, reported in 2012 that:

> [The police have] got that [more] friendly approach than they normally do because they know the tourists are here. That's why you know, they can't be stopping people all the time, asking questions. It's not going to be a good image for them. So they've probably been told you know don't be so harsh, unless they see you're doing something wrong, then obviously you know, but yeah they've been okay.

The loss of their friend Jonathan reinforced for many of the youth the feeling that the intensified policing that was a result of the Olympic Games was not of benefit to themselves and their friends. Though none told us that they had participated in the riots, most were sympathetic to the anger at police that they identified as the cause. When Jonathan was murdered at neighbouring Westfield, the youth were quick to notice that, despite the enormous security presence at the mall and in their neighbourhood, they and their friends were still vulnerable to such violence. After years of being unfairly stopped and harassed by police, all of these experiences combined to suggest to the youth that the police presence in their neighbourhood was not to protect them, but rather to ensure the safety of tourists coming to the area for the Olympic Games.

Conclusions

In 2006, the Chief Inspector of the Metropolitan Police announced that "we want the security legacy to be us leaving a safe and secure environment for the communities of East London after the Games" (as cited in Coaffee, Fussey and Moore 2011, 3322). From the experiences of the youth in our study, this would appear to be another in a long list of failed legacy promises. The presence of the Olympics triggered the implementation of dispersal orders that restricted their freedom of movement and assembly within their own neighbourhood; the policing of their neighbourhood during and after the 2011 riots resulted in increased unease about the police, particularly for the Black men in our study, and saw one of our participants being unjustly jailed for almost six months. The increased police presence in itself made many of the youth feel unsafe, as they were often the targets of police attention. With the knifing death of their friend at the neighbouring Westfield mall, the sense of unease was even further amplified. The youth could not make sense of the fact that there were so many more police around, plus security guards and cameras at the mall, and yet still one of their own could be stabbed to death in such a public place. This highlighted for them the feeling that the enhanced police and security for the duration of the Olympics was designed not for them, but for foreign visitors and also for the new residents of the 'other Stratford' that had sprung up in the wake of the Olympic-led regeneration strategies (see also Coaffee, Fussey and Moore 2011).

Bibliography

All website URLs were accessed between September 2014 and December 2015.

Beckford, Martin. 2012. "Riots: Police to Step up Monitoring of Twitter ahead of Olympics," March 14 (section: News). www.telegraph.co.uk/news/uknews/law-and-order/9141918/Riots-Police-to-step-up-monitoring-of-Twitter-ahead-of-Olympics.html.

Boykoff, Jules, and Pete Fussey. 2013. "London's Shadow Legacies: Security and Activism at the 2012 Olympics." *Contemporary Social Science* 9 (2): 253–70. doi:10.1080/2158 2041.2013.838292.

Bridges, Lee. 2012. "Four Days in August: The UK Riots." *Race & Class* 54 (1): 1–12. doi:10.1177/0306396812446564.

Cavanagh, Allison, and Alex Dennis. 2012. "Framing the Riots." *Capital & Class* 36 (3): 375–81.

Coaffee, Jon, Pete Fussey, and Cerwyn Moore. 2011. "Laminated Security for London 2012: Enhancing Security Infrastructures to Defend Mega Sporting Events." *Urban Studies* 48 (15): 3311–27. doi:10.1177/0042098011422398.

Crawford, Adam. 2008. "Dispersal Powers and the Symbolic Role of Anti-Social Behaviour Legislation." *Modern Law Review* 71 (5): 753–84.

Fekete, Liz. 2013. "Total Policing: Reflections from the Frontline." *Race & Class* 54 (3): 65–76. doi:10.1177/0306396812464159.

Fussey, Pete, and Jon Coaffee. 2012. "Balancing Local and Global Security Leitmotifs: Counter-Terrorism and the Spectacle of Sporting Mega-Events." *International Review for the Sociology of Sport* 47 (3): 268–85.

Fussey, Pete, Jon Coaffee, Gary Armstrong, and Dick Hobbs. 2012. "The Regeneration Games: Purity and Security in the Olympic City." *The British Journal of Sociology* 63 (2): 260–84. doi:10.1111/j.1468-4446.2012.01409.x.

Ginsberg, Jodie. 2011. "Six Times the Usual Number of Police to Patrol London's Streets Friday." *National Post*, August 12. www.nationalpost.com/m/wp/blog.html?b=news. nationalpost.com/2011/08/12/six-times-the-usual-number-of-police-to-patrol-londons-streets-friday.

Hill, Dave. 2011. "London Riots: Pressure Grows to Show That the 2012 Olympics Will Be Safe." *The Guardian*. August 9. www.theguardian.com/uk/davehillblog/2011/aug/09/london-riots-2012-olympic-safety-fears.

Jamieson, Janet. 2012. "Bleak Times for Children? The Anti-Social Behaviour Agenda and the Criminalization of Social Policy." *Social Policy & Administration* 46 (4): 448–64. doi:10.1111/j.1467-9515.2012.00843.x.

Lightowlers, Carly L. 2015. "Let's Get Real About the 'Riots': Exploring the Relationship between Deprivation and the English Summer Disturbances of 2011." *Critical Social Policy* 35 (1): 89–109. doi:10.1177/0261018314545597.

MacDonald, Malcolm, and Duncan Hunter. 2013. "The Discourse of Olympic Security: London 2012." *Discourse & Society* 24 (1): 66–88. doi:10.1177/0957926512474148.

Manley, Andrew, and Michael Silk. 2013. "Liquid London: Sporting Spectacle, Britishness and Ban-Optic Surveillance." *Surveillance & Society* 11 (4): 360–76.

Raine, Robert. 2015. "Reflections on Security at the 2012 Olympics." *Intelligence and National Security* 30 (4): 422–33.

Squires, Peter. 2008. "The Politics of Anti-Social Behaviour." *British Politics* 3 (3): 300–323. doi:http://dx.doi.org.proxy.library.carleton.ca/10.1057/bp.2008.16.

Walsh, Charlotte. 2003. "Dispersal of Rights: A Critical Comment on Specified Provisions of the Anti-Social Behaviour Bill." *Youth Justice* 3 (2): 104–11. doi:10.1177/147322540300300204.

Whelan, Chad. 2013. "Surveillance, Security and Sports Mega Events: Toward a Research Agenda on the Organisation of Security Networks." *Surveillance & Society* 11 (4): 392–404.

Conclusions

These Games are not for you

Olympic promises, Olympic legacies, and marginalized youth in Olympic cities

In 2014, Rio mayor Eduardo Paes claimed that "The Olympics are being done, above all, to change the lives of people of this city for the better"; yet Rio's poorest have been subject to intensive displacement and gentrification of the city in the lead-up to the 2016 Summer Games (Tavener 2015). The 2018 Winter Olympics in PyeongChang, Korea, have been promoted to the local population with the claim that they will create 230,000 jobs and generate US$20 billion in investments and consumption (Sang-hun 2011). Given that the population of PyeongChang is only 50,000 strong, these numbers defy belief. In Tokyo, host to the 2020 Summer Games, plans are already underway for massive security spending, including the mobilization of 50,000 police and other security officials ("2020 Olympic Planners Gear up for High-Tech Security" 2015). While the focus is on 'fighting terrorism,' evidence from previous Games suggest that local marginalized people, such as ethnic minority youth and the homeless, will also become likely targets. In each of these cities, lip service has been paid to their Olympic Games serving as an 'inspiration' to a generation of young people, just as has been claimed since the inception of the modern Games in 1896.

Olympic proponents continue to claim social benefits from the Games, yet the checks and balances that might ensure such outcomes are noticeably lacking. Meanwhile, local marginalized populations are forced to contend with the shadow legacy of Olympic security. Young people continue to represent the symbolic recipient of Olympic largesse, in word if not in deed. Here, an essential question must be asked: if cities require social goods such as housing, employment, and opportunities for the young, why are they turning to the Olympics in order to gain them? This is particularly pertinent given that the majority of funding for Olympic Games now comes from the public purse. Why spend public money on giant sporting events that last only three to six weeks when that money could be dedicated to actually tackling social problems within the city?

The answer is that the Olympics – or what Helen Lenskyj calls 'the Olympic industry' – is not primarily concerned with social legacies. Rather, as I have argued throughout, Olympic proponents make use of the *language* of social legacy in order to persuade local populations to support their bids. The IOC looks favourably on bids that incorporate social legacy components because they have been the subject of substantial public scrutiny and embarrassment, most notably through critical reports authored by the UN Rapporteur on Housing and the Centre on Housing Rights and Evictions (COHRE). But the interests of the Olympics are not the interests of local marginalized populations. As economist Andrew Zimbalist (2015, 121) notes, "In either democratic or authoritarian countries, the tendency is for event planning to hew closely to the interests of the local business elite. Construction companies, their unions (if there are any), insurance companies, architectural firms, media companies, investment bankers (who float the bonds), lawyers, and perhaps some hotel or restaurant interests get behind the Olympic or World Cup project. All stand to gain handsomely from the massive public funding."

Some commentators on the effects of the Olympics on marginalized populations suggest that the negative impacts of the Games need to be addressed because they "tarnish the legacy of the Games" (Dahill, 2010–11, p. 1128). Such analyses assume that the Olympics is a positive institution whose errors can be rectified in order to properly distribute the positive opportunities that accompany hosting the Olympic Games. I find this assessment difficult to accept. After five years spent with homeless and marginally housed young people living in Olympic cities, witnessing their struggles for housing, jobs, safety and dignity, I do not see the Olympics as being the solution to their troubles. Rather, the Games have largely exacerbated the problems they already faced. From what I have seen, the solution to the negative social legacy impacts of Olympic Games is simply to prohibit them from taking place, at least at the size and scale and with the same footloose propensity that currently characterize them.

Since this is not likely to happen, at least in the foreseeable future, some suggestions for ameliorating the worst of the negative effects are in order. I draw here on the work of other critical Olympics scholars, as well as the reports authored by COHRE and the Special Rapporteur on Adequate Housing, reiterating the suggestions with which I agree, and adding a few of my own. An important place to start is with introducing real accountability measures into the bidding process, so that organizing committees cannot simply use social legacy goals to promote their bid without being held responsible for ensuring their implementation. Both Raquel Rolnik and Helen Jefferson Lenskyj suggest that the IOC incorporate mechanisms into the bidding process that would ensure social legacy goals are actually met. As Lenskyj (2008, 152) points out, the IOC already has the basic template for such a mechanism in the form of their *Agenda 21: Sport for Sustainable Development*: "It would be a relatively simple step to make *Agenda 21* a binding instrument and thus a key criterion in the evaluation of future Olympic bids." However, she notes her pessimism about the likelihood of this occurring, given that it contradicts "the profit-making motives of multinational corporate sponsors of the Olympics." Rolnik (2009, 20) recommends that the IOC "evaluate the bid candidatures against compliance with international standards on the right to adequate housing and guarantee that only those in conformity with the standards are selected." COHRE reiterates this recommendation, as their first of ten guidelines for promoting and protecting housing rights in the context of a mega-event: "Respect, ensure respect for, and implement all international housing rights laws and standards in all aspects of hosting a mega-event" (COHRE 2007, 208). From an economic perspective, Andrew Zimbalist (2015, 130) suggests that the IOC accept the use of "older, more modest stadiums," encourage "repeat hosting," and make "a more serious and professional effort to identify which bids made the most sense for a city's development." He also suggests that the IOC could "opt to share more of the generated revenue from the games with the host city or country" (131).

At the bidding stage, I would add the following recommendations: since "one of the explicit selection criterion in the IOC's rule book is broad support from the local population," (Zimbalist 2015, 125), each host city should be required to hold a referendum for *all residents* (not just citizens) about whether they are willing to host the Olympics. Importantly, *both* sides ought to have equal resources to make their case. As it currently stands, the big-money interests tend to align with the Yes side, and are able to fund splashy campaigns to persuade populations of the value of the Games, as happened in the Vancouver plebiscite in 2003. The No side gets scraped together by activists and concerned citizens, generally without deep pockets. If both sides were to have equal resources, perhaps there would be an opportunity for a genuine public debate about the relative merits and limitations to the Games. As one part of this educated debate, funds ought to be made available for a non-interested economic impact statement to be prepared, one that is not prone to the 'mischievous practices' that plagued Vancouver's and London's economic impact studies. Likewise, realistic assessments of the actual numbers of jobs that will be created, and for whom, ought to be part of the discussion, alongside discussions about opportunity costs (i.e. what is lost by spending public money on the Olympics, in lieu of other important social priorities). Finally, serious scrutiny of plans for security and its costs ought to be carried out, including an assessment of the long-term impacts of expanded security infrastructure on host city residents, particularly marginalized populations.

The above are a minimum set of requirements if the Olympics are to continue to draw 60% (as in Vancouver) to 85% (as in London) of their funding from the public purse. But another recommendation that ought to be seriously considered is in many ways much easier: do not permit public money to be spent on the Olympics. The 1984 Los Angeles Games were able to do this (though some public funds were still dedicated to infrastructure repair projects); with the level of corporate sponsorship that the Olympics now boasts, surely it is possible for the Games to be a private venture that is privately funded? This, at least, would remove the temptation to farcically claim that social legacies are a likely outcome of the Games, and might even force Olympic organizers to work within their budgets. Public funding must also be removed from the policing of the Games, since security budgets alone account for a huge portion of public expenditures.

In addition to the above broad recommendations about the Olympics, I have specific recommendations for researchers, civil society, and residents of future bid and host cities. These can be summarized as follows.

• For researchers: develop long term, qualitative research that works with marginalized populations in Olympic host cities.

- For civil society: beware of co-optation by the Olympic industry.
- For bid city residents: if you don't want the Olympics in your town, make a lot of noise about it.
- For host city residents: hold your government to account for commitments to social legacies and over-spending on the Olympics.

Each of these is expanded below.

Recommendation 1: Conduct qualitative research with marginalized residents

There is a serious dearth of sustained qualitative research with Olympic host city residents; while studies such as mine can fill in some of the gaps in our knowledge, there is a great deal we do not know. Other people who are known to be negatively impacted by the Games include sex trade workers, homeless adults, poor and working class communities, Roma, indigenous peoples, and other ethnic minority groups. Long-term, high-quality, ethnographic research with these communities in Olympic host cities would provide us with a much broader base of insight from which to work in mitigating the negative social consequences of the Olympics. Ongoing social scientific research on the impacts of the Olympics for marginalized residents can also better shape other research initiatives designed to ameliorate the worst of the effects. Importantly, the research needs to be more than a short snapshot approach – sustained engagement with the populations in question will yield much more useful, and accurate, information. For instance, a 2012 article in the *International Journal of Drug Policy* reports on a qualitative research study designed by members of the BC Centre for Excellence in HIV/AIDS and the Department of Medicine at UBC. The study sought to determine whether the increased numbers of police in Vancouver during the Olympics had a negative health impact on injection drug users. The study was a direct result of critical Olympics research that had documented the likelihood that marginalized populations were more likely to be targeted by police and security personnel during the Games. However, the study focused *only* on the period during the Games; its conclusion was that the police were suitably restrained and that their presence did not negatively impact injection drug users. What the study misses was the impact of policing in the year *prior* to the Games, when, according to my study, the majority of negative police interactions occurred for marginalized residents.

Gaps in our knowledge about the impacts of the Games for marginalized host city residents include details about employment, the effects of the Games on housing and in producing gentrification pressures, and the timing and nature of marginalized residents' interactions with police and security personnel. Employment questions raised by my study include: who is getting what kinds of jobs? How are the jobs divided by gender? How many of the jobs are going to the long-term unemployed? How many are going to young people? How many of the jobs are short-term and how many lead to longer term employment? For housing, how do pre-existing policy trajectories get amplified and accelerated when the

Olympics come to town? What are the longer-term impacts in terms of affordability and what are the displacement pressures created by gentrification? Questions about policing and security include the longer term impacts of amplified policing for marginalized residents, not only during the Games but also before and after. What pre-existing incursions on civil liberties get rallied for the Olympics security cause (such as the dispersal laws in London), and what does this mean for the people who are targets of these laws? More sustained research on topics such as these will build a powerful evidence base that can be drawn upon by civil society, social movements, and policy actors in their efforts to prevent the Olympics from happening in their own city, or at least in mitigating the worst of the social impacts.

The importance of research with marginalized populations is not only one of providing empirical evidence about the actual effects of the Games. There is also a moral and ethical imperative to provide space for those who do not often get space, to speak their experiences and share their truths. The youth in my study discussed this in our final round of focus groups in London, in 2013:

Respondent 1: Yeah, what you've been doing, I think it's good because it's like you get to hear from the young people, how they're actually feeling.

Respondent 2: If only the actual [housing] council did things like this.

Respondent 1: It's mad because as much as you probably won't believe, but you make us feel like we matter, we count, our opinions matter and how we feel actually matters.

Respondent 2: I hope the research goes to good use and they read about it or something.

Interviewer: Do you feel that people listen, that you have a voice?

Respondent 1: No, not in here.

Respondent 2: No.

Respondent 3: Not at all, not even the key workers.

Respondent 1: You don't get a voice, I think in London, the youth don't have a voice at all, I'd love to be the voice of the youth, because I've got so much I could say . . . We need to be heard because it's like they wake up and I think they think like this, "When I was a youth I wanted a park, when I was a youth I wanted to ride a bike so let's put the Barclays Bike there so they can ride it" or "let's add another park there," you know, "let's add some shops there," you know, that's not what we want, how about you come and talk to us, find out how we are and what we want.

It is important not to romanticize 'youth voice' or the voices of marginalized people, nor our own role as researchers and the process of translation. Nonetheless, there is both a pragmatic and ethical dimension to ensuring that long-term, high quality research is conducted, which engages with the experiences of those most affected by the Olympics in host cities.

Recommendation 2: Beware civil society co-optation by the Olympic industry

In both Vancouver and London, well-organized elements of civil society worked with the Olympics bid committees to ensure that social legacy goals were incorporated into the bid – yet ultimately, while these collaborations and commitments helped the bid committees win, there were no mechanisms in place to ensure that the commitments were met. In other words, civil society organizations, in collaborating with the Olympics with the well-intended desire to leverage the Games for social goods, may end up being co-opted by the Games and not produce the social legacy benefits they so desire. Leveraging the Olympics is a risky business, and has no guarantee of success. A better strategy, as happened in Chicago and Boston,[1] is to work collaboratively with other civil society and activist organizations to prevent the Olympics from happening in your city – because the IOC doesn't want to grant it to a city where significant protests are likely to occur. These collaborations can then become the basis for ongoing pressure applied to city and national governments to address the actual social needs of your communities.

Recommendation 3: If you don't want the Olympics, make a lot of noise

For residents of cities who are considering bidding for the Games, the best way to prevent this from happening is to create a massive spectacle of opposition. The IOC does not want to award the Games to cities where it will face opposition; so the best strategy before the bid is won is to create a great deal of opposition. Street rallies, letters to the editor, letters to politicians, letters to the IOC – even visiting the IOC, as No Games Chicago did – these are all strategies for preventing your city from winning an Olympic bid. Be persuasive and factual; there is a great deal of evidence available now, through books and the internet, to build a well-researched case about why the Olympics will be bad for your city. Use this to win popular support, and demonstrate that popular support however you can. Build coalitions across diverse interests to oppose the Games, and be sure to incorporate the voices and perspectives of those who will be most negatively affected, such as homeless people, sex trade workers, and indigenous peoples. A broad-based coalition can then be transformed into an effective political alliance for advocating for the types of social changes that are needed within your city.

Recommendation 4: If your city is hosting the Olympics, hold your government to account

Chances are, if you are a resident of a host city for a future Olympic Games, the bid committee made promises to the IOC about benefits that would accrue to the city in terms of jobs, housing, transit and the like. Find out what those commitments were (many bid documents and the IOC reports can be accessed through the olympic.org website), and hold your government to account for keeping those promises. Work in solidarity with marginalized populations to try to prevent displacement, either forcibly or under secret cover such as police sweeps before the Games begin. Keep the media apprised of your efforts. Don't expect the Olympic organizing committee or your government to be sympathetic.

The way forward

At this point in time, I do not expect that either my more radical (ban the Olympics) or more moderate (ban public funding of the Olympics) recommendations will be taken up. As Jules Boykoff (2014) notes, the political opportunity structure necessary to effectively oppose the Olympics is not currently in place – though it is shifting. We can see this in the plethora of critical scholarship emerging about the Games, the fact that bids for future Games are declining, and the vivacity of 'No Games' campaigns in Chicago (candidate city for 2016) and Boston (seeking candidacy for 2024).

While the focus of this book has been the impact of the Olympics on marginalized youth, it is also important to reiterate that the conditions they face were not wrought by the Games. While my study suggests that the Olympics exacerbated many of the poor conditions that they already faced (such as lack of housing, poor prospects for decent employment, and targeted policing), it was not the Olympics that created these conditions in the first place. We must look to the wider contexts of capitalism and neoliberalism, decades-long retrenchment of social safety nets, and the recent imposition of severe austerity measures since the 2008 economic crash, in order to understand the causes of their marginalization in the first place. Inequality is growing, and while the Olympics demonstrably makes such inequality worse in many ways, it is not the Olympics that created it.

I have sought to make the case throughout that the Olympics draws on discourses of social legacy in order to justify itself, and, increasingly, its use of public funds. But we need to take a step back from this argument to ask: why does it take a mega-event to mobilize support for social commitments? Citizens and city councils ought not to require corporate-driven mega-events in order to 'leverage' public funds for transport systems, housing, and infrastructure spending. This money is public money for a reason – it ought to be used for public benefit. Something has gone very wrong when government funding can only be assured if a city takes on the enormous risks and hassles of hosting a gigantic sporting event. To move forward from here, we will need to direct concerted effort and attention towards shifting the conditions that have brought us to this unfortunate place.

Note

1 For more on the successful No Games Chicago campaign, see https://nogames. wordpress.com. For more on the successful No Games Boston campaign, see www. nobostonolympics.org.

Bibliography

All website URLs were accessed between September 2014 and December 2015.

"2020 Olympic Planners Gear up for High-Tech Security." 2015. Japan Today. January 10. www.japantoday.com/category/kuchikomi/view/2020-olympic-planners-gear-up-for-high-tech-security.

Boykoff, Jules. 2014. *Activism And The Olympics: Dissent At The Games In Vancouver And London*. New Brunswick, New Jersey: Rutgers University Press.

COHRE. 2007. "Fair Play for Housing Rights: Mega-Events, Olympic Games and Housing Rights." Centre On Housing Rights and Evictions (COHRE). www.ruig-gian.org/ressources/Report%20Fair%20Play%20FINAL%20FINAL%20070531.pdf.

Dahill, Elizabeth Hart. 2010. "Hosting the Games for All and by All: The Right to Adequate Housing in Olympic Host Cities." *Brooklyn Journal of International Law* 36: 1128.

Lenskyj, Helen Jefferson. 2008. Olympic Industry Resistance: Challenging Olympic Power and Propaganda. Albany: State University of New York Press.

Rolnik, Raquel. 2009. "Special Rapporteur on Adequate Housing as a Component of the Right to an Adequate Standard of Living, and on the Right to Non-Discrimination in This Context." United Nations General Assembly. www.ohchr.org/en/issues/housing/pages/housingindex.aspx.

Sang-hun, Choe. 2011. "Pyeongchang, Sleepy South Korean Town, Was Built Into Olympic Host." *The New York Times*, July 7. www.nytimes.com/2011/07/08/sports/olympics/08iht-oly08.html.

Tavener, Ben. 2015. "The Olympics Are Screwing Rio de Janeiro's Poorest Citizens Out of Housing." *VICE News*. April 16. https://news.vice.com/article/the-olympics-are-screwing-rio-de-janeiros-poorest-citizens-out-of-housing.

Zimbalist, Andrew. 2015. *Circus Maximus: The Economic Gamble Behind Hosting the Olympics and the World Cup*. Washington, D.C.: Brookings Institution Press.

Index